Java™
After Hours

10 Projects
You'll Never Do at Work

Steven Holzner

SAMS

800 East 96th Street, Indianapolis, Indiana 46240

Java After Hours:
10 Projects You'll Never Do at Work

International Standard Book Number: 0-672-32747-3

Library of Congress Catalog Card Number: 2005901842

Printed in the United States of America

First Printing: June 2005

08   07   06   05   4   3   2   1

Trademarks

All terms mentioned in this book that are known to be trademarks or service marks have been appropriately capitalized. Sams Publishing cannot attest to the accuracy of this information. Use of a term in this book should not be regarded as affecting the validity of any trademark or service mark.

Warning and Disclaimer

Every effort has been made to make this book as complete and as accurate as possible, but no warranty or fitness is implied. The information provided is on an "as is" basis.

Bulk Sales

Sams Publishing offers excellent discounts on this book when ordered in quantity for bulk purchases or special sales. For more information, please contact

  U.S. Corporate and Government Sales
  1-800-382-3419
  corpsales@pearsontechgroup.com

For sales outside of the U.S., please contact

  International Sales
  international@pearsoned.com

Acquisitions Editor
Loretta Yates

Development Editor
Songlin Qiu

Managing Editor
Charlotte Clapp

Project Editor
George E. Nedeff

Copy Editor
Bart Reed

Indexer
Sharon Shock

Proofreader
Susan Eldridge

Technical Editor
Christian Kenyeres

Publishing Coordinator
Cindy Teeters

Book Designer
Gary Adair

Page Layout
Bronkella Publishing
Stacey Richwine-DeRome

Contents at a Glance

Table of Contents

About the Author

Steve Holzner has been writing about Java for as long as Java has been around—nearly two dozen books over many years. He has written a total of 92 books, which have sold more than two million copies in 18 languages. He has also been a contributing editor at *PC Magazine* and has been on the faculty of MIT and Cornell University. He runs his own training company, Onsite Global, for corporate programmers at www.onsiteglobal.com, teaching nearly all current programming topics.

Dedication

To Nancy, of course.

Acknowledgments

Thanks to acquisitions editor Loretta Yates, development editor Songlin Qiu, project editor George Nedeff, copy editor Bart Reed, and technical editor Christian Kenyeres.

We Want to Hear from You!

As the reader of this book, *you* are our most important critic and commentator. We value your opinion and want to know what we're doing right, what we could do better, what areas you'd like to see us publish in, and any other words of wisdom you're willing to pass our way.

As the publisher for Sams Publishing, I welcome your comments. You can email or write me directly to let me know what you did or didn't like about this book—as well as what we can do to make our books better.

Please note that I cannot help you with technical problems related to the topic of this book. We do have a User Services group, however, where I will forward specific technical questions related to the book.

When you write, please be sure to include this book's title and author as well as your name, email address, and phone number. I will carefully review your comments and share them with the author and editors who worked on the book.

Email: feedback@samspublishing.com

Mail: Paul Boger
Sams Publishing
800 East 96th Street
Indianapolis, IN 46240 USA

For more information about this book or another Sams Publishing title, visit our website at www.samspublishing.com. Type the ISBN (0672327473) or the title of a book in the Search field to find the page you're looking for.

Introduction

Welcome to *Java After Hours: 10 Projects You'll Never Do at Work*, the book that lets you kick back and take control of Java. This book is not to be taken too seriously—it's meant to be *fun*. So relax; you're in the driver's seat here. This is where you get to make Java do some outrageous things for *you*.

Why Is This Book Unique?

If you're a programmer, too many of the programming books you've read have probably not been much fun at all. In fact, many of them are grim slogs.

Not this one. This is designed to be the computer book for the rest of us who just want to kick back and get a little enjoyment out of what we do everyday.

That's not to say that the programs you're going to find here aren't powerful and that you can't learn some interesting techniques from them—you can. There's all kinds of cool stuff in here, from creating a multithreaded hockey game to an online chat room, from an Internet-based intercom to a temperature forecaster that draws JPEG images online and sends them to browsers.

There's a lot packed in here, and as the book's author, my hope is that at least some of it will make you take a second look and say, "Cool!"

Who Is This Book For?

This book is for you if you're a Java programmer and you're tired of the usual run-of-the-mill stuff.

This book is also for you if you want to learn some of the techniques involved: sending JPEGs back from a web server, grabbing web pages from Java code, creating drop shadows in Java2D, using online filters, controlling any other program robotically, and more.

About the Book's Code

This book contains 10 projects, along with some minor projects used for illustration purposes (one of these subprojects builds an entire web server you can run from your desktop, given an Internet connection and a fixed IP address, which you probably have if you have a broadband connection).

Here's an overview of the code in this book:

- **Chapter 1: Aquarium**—A multithreaded fish-swimming project with fish that swim realistically against a bubbly background.

- **Chapter 2: Slapshot!**—A multithreaded hockey game that *moves*. You play against the computer and set the speed. And when you set the speed in the upper 90s, you've got a good chance of losing.

- **Chapter 3: The Graphicizer**—An image-editing and conversion tool. This one lets you read in JPG, PNG, or GIF files and save images in JPG or PNG format. You can work with images pixel by pixel, embossing them, sharpening them, brightening them, blurring them, reducing them, and so on. And you can even undo the most recent change.

- **Chapter 4: Painter**—Lets you draw your own images from scratch—ellipses, rectangles, lines, and so on. You can even draw freehand with the mouse. You can also draw each shape open or filled, using a texture fill, a solid color fill, or a gradient fill. You can draw text. You can give shapes a drop shadow, or make them transparent. You can draw using thin lines or thick lines. You can set the drawing color. And not only can you save your work when done, you can also read in images and work on them, annotating them with text or adding your own graphics.

- **Chapter 5: The Chat project**—In this project you create your own private Internet chat room that will keep you in touch with anyone over the Internet. All you need is Internet access and a Java-enabled web server. You can have as many people in your chat room as you like. What they type, you can see, and what you type, they can see. Type all you like—all you're paying for is the local Internet connection.

- **Chapter 6: WebLogger**—Log access to your website. This project lets you log users who access your website by access time, authentication type, username (if they've logged in), user IP address, the URL they accessed on your site, their browser type, the milliseconds they were there for, and so on. All without their knowledge.

- **Chapter 7: The Robot project**—Another cool one. This project lets you control any other program by remote control; just tell it what to do. You can send text to the other program you're controlling. You can use the Alt and Ctrl keys. You can send tab characters, the Enter key, or the Esc key. You can also use the mouse—just enter the screen location (in pixels) where you want the mouse to move to. Then click the mouse, right-click it, or double-click it. You can also take screen captures. Want to automate working with any program? The Robot will do it.

- **Chapter 8: The Browser project**—This project lets you create a fully featured browser (subclassing Microsoft Internet Explorer) in your Java applications.

- **Chapter 9: The Intercom project**—This project lets two people type across the Internet. You just start up the project, connect with the click of a button, and you've got your own connection: Everything you type into the Intercom, the other use can see, and everything the other user types, you can see. This one is a client/server application and connects directly across the Internet using its own protocol—unlike the Chat project, no Java-enabled web server is needed here at all.

- **Chapter 10: The Forecaster project**—Displays a four-day temperature forecast for your area, starting with today's high and low temperatures. All you've got to do is to tell the Forecaster your ZIP Code, and it'll give you the forecast by reading its data from the National Weather Service and sending a JPEG image from the server back to the browser.

You can download all the code used throughout this book from the Sams website at http://www.samspublishing.com. Enter this book's ISBN (without the hyphens) in the Search box and click Search. When the book's title is displayed, click the title to go to a page where you can download the code.

Conventions Used in This Book

This book uses various typefaces:

- A special monospace font is used to help you distinguish code-related terms from regular English, for. Here's an example: The actionPerformed method handles menu selections, setting the appropriate drawing flags as needed.

- As I develop the code in this book, the new code being added will appear this way:

```
import java.awt.*;
import java.awt.event.*;

public class Intercom1 extends Frame implements Runnable, ActionListener
{
    public static void main(String[] args)
    {
        new Intercom1();
    }
    .
    .
    .
}
```

- Each chapter has a real-world scenario, which looks like this:

REAL-WORLD SCENARIO

You're going to find real-world experience and insights in real-world scenarios like this one. These track what's going on in the computer industry, in the technology under discussion, or just generally in programmer's lives these days.

- Notes, tips, and cautions look like this:

NOTE

Notes provide additional information related to the surrounding topics.

TIP

Tips provide shortcuts to make a task or better ways to accomplish certain features.

CAUTION

Cautions alert you to potential problems, or to common pitfalls you should avoid.

And that's all you need. Get ready and turn to Chapter 1, "Making Fish Swim in the Multithreaded Aquarium," to crank things up and make those fish swim.

CHAPTER 1

Making Fish Swim in the Multithreaded Aquarium

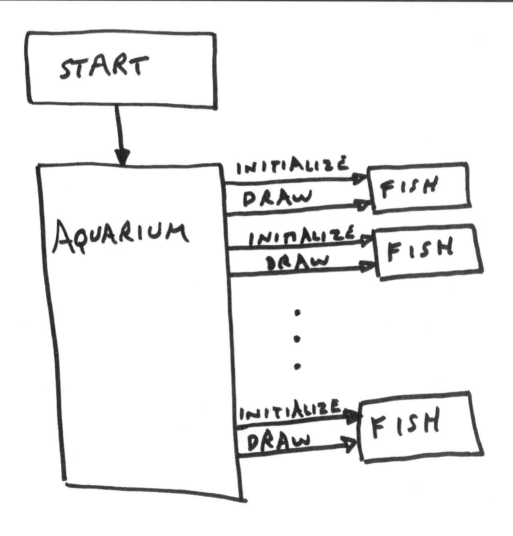

The Aquarium application.

This first project is purely for fun—a working, multithreaded aquarium where the fish actually swim around and bounce off the walls. We're going to create a dozen fish objects and turn them loose in the aquarium, where they're going to do their own thing as you'd expect fish to do.

You can see what the aquarium looks like in Figure 1.1; although you can't see the colors in the figure, the dozen fish are bright green and swimming at much the same speed that real fish would. When they hit the edge of the aquarium, they reverse direction, and every so often, they change their velocity at random to keep everything lively. The only thing they don't do is need to be fed.

FIGURE 1.1 Fish swimming in the aquarium.

This application makes a soothing backdrop as the fish wander around, swimming leisurely. You can tweak their speed and how often they change direction in the code, as well as make the aquarium larger or smaller to fit your taste. You can even use your own background image (imagine your boss's face there).

This application contains a certain amount of sophistication, despite its apparent simplicity; the fish are drawn as multithreaded sprites, each of which is its own object that knows how to move and draw itself. Here are some of the things this application does:

- Creates a sprite class (called `Fish`) whose objects can move and draw themselves on the screen as needed

- Animates the sprites, moving them around and bouncing them off the walls when they get too close to the edges

- Uses double buffering to avoid making the onscreen image flicker

- Uses a separate thread to move the sprites around

So how do you create this application? First, you've got to build the aquarium to give the fish a home.

Building the Aquarium

This application doesn't need a lot of sophisticated windowing techniques or controls, so it draws itself in a straightforward way using the Java Abstract Windowing Toolkit, also known as the AWT (some of the upcoming applications that need to be more powerful will use Swing). The main class in this application is Aquarium, and you need to base it on a class that can display the aquarium, which means using a class such as Frame in the AWT:

```
import java.awt.*;


public class Aquarium extends Frame
{
    .
    .
    .
```

This class relies on the Frame class (full name java.awt.Frame), and you can find the significant methods of this class in Table 1.1.

TABLE 1.1   The Significant Methods of the *java.awt.Frame* **Class**

Method	Does This
void addNotify()	Connects this frame window to a native screen resource
int getCursorType()	Deprecated. Used to get the type of cursor in this frame, but now you should use Component.getCursor()
int getExtendedState()	Returns the full extended state of this frame
static Frame[] getFrames()	Returns an array that holds all the Frame objects the application has created
Image getIconImage()	Returns the icon used for this frame—this is the image used when the frame is minimized
Rectangle getMaximizedBounds()	Returns the bounding rectangle for this frame if it is maximized
MenuBar getMenuBar()	Returns the menu bar used in this frame, if there is one
int getState()	Returns the state of this frame. Note that this method is considered obsolete
String getTitle()	Returns the title used in the frame
boolean isResizable()	Returns a value of true if this frame may be resized
boolean isUndecorated()	Returns a value of true if this frame is not decorated
protected String paramString()	Returns a parameter string that specifies the state of this frame

TABLE 1.1   Continued

Method	Does This
`void remove(MenuComponent m)`	Removes the menu bar from this frame and disposes of it
`void removeNotify()`	Disconnects this frame from its native screen resource, which means it cannot be displayed
`void setCursor(int cursorType)`	**Deprecated. Use** `Component.setCursor(Cursor)` **instead**
`void setExtendedState(int state)`	Specifies the extended state of this frame
`void setIconImage(Image image)`	Specifies the icon that will be displayed when this frame is minimized
`void setMaximizedBounds(Rectangle bounds)`	Specifies the rectangle corresponding to the maximum bounds for this frame
`void setMenuBar(MenuBar mb)`	Specifies the menu bar you want to use in this frame
`void setResizable(boolean resizable)`	Specifies whether this frame may be resizable
`void setState(int state)`	Specifies the state of this frame. Note that this method is now obsolete
`void setTitle(String title)`	Specifies the title you want to use in this frame
`void setUndecorated(boolean undecorated)`	Specifies whether you want to use decorations in this frame

All this window has to do is to open when the application starts and display a background of bubbles, as shown in Figure 1.1, as well as the fish. When the Aquarium application first runs, its `main` method will be called, but that's a static method with many restrictions on the data you can work with, so it's a good idea to create a new `Aquarium` object in `main`, because the new object will not suffer those restrictions:

```java
import java.awt.*;

public class Aquarium extends Frame
{
    public static void main(String[] args)
    {
        new Aquarium();
    }
        .
        .
        .
}
```

The new `Aquarium` object's constructor will be where the action is. In this constructor, you can set the title of the `Frame` window using the `setTitle` method, and this window will be titled "The Aquarium," as shown in Figure 1.1. To close the window, you need to catch the window close event that occurs when the user clicks the close button at upper-right corner of the window. The AWT uses listener classes to catch events such as this one. Here's how you typically handle the closing of a window, using System.exit(0) to end the application:

```java
import java.awt.*;
import java.awt.event.*;

public class Aquarium extends Frame
{
    Aquarium()
    {
        setTitle("The Aquarium");
        .
        .
        .
        this.addWindowListener(new WindowAdapter(){
            public void windowClosing(
                WindowEvent windowEvent){
                    System.exit(0);
                }
            }
        );
    }

    public static void main(String[] args)
    {
        new Aquarium();
    }
    .
    .
    .
}
```

That takes care of the rudiments of creating and closing the tank in which the fish will swim. Now what about the getting the fish into the action?

Loading the Fish

The two fish images are fish1.gif, which points to the left, and fish2.gif, which points to the right. GIF images are a good choice here, because you can draw your images on a transparent background; as the fish move around, the square background on which they're drawn will not appear, because it's transparent—only the fish image will be visible. That means the fish will actually look like fish, not boxes, swimming around.

Besides loading the fish images, this is a good time to load the background image of bubbles, because the application needs to know how large that image is so it can size the window correctly. This application comes with a file named bubbles.gif that you can see as the background, as shown in Figure 1.1. However, you can use your own image instead—the possibilities are endless.

To make sure the images are loaded correctly, Aquarium uses a MediaTracker object, which will alert the user if there are problems in loading fish1.gif, fish2.gif, and the background image, bubbles.gif. Here's how the MediaTracker object, tracker, is set up:

```java
import java.awt.*;
import java.awt.event.*;

public class Aquarium extends Frame
{
    MediaTracker tracker;

    Aquarium()
    {
        setTitle("The Aquarium");

        tracker = new MediaTracker(this);
            .
            .
            .
        this.addWindowListener(new WindowAdapter(){
            public void windowClosing(
                WindowEvent windowEvent){
                    System.exit(0);
                }
            }
        );
    }
        .
        .
        .
}
```

This application stores the fish and background images in objects of the java.awt.Image class, which is going to be used extensively throughout the chapter. The significant methods of this class appear in Table 1.2.

TABLE 1.2   The Significant Methods of the *java.awt.Image* Class

Method	Does This
abstract void flush()	**Deallocates all resources currently used by the** Image **object**
ImageCapabilities getCapabilities(GraphicsConfiguration gc)	**Returns an object of the** ImageCapabilities **class, which contains information about the capabilities of this image**
abstract Graphics getGraphics()	**Returns a graphics context that you can use to draw in this image**
abstract int getHeight(ImageObserver observer)	**Returns the height of the image, in pixels**
abstract Object getProperty(String name, ImageObserver observer)	**Returns the value of a property of this image, which you specify by name**
Image getScaledInstance(int width, int height, int hints)	**Returns a scaled version of the current image, with the specified height and width**
abstract ImageProducer getSource()	**Returns the actual object used to create the pixels in this image**
abstract int getWidth(ImageObserver observer)	**Returns the width of this image**

To load in the images, you can use the getImage method of the AWT's toolkit, a built-in treasure chest of helpful functions. The Toolkit class is abstract and can't be instantiated directly, but you can use the Toolkit class's static method getDefaultToolkit to get a working toolkit object for the current application. Here's how you can load in the images the application needs, storing the fish images in an array named fishImages and the background image in an image named aquariumImage:

```
import java.awt.*;
import java.awt.event.*;

public class Aquarium extends Frame
{
    Image aquariumImage;
    Image[] fishImages = new Image[2];
    MediaTracker tracker;

    Aquarium()
    {
        setTitle("The Aquarium");

        tracker = new MediaTracker(this);

        fishImages[0] = Toolkit.getDefaultToolkit().getImage
            ("fish1.gif");
        tracker.addImage(fishImages[0], 0);
```

```
      fishImages[1] = Toolkit.getDefaultToolkit().getImage
         ("fish2.gif");
      tracker.addImage(fishImages[1], 0);


      aquariumImage = Toolkit.getDefaultToolkit().getImage
         ("bubbles.gif");
      tracker.addImage(aquariumImage, 0);


      try {
         tracker.waitForID(0);
      }catch (Exception ex) {
         System.out.println(ex.getMessage());
      }
         .
         .
         .

   this.addWindowListener(new WindowAdapter(){
      public void windowClosing(
         WindowEvent windowEvent){
            System.exit(0);
         }
      }
   );
}
   .
   .
   .

}
```

Now the fish and background images are available in code. You can size the window to match the background image with the setSize method, make sure the window can't be resized (because the background image is of a fixed size) with the setResizable method, and show the window on the screen with the window's setVisible method, as shown in the following code:

```
import java.awt.*;
import java.awt.event.*;

public class Aquarium extends Frame
{
    Image aquariumImage;
    Image[] fishImages = new Image[2];
    MediaTracker tracker;
```

```
Aquarium()
{
    setTitle("The Aquarium");
    .
    .
    .
    try {
        tracker.waitForID(0);
    }catch (Exception ex) {
        System.out.println(ex.getMessage());
    }

    setSize(aquariumImage.getWidth(this), aquariumImage.getHeight(this));

    setResizable(false);

    setVisible(true);
    .
    .
    .
    this.addWindowListener(new WindowAdapter(){
        public void windowClosing(
            WindowEvent windowEvent){
                System.exit(0);
            }
        }
    );
}
    .
    .
    .

}
```

This application will use one more Image object besides the three it already has—memoryImage. This is where double buffering comes into play; to avoid making the image of the aquarium flicker, the application draws its visual display offscreen and then draws the completed scene on the screen all at once. This means Java can avoid drawing a fish, updating the entire display, drawing another fish, updating the entire display, and so on, which would make the aquarium flicker.

You can create this offscreen Image object, memoryImage, in memory. In addition, the application creates a Graphics object, called memoryGraphics, that can be used to draw in the new memory image this way:

```
import java.awt.*;
import java.awt.event.*;
```

```
public class Aquarium extends Frame
{
    Image aquariumImage, memoryImage;
    Graphics memoryGraphics;
    Image[] fishImages = new Image[2];
    MediaTracker tracker;

    Aquarium()
    {
        .
        .
        .
        setSize(aquariumImage.getWidth(this), aquariumImage.getHeight(this));

        setResizable(false);

        setVisible(true);

        memoryImage = createImage(getSize().width, getSize().height);
        memoryGraphics = memoryImage.getGraphics();

        this.addWindowListener(new WindowAdapter(){
            public void windowClosing(
                WindowEvent windowEvent){
                    System.exit(0);
                }
            }
        );
    }
    .
    .
    .
}
```

The Graphics class is what lets you do all the drawing in this application, and the significant methods of this class (that is, the ones you'll see later in this book) appear in Table 1.3.

TABLE 1.3   The Significant Methods of the *java.awt.Graphics* **Class**

Method	Does This
void draw3DRect(int x, int y, int width, int height, boolean raised)	**Draws a 3D rectangle in outline**
abstract void drawArc(int x, int y, int width, int height, int startAngle, int arcAngle)	**Draws an arc, in outline, inside the specified rectangle**

TABLE 1.3   Continued

Method	Does This
`void drawChars(char[] data, int offset, int length, int x, int y)`	Draws the text given by the given character array
`abstract boolean drawImage(Image img, int x, int y, ImageObserver observer)`	Draws an image in the graphics object
`abstract void drawLine(int x1, int y1, int x2, int y2)`	Draws a line connecting (x1, y1) and (x2, y2), using the current drawing color
`abstract void drawOval(int x, int y, int width, int height)`	Draws an oval, in outline, using the current drawing color
`abstract void drawPolygon(int[] xPoints, int[] yPoints, int nPoints)`	Draws a polygon, in outline, whose vertices are defined by arrays of x and y coordinates
`abstract void drawPolyline(int[] xPoints, int[] yPoints, int nPoints)`	Draws lines connecting the points in the given arrays of both x and y coordinates
`void drawRect(int x, int y, int width, int height)`	Draws the given rectangle, in outline
`abstract void drawRoundRect(int x, int y, int width, int height, int arcWidth, int arcHeight)`	Draws a rectangle with round corners, in outline, with the current color
`abstract void drawString(String str, int x, int y)`	Draws the given text using the `Graphics` object's current font and color
`void fill3DRect(int x, int y, int width, int height, boolean raised)`	Draws a filled 3D rectangle using the current color
`abstract void fillArc(int x, int y, int width, int height, int startAngle, int arcAngle)`	Draws a filled elliptical arc inside the given rectangle using the current color
`abstract void fillOval(int x, int y, int width, int height)`	Draws a filled oval inside the given rectangle using the current color
`abstract void fillPolygon(int[] xPoints, int[] yPoints, int nPoints)`	Draws a filled polygon, as defined by the given arrays of x and y coordinates, using the current color
`void fillPolygon(Polygon p)`	Draws a filled polygon, as defined by the given `Polygon` object, using the current color
`abstract void fillRect(int x, int y, int width, int height)`	Draws a filled rectangle using the current color
`abstract void fillRoundRect(int x, int y, int width, int height, int arcWidth, int arcHeight)`	Draws a filled rounded corner rectangle using the current color
`abstract Color getColor()`	Returns this `Graphics` object's current color
`abstract Font getFont()`	Returns this `Graphics` object's current font
`abstract void setColor(Color c)`	Sets this `Graphics` object's color to the given color
`abstract void setFont(Font font)`	Sets this `Graphics` object's font to the specified font

Okay, the setup is complete; the images are ready to go, and the window is ready to be used. What about getting the fish to actually start doing something?

Moving Those Fish

Applications that draw using sprites often do their drawing in a new execution stream—that is, a new thread. The reason for this is because while the new thread draws the sprites and moves them around, the main thread in the application can be doing other things—such as, in this application, closing the window when the user clicks the close button.

The drawing and graphics work that goes on behind the scenes will take place in this new thread. To handle a new thread, you make sure that an application implements the Runnable interface:

```
import java.awt.*;
import java.awt.event.*;

public class Aquarium extends Frame implements Runnable
{
            .
            .
            .
}
```

The Runnable interface has only one method, run, which is called when you start a new Thread object connected to the current object. Here's how you create and start that new thread, a Thread object named thread:

```
import java.awt.*;
import java.awt.event.*;

public class Aquarium extends Frame implements Runnable
{
    Image aquariumImage, memoryImage;
    Image[] fishImages = new Image[2];
    MediaTracker tracker;
    Thread thread;

    Aquarium()
    {
        setTitle("The Aquarium");
            .
            .
            .
```

```
memoryImage = createImage(getSize().width, getSize().height);
memoryGraphics = memoryImage.getGraphics();

thread = new Thread(this);
thread.start();

this.addWindowListener(new WindowAdapter(){
    public void windowClosing(
        WindowEvent windowEvent){
            System.exit(0);
        }
    }
);
}
.
.
.
.
}
```

You can see the significant methods of the `Thread` class in Table 1.4.

TABLE 1.4   The Significant Methods of the `java.lang.Thread` Class

Method	Does This
`static int activeCount()`	Returns the number of threads that are active in this thread's thread group
`void checkAccess()`	Checks to see if the current running thread can modify a specific thread
`static Thread currentThread()`	Returns a reference to the current `Thread` object
`void destroy()`	Deprecated. This method was supposed to destroy a thread. However, it was decided that doing so could leave system resources locked by this thread being inaccessible. See the discussion in the text for an alternative
`static void dumpStack()`	Displays a stack trace showing stack use by the current thread
`static Map<Thread,StackTraceElement[]> getAllStackTraces()`	Returns stack traces for all active threads
`static Thread.UncaughtExceptionHandler getDefaultUncaughtExceptionHandler()`	Returns the default exception handler used when a thread terminates because an exception was not caught
`long getId()`	Returns the ID of this thread, allowing you to identify it

TABLE 1.4   Continued

Method	Does This
`String getName()`	Returns the name of this thread
`int getPriority()`	Returns the priority of this thread
`Thread.State getState()`	Returns the current state of this thread
`ThreadGroup getThreadGroup()`	Returns the thread group this thread is a member of
`Thread.UncaughtExceptionHandler getUncaughtExceptionHandler()`	Returns the exception handler used when a thread terminates because an exception was not caught
`static boolean holdsLock(Object obj)`	Returns a value of `true` if the current thread has a lock on the given object
`void interrupt()`	Interrupts the thread
`static boolean interrupted()`	Returns `true` if the current thread has been interrupted
`boolean isAlive()`	Returns `true` if this thread is alive
`boolean isDaemon()`	Returns `true` if this thread is a daemon thread
`boolean isInterrupted()`	Returns `true` if this thread has been interrupted
`void join()`	Lets you join execution streams by waiting for this thread to die
`void join(long millis)`	Lets you join execution streams by waiting at most the given number of milliseconds for this thread to die
`void join(long millis, int nanos)`	Lets you join execution streams by waiting at most the given number of milliseconds plus the given number of nanoseconds for this thread to die
`void resume()`	Deprecated. This method originally was supposed to suspend the execution of a thread. However, it was decided that doing so could leave system resources locked by this thread being inaccessible. See the discussion in the text for an alternative
`void run()`	Executes the `run` method if the objected used to construct this thread implements the `Runnable` interface
`static void setDefaultUncaughtExceptionHandler (Thread.UncaughtExceptionHandler eh)`	Sets the default handler used when a thread terminates because of an uncaught exception
`void setName(String name)`	Sets the name of this thread to the given name
`void setPriority(int newPriority)`	Sets the priority of the thread

TABLE 1.4   Continued

Method	Does This
`void setUncaughtExceptionHandler(Thread.UncaughtExceptionHandler eh)`	Sets the exception handler to use when this thread terminates because of an uncaught exception
`static void sleep(long millis)`	Makes the thread temporarily suspend execution for the given number of milliseconds
`static void sleep(long millis, int nanos)`	Makes the thread temporarily suspend execution for the given number of milliseconds plus the given number of nanosecond
`void start()`	Executes the thread's code by making Java call the thread's `run` method
`void stop()`	Deprecated. This method was originally supposed to stop a thread. However, it was decided that doing so could leave system resources locked by this thread being inaccessible. See the discussion in the text for an alternative
`void stop(Throwable obj)`	Deprecated. This method was originally supposed to stop a thread. However, it was decided that doing so could leave system resources locked by this thread being inaccessible. See the discussion in the text for an alternative
`void suspend()`	Deprecated. This method was originally supposed to suspend a thread's execution. However, it was decided that doing so could leave system resources locked by this thread being inaccessible. See the discussion in the text for an alternative
`static void yield()`	Makes this thread pause and yield control temporarily to other threads, letting them execute

To implement the `Runnable` interface and support the new thread, you have to add a run method with the code you want to execute in the new thread to the current object. When the `thread.start` method is called, the `run` method is called, executing the thread's code.

To create and draw the sprites in this application, add the run method to the `Aquarium` class. To initialize the fish sprites, the code starts by determining the actual edges of the container they're in, which means determining the dimensions of the client window (the area inside all the toolbars and borders) of the current window. You can determine that area using various methods inherited by the `Frame` class—`java.awt.Frame` is built on top of `java.awt.Window`, which is built on top of java.awt.Container, which in turn is built on top of java.awt.Component. In this case, you can use the Component method getSize and the Container method getInsets to determine the actual dimensions in which the fish have to swim around, which is stored in a Java Rectangle object named edges:

```java
public class Aquarium extends Frame implements Runnable
{
    Image aquariumImage, memoryImage;
    Image[] fishImages = new Image[2];
    Thread thread;
    MediaTracker tracker;
    Graphics memoryGraphics;

    Aquarium()
    {
        .
        .
        .
    }

    public void run()
    {
        Rectangle edges = new Rectangle(0 + getInsets().left, 0
            + getInsets().top, getSize().width - (getInsets().left
            + getInsets().right), getSize().height - (getInsets().top
            + getInsets().bottom));

        .
        .
        .

}
```

Next in run, the code creates the fish sprites. Each fish will be represented by a Fish object that will do all the fish needs to do—swim and draw itself in the aquarium. To keep track of the Fish objects, you'll need to store them in a Java Vector object named fishes, and the number of fish will be stored in an int named numberFishes:

```java
public class Aquarium extends Frame implements Runnable
{
    Image aquariumImage, memoryImage;
    Image[] fishImages = new Image[2];
    Thread thread;
    MediaTracker tracker;
    Graphics memoryGraphics;
    int numberFish = 12;
    Vector<Fish> fishes = new Vector<Fish>();
```

.
.
.

That's how things look if you're using Java 1.5 (the default for this book), where you need to specify the type of objects in a Vector; if you're using Java 1.4, declare the fishes vector this way:

```
Vector fishes = new Vector();
```

Next, you create all the fish. The Fish class's constructor needs the two images for each fish (left-pointing and right-pointing), the edges rectangle so the fish knows the bounds of the aquarium, and a pointer to the Aquarium object itself so the fish knows where it's supposed to draw itself. Here's how the run method creates the fish, passing those values to the Fish class's constructor:

```
public void run()
    {
        for (int loopIndex = 0; loopIndex < numberFish; loopIndex++){
            Rectangle edges = new Rectangle(0 + getInsets().left, 0
                + getInsets().top, getSize().width - (getInsets().left
                + getInsets().right), getSize().height - (getInsets().top
                + getInsets().bottom));

        for (int loopIndex = 0; loopIndex < numberFish; loopIndex++){
            fishes.add(new Fish(fishImages[0], fishImages[1], edges, this));
            try {
                Thread.sleep(20);
            }
            catch (Exception exp) {
                System.out.println(exp.getMessage());
            }
        }

.
.
.

}
```

That's the loop that actually creates the Fish objects. Want more fish? Just change the value assigned to numberFish in that variable's declaration. Try this for a blast:

```
int numberFish = 120;
```

Note also that after each fish is created and added to the fishes vector, the code calls the Thread.sleep method. This method makes the thread pause by the number of milliseconds you pass—in this case, that's 20 milliseconds. The code pauses for 20 milliseconds between creating various fish because each fish uses the system time to generate its random position and velocity, and some systems can't resolve time periods less than this—if you simply created one fish immediately after the other, some would end up with exactly the same coordinates and velocity (which means one fish might be hidden behind another, even after they bounced off walls and kept moving around the aquarium).

After the fish are created, all you have to do is to keep calling their swim method to have them move around the tank. Here's what that looks like—note that you can adjust how fast the fish move by changing the value assigned to the sleepTime variable, which is how long the thread sleeps between moving individual fish:

```
public class Aquarium extends Frame implements Runnable
{
    Image aquariumImage, memoryImage;
    Image[] fishImages = new Image[2];
    Thread thread;
    MediaTracker tracker;
    Graphics memoryGraphics;
    int numberFish = 12;
    int sleepTime = 110;
    Vector<Fish> fishes = new Vector<Fish>();
            .
            .
            .
public void run()
    {
    for (int loopIndex = 0; loopIndex < numberFish; loopIndex++){
            Rectangle edges = new Rectangle(0 + getInsets().left, 0
            + getInsets().top, getSize().width - (getInsets().left
```

REAL-WORLD SCENARIO: TYING UP LOOSE THREADS

Threads are handled differently on different systems, and unless you make some provision for ending a thread, it can hang around forever—and if you get enough of them, the Java runtime will run out of heap space, and the system may even hang, or at least slow waaaaay down.

In the old days, you could stop a thread using its stop method (there were also plans for a destroy method, but that method was never implemented), but that method is now deprecated. The reason is that the creators of Java were concerned that if the thread tied up some system resource, such as a file, and then was stopped, there would no longer be any way to reach that resource.

Their solution was to say that the programmer is responsible for stopping the thread, and that's done by having control return from the run method. In the same way, the suspend and resume methods, which paused and restarted threads, were deprecated. Now the programmer is responsible for pausing and restarting threads himself, which is typically done by setting Boolean variables and making the thread stop working temporarily if so required.

continues

```
            + getInsets().right), getSize().height - (getInsets().top
            + getInsets().bottom));

        fishes.add(new Fish(fishImages[0], fishImages[1], edges, this));
        try {
            Thread.sleep(20);
        }
        catch (Exception exp) {
            System.out.println(exp.getMessage());
        }
    }
}

Fish fish;

while (runOK) {
        for (int loopIndex = 0; loopIndex < numberFish; loopIndex++){
        fish = (Fish)fishes.elementAt(loopIndex);
        fish.swim();
    }

    try {
        Thread.sleep(sleepTime);
    }
    catch (Exception exp) {
        System.out.println(exp.getMessage());
    }
```

REAL-WORLD SCENARIO: TYING UP LOOSE THREADS *continued*

On some systems, threads are launched as their own processes, and sometimes, they can get away from you if you're not careful. Some years ago, I was working on my own commercial site, on one of the major hosting companies, and I wrote some code that intentionally spawned new processes. The problem was that they were never ended properly (even though the code intended to end them when they were done, it didn't terminate them as it should), so my applications just happily went on spawning endless new processes.

That was on Friday night. When I came back to take a look on Sunday, I found that my code had single-handedly brought down the entire machine over the weekend—and the server was the host for two international banks, as well as a major airline.

Ah, well!

The moral is, if you don't want your account locked, all your files disabled, and a lot of nasty, frantic emails from system operators threatening legal action, be careful about what you do with threads and not ending spawned processes.

```
        repaint();
    }
}
```

Note the runOK variable here—the while loop keeps calling the swim method of each fish while this variable is true. What's runOK all about? It's the variable used to end the thread when the application is ended. You add the declaration of this variable to the code this way:

```
public class Aquarium extends Frame implements Runnable
{
    Image aquariumImage, memoryImage;
    Image[] fishImages = new Image[2];
    Thread thread;
    MediaTracker tracker;
    Graphics memoryGraphics;
    int numberFish = 12;
    int sleepTime = 110;
    Vector<Fish> fishes = new Vector<Fish>();
    boolean runOK = true;
        .
        .
        .
```

And when the user closes the window, the application will set runOK to false before actually ending. Therefore, add the following code:

```
        this.addWindowListener(new WindowAdapter(){
            public void windowClosing(
                WindowEvent windowEvent){
                    runOK = false;
                    System.exit(0);
                }
            }
        );
```

That'll end the thread simply by making the run method finish and return. This way, we get rid of the thread when the application ends.

Double-Buffering the Drawing

Besides the swim method, the Fish class also has a drawFishImage method, which will draw the fish. Note that the last line in the run method, after each fish has been moved to a new position by the swim method, calls the window's repaint method to redraw the aquarium:

```
while (runOK) {
    for (int loopIndex = 0; loopIndex < numberFish; loopIndex++){
        fish = (Fish)fishes.elementAt(loopIndex);
        fish.swim();
    }

    try {
        Thread.sleep(sleepTime);
    }
    catch (Exception exp) {
        System.out.println(exp.getMessage());
    }

    repaint();

}
```

The `repaint` method calls the `update` method, which is where flickering usually happens, because by default the `update` method first redraws the entire window using the background window color. To avoid that flickering, this application overloads the `update` method itself, drawing everything in the offscreen memory-based image `memoryImage` and then drawing the completed image onscreen.

The overridden `update` method is passed the `Graphics` object it should use to draw in the main window. In the Aquarium application, the code starts by drawing the background image using the `Graphics` object corresponding to the memory image, *not* to the main window. You can draw the background image in the memory image with the `drawImage` method by passing it the image to draw, the X and Y location at which to draw the new image, and an object that acts as an image observer in case you want to be notified of the events that happen as the image is loaded (Aquarium doesn't make use of these events, so the code simply passes the current object as the image observer):

```
public void update(Graphics g)
{
    memoryGraphics.drawImage(aquariumImage, 0, 0, this);
        .
        .
        .
}
```

And you can draw each fish in the memory image simply by calling each fish's `drawFishImage` method:

```
public void update(Graphics g)
{
    memoryGraphics.drawImage(aquariumImage, 0, 0, this);
```

```
    for (int loopIndex = 0; loopIndex < numberFish; loopIndex++){
        ((Fish)fishes.elementAt(loopIndex)).drawFishImage
            (memoryGraphics);
    }
        .
        .
        .
}
```

Now that the offscreen image is complete, you can flash it onto the screen with minimum flicker, like so:

```
public void update(Graphics g)
{
    memoryGraphics.drawImage(aquariumImage, 0, 0, this);

    for (int loopIndex = 0; loopIndex < numberFish; loopIndex++){
        ((Fish)fishes.elementAt(loopIndex)).drawFishImage
            (memoryGraphics);
    }

    g.drawImage(memoryImage, 0, 0, this);
}
```

That completes everything except creating the actual Fish objects with their constructors, the swim and drawImage methods. That's coming up next.

Creating the Fish

Each Fish object has three methods—a constructor, a swim method that moves the fish, and a drawImage method that draws the fish using the Graphics object you pass it.

The constructor's job is to store what's passed to it—the two fish images, the bounding rectangle of the aquarium, and the object that corresponds to the tank itself. In addition, the constructor creates a random number generator seeded with the current system time in milliseconds (returned by the System.currentTimeMillis method), and it uses this random number generator to create a random location and velocity for the fish. After the random number generator is seeded, every time you call its nextInt method, you'll get a new, random integer from 0 to 2^{32}.

Both the fish's location and velocity are stored in Java Point objects, which have x and y members; all values are stored in pixels. The location variable holds the position of the upper-left corner of the fish image, and the velocity variable holds the X and Y number of pixels that will be added to the fish's location each time the swim method is called. Here's what the Fish class's constructor looks like:

```
class Fish
{
    Component tank;
    Image image1;
    Image image2;
    Point location;
    Point velocity;
    Rectangle edges;
    Random random;

    public Fish(Image image1, Image image2, Rectangle edges,
        Component tank)
    {
        random = new Random(System.currentTimeMillis());
        this.tank = tank;
        this.image1 = image1;
        this.image2 = image2;
        this.edges = edges;
        this.location = new Point(100
            + (Math.abs(random.nextInt()) % 300),
            100 + (Math.abs(100 + random.nextInt()) % 100));

        this.velocity = new Point(random.nextInt() % 8, random.nextInt() % 8);
    }
    .
    .
    .
}
```

That initializes the fish; how about making them *do* something?

Making the Fish Swim

The swim method is what gets those fish to go. It does this by incrementing the location x and y coordinates by adding the x and y values stored in the velocity variable each time swim is called.

Every so often, the fish should change direction, just as fish in an aquarium might. Here's how that works in the swim method, which, every now and then, adds new random numbers to the x and y component of the velocity and then makes sure no velocity component exceeds an absolute magnitude of 8:

```
public void swim()
    {
    if(random.nextInt() % 7 <= 1){
```

```
        velocity.x += random.nextInt() % 4;

        velocity.x = Math.min(velocity.x, 8);
        velocity.x = Math.max(velocity.x, -8);

        velocity.y += random.nextInt() % 4;

        velocity.y = Math.min(velocity.y, 8);
        velocity.y = Math.max(velocity.y, -8);
    }
    .
    .
    .
```

Next, the code adds the x and y components of the fish's velocity to move the fish to a new position:

```
location.x += velocity.x;
location.y += velocity.y;
```

All that's left to do is to determine if updating the fish's position has put it beyond the edge of the aquarium, in which case the fish should bounce off the edge of the tank, which you can make happen by reversing the sign of its x or y velocity, like this:

```
if (location.x < edges.x) {
    location.x = edges.x;
    velocity.x = -velocity.x;
}

if ((location.x + image1.getWidth(tank))
    > (edges.x + edges.width)){
    location.x = edges.x + edges.width - image1.getWidth(tank);
    velocity.x = -velocity.x;
}

if (location.y < edges.y){
    location.y = edges.y;
    velocity.y = -velocity.y;
}

if ((location.y + image1.getHeight(tank))
    > (edges.y + edges.height)){
    location.y = edges.y + edges.height - image1.getHeight(tank);
    velocity.y = -velocity.y;
}
}
```

That completes the swim method, which updates the fish's position each time it's called. The last thing to do is to actually draw the fish when needed, and that's done by the drawFishImage method.

Drawing the Fish

The drawFishImage method draws the fish when needed in the memory-based image before that image is flashed onto the screen. This method is passed the Graphics object it should use to draw the fish.

Drawing the image isn't hard; all you need to do is to use the Graphics object's drawImage method to draw the fish at its position as given by its location object. The only subtlety here is that you should draw the image of the fish going to the left if its x velocity is negative, and going to the right if its x velocity is positive. Here's what it looks like in the drawFishImage method:

```
public void drawFishImage(Graphics g)
{
    if(velocity.x < 0) {
        g.drawImage(image1, location.x, location.y, tank);
    }
    else {
        g.drawImage(image2, location.x, location.y, tank);
    }
}
```

That completes the entire Aquarium application, and it's ready to roll.

NOTE

Download the complete source code for the Aquarium project, Aquarium.java, at the Sams website. All you need to do is to compile it as discussed next and run it to get it going.

If you're using Java 1.5, which you can get from http://java.sun.com, compile this application, as follows, using the Java compiler, javac, to create the Aquarium.class file that you'll actually run:

CAUTION

If javac isn't in your path, you'll have to preface it with the correct path—something like c:\jdk1.5\bin\javac in Windows.

```
%javac Aquarium.java
```

Then make sure the needed image files (bubble.gif, fish1.gif, and fish2.gif) are in the same directory as Aquarium.class and run the application this way (preface the java command with the correct path, if needed):

```
%java Aquarium
```

The results appear in Figure 1.1. If you're using Java 1.4, follow the same steps, but make sure you've changed the line

```
Vector<Fish> fishes = new Vector<Fish>();
```

at the beginning of the code, to this:

```
Vector fishes = new Vector();
```

Conclusion

This first project was for fun, displaying an aquarium full of fish swimming around using multithreaded sprite animation. What could be more fun than a dozen bright green guppies floating around on your computer? It's suitable when you need a quick break from work, as a backdrop on your desktop, something to perk you up, or just anytime you need an aquarium.

This application used a fair number of sophisticated techniques in order to get its fish to swim. The fish images are GIF files specially created with transparent areas to make sure they look like fish swimming around, not small white boxes. The MediaTracker object in this application read in the fish images and stored them as graphics sprites. The sprites were animated with a new thread, which the application took care to end when the main window was closed. The fish were implemented as objects, and each knows how to swim around the tank as well as when to bounce off the edges, as required. Also, the application took care of flickering by using double buffering.

The result of all this work was a pleasing aquarium application. The coming chapters will get into more powerful applications, of course—Internet intercoms, chat rooms, online JPEG factories, and so on, but it doesn't hurt to start with a little fun.

CHAPTER 2

Slapshot! The Interactive Hockey Game

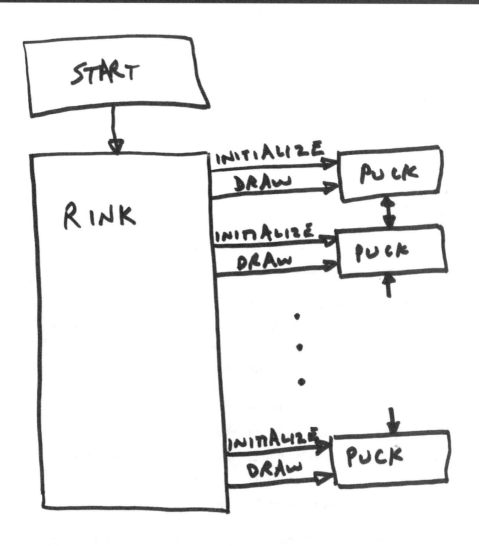

The Slapshot! application.

Let's get *interactive*. Chapter 1, "Making Fish Swim in the Multithreaded Aquarium," was all about the Aquarium application, which is nice to watch but doesn't really let you get in on the action. This chapter is on Slapshot!, an interactive hockey game, where you actually have to do something active, or you'll lose. The code developed in Chapter 1 is going to be leveraged for this chapter, because Slapshot! uses hockey puck sprites, much like the fish in the aquarium—only the pucks move faster.

You can see what this game looks like in Figure 2.1. The pucks shown in this figure are zooming around the ice at the speed you choose (varies from very slow to just about unbeatably fast). Your job is to use the mouse with the blocker on the left, as you see in the figure, to keep the pucks out of the goal (represented as a thick red vertical line in the app). The computer's going to play against you on this one—the blocker in front of the goal on the right is run by the code. The score appears near the bottom of the game's window. Can you beat the game? Probably. Until you start increasing the speed anyway....

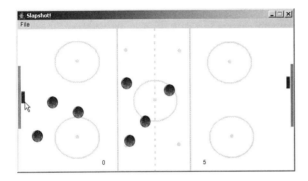

FIGURE 2.1   **The Slapshot! game in action.**

Here are some of the things this application does:

- Creates a sprite class (called `Puck`) whose objects can move and draw themselves on the screen as needed
- Animates the sprites, moving them around and bouncing them off both each other and the walls of the rink as needed
- Uses double buffering to avoid making the onscreen image flicker
- Uses the mouse to let you block pucks from your goal
- Uses a menu system to let users start and stop games, set the speed, and exit
- Displays a dialog box on command to let you set the speed
- Uses a separate thread to move the pucks around

So how do you create this game and get it running? The first step, as you might expect, is to build the rink.

Creating the Rink

Like the Aquarium application, where the tank was created in the constructor, the hockey rink is created in Slapshot!'s constructor. Some of this constructor will be familiar from the Aquarium project in the previous chapter, but there's a lot more going on here.

To let the user select options—starting a game, ending one, setting the speed, and so on—this application uses a menu system. After creating a menu bar, the code creates a File menu and stocks it with items such as Start, End, Set Speed..., and Exit. These menu items are connected to the code using an action listener, which means the Slapshot class must implement the ActionListener interface and add an actionPerformed method to handle menu selections. The menu items are added to a menu, which is then added to the menu bar, which in turn is added to the application itself, as shown here:

```
public class Slapshot extends Frame implements ActionListener, Runnable
{
        .
        .
        .

Slapshot()
{
    menubar = new MenuBar();

    menu1 = new Menu("File");

    menuitem0 = new MenuItem("Start");
    menu1.add(menuitem0);
    menuitem0.addActionListener(this);

    menuitem1 = new MenuItem("End");
    menu1.add(menuitem1);
    menuitem1.addActionListener(this);

    menuitem2 = new MenuItem("Set speed...");
    menu1.add(menuitem2);
    menuitem2.addActionListener(this);

    menuitem3 = new MenuItem("Exit");
    menu1.add(menuitem3);
    menuitem3.addActionListener(this);

    menubar.add(menu1);
    setMenuBar(menubar);
        .
        .
        .
```

The significant methods of the Menu class appear in Table 2.1, and the significant methods of the MenuItem class appear in Table 2.2.

TABLE 2.1   The Significant Methods of the *java.awt.Menu* **Class**

Method	Does This
MenuItem add(MenuItem mi)	Adds a new menu item to the current menu
void addSeparator()	Adds a line used to separate items within the menu
int countItems()	Deprecated. Use getItemCount() instead of this method
MenuItem getItem(int index)	Returns the item at the given index of this menu.
int getItemCount()	Returns the number of items currently in this menu
void insert(MenuItem menuitem, int index)	Places a menu item in this menu at the given position
boolean isTearOff()	Returns true if this menu is a tear-off menu
void remove(int index)	Deletes the menu item at the given index from this menu
void remove(MenuComponent item)	Deletes the given menu item from this menu
void removeAll()	Deletes all the items in this menu

TABLE 2.2   The Significant Methods of the *java.awt.MenuItem* **Class**

Method	Does This
void addActionListener (ActionListener l)	Adds an action listener so that you can get menu item selection events
void disable()	Deprecated. Use the setEnabled(boolean) method instead
void enable()	Deprecated. Use the setEnabled(boolean) method instead
void enable(boolean b)	Deprecated. Use the setEnabled(boolean) method instead
ActionListener[] getActionListeners()	Returns an array containing the action listeners listening to this menu item
String getLabel()	Returns the label of this menu item
MenuShortcut getShortcut()	Returns the MenuShortcut object for this menu item
boolean isEnabled()	Returns true if this menu item is enabled
void removeActionListener (ActionListener l)	Removes the given action listener, which means it will no longer get events from this menu item
void setEnabled(boolean b)	Specifies whether or not this menu item is enabled and therefore can be selected by the user
void setLabel(String label)	Sets the label for this menu item to the text you pass
void setShortcut(MenuShortcut s)	Sets a MenuShortcut object for this menu item

The constructor next adds a MouseListener and MouseMotionListener to the application to let the user move his blocker with the mouse, and it also implements the MouseListener and MouseMotionListener interfaces. In addition, it creates a dialog box of the OkCancelDialog class (discussed later in the chapter) that's used to let the user enter a new speed:

```
public class Slapshot extends Frame implements ActionListener,
➥MouseListener, MouseMotionListener, Runnable
    OkCancelDialog textDialog;
        .
        .
        .
{
    menubar = new MenuBar();
        .
        .
        .
    addMouseListener(this);
    addMouseMotionListener(this);

    textDialog = new OkCancelDialog(this,
        "Set speed (1-100)", true);
        .
        .
        .
```

Slapshot! also needs to display the user's score and the computer's score, and it'll use two AWT Label controls for that. After setting the AWT layout to null, you can use the label's setBounds method to place the labels where you want them:

```
    setLayout(null);

    label1 = new Label();
    label1.setText("0");
    label1.setBounds(180, 310, 20, 20);
    label1.setVisible(false);
    add(label1);

    label2 = new Label();
    label2.setText("0");
    label2.setBounds(400, 310, 20, 20);
    label2.setVisible(false);
    add(label2);
        .
        .
        .
```

You can see the methods of the Label class in Table 2.3.

TABLE 2.3   The Significant Methods of the *java.awt.Label* Class

Method	Does This
int getAlignment()	Returns the alignment setting of this label
String getText()	Returns the text currently stored in this label
void setAlignment(int alignment)	Sets the alignment of this label to the given value
void setText(String text)	Sets the text stored in this label to the text you pass

Next, a media tracker monitors the loading the images needed—the rink itself, the puck image, and the blocker image (a short upright bar). After that, the main window is sized and displayed:

```
tracker = new MediaTracker(this);
backGroundImage = Toolkit.getDefaultToolkit().
    getImage("rink.gif");
tracker.addImage(backGroundImage, 0);

gifImages[0] = Toolkit.getDefaultToolkit().
    getImage("puck.gif");
tracker.addImage(gifImages[0], 0);

gifImages[1] = Toolkit.getDefaultToolkit().
    getImage("blocker.gif");
tracker.addImage(gifImages[1], 0);

try {
    tracker.waitForID(0);
}catch (InterruptedException e) {
    System.out.println(e);
}

setTitle("Slapshot!");

setResizable(false);

setSize(backGroundImage.getWidth(this),
    backGroundImage.getHeight(this));

setVisible(true);
    .
    .
    .
```

Finally, the constructor creates a memory image for double buffering, creates and starts the new thread that will move the pucks, and adds a window listener to handle window-closing events:

```
memoryImage = createImage(getSize().width, getSize
    ().height);
memoryGraphics = memoryImage.getGraphics();

thread = new Thread(this);
thread.start();

this.addWindowListener(new WindowAdapter(){
    public void windowClosing(
        WindowEvent e){
            runOK = false;
            System.exit(0);
        }
    }
);
}
```

When the application starts, the constructor runs and the hockey rink appears; to make something actually *happen*, you have to select the Start item in the File menu.

Starting a Game

Because the code has connected the menu items to an action listener, the application will use a method named actionPerformed that's called when the user makes a menu selection. This method is passed an ActionEvent object, whose getSource method returns the menu item the user selected. When the user selects the Start item, menuitem0, the application should begin a new game by telling the new thread to get things started.

The standard technique for communicating with threads is with Boolean flags, and that's how you start a new game. In this case, the worker thread waits until a flag named stop is set to true before running the game. The user may have decided to start a new game in the middle of a current game, so the first order of business is to stop the current game if it's going and then redraw the empty hockey rink without any pucks—here's what that looks like when the user selects the Start menu item:

```
public void actionPerformed(ActionEvent e)
{
    if(e.getSource() == menuitem0){
        if(!stop){
            stop = true;
            repaint();
```

```
        }
        .
        .
        .
}
```

After stopping the current game (if there is one), the code calls a method named init (coming up next) to set up the new game. It also sets the stop flag to false to let the thread start running the game and then clears the scores in the two labels:

```
public void actionPerformed(ActionEvent e)
{
    if(e.getSource() == menuitem0){
        if(!stop){
            stop = true;
            repaint();
        }
        init();
        label1.setVisible(true);
        label2.setVisible(true);
        stop = false;
        label1.setText("0");
        label2.setText("0");
        yourScore = 0;
        theirScore = 0;
    }
    .
    .
    .
}
```

The init method creates a new vector of Puck objects, called pucks, stores the locations of the boundaries of the rink in a Rectangle object named edges, and creates all 12 pucks, numbered 0 to 11—just as the fish in Aquarium were stored in a vector named fishes, so the pucks in Slapshot! are stored in a vector named pucks:

CAUTION

If you're using Java 1.4 instead of Java 1.5, omit the "<Puck>" part in the declaration of pucks.

```
public class Slapshot extends Frame implements ActionListener,
➡MouseListener, MouseMotionListener, Runnable
{
    .
    .
    .
```

```
    Vector<Puck> pucks = new Vector<Puck>();

public void init()
{
    Point position, velocity;
    pucks = new Vector<Puck>();

    Rectangle edges = new Rectangle(10 + getInsets().left, getInsets().top,
        getSize().width - (getInsets().left + getInsets().right),
        getSize().height - (getInsets().top + getInsets().bottom));

    for (int loopIndex = 0; loopIndex < 12; loopIndex++){
        pucks.add(new Puck(gifImages[0], 0, maxVelocity, edges, this));

        try {
            Thread.sleep(20);
        }
        catch (Exception exp) {
            System.out.println(exp.getMessage());
        }
    }
    .
    .
    .
}
```

This method also creates two special pucks—the computer's blocker, which it uses to fend off pucks, and the user's blocker, which the user can move with the mouse. These blockers are also Puck objects, which makes the logic where the various pucks bounce off other pucks—and the blockers—much easier to write.

However, you'll need to give the blockers a different behavior than the pucks, because the computer moves one blocker and the user moves the other. For that reason, each Puck object has a type that you can set—standard pucks are type 0, the computer's blocker is type 1, and the user's is type 2. The difference is that blockers are not moveable by the puck-moving code, whereas pucks are, so the Puck method immovable returns false for pucks but true for blockers. This way, blockers are not inadvertently moved along with all the pucks. The type is passed to the Puck constructor as the second argument, like this, in init:

```
public void init()
{
    .
    .
    .
    for (int loopIndex = 0; loopIndex < 12; loopIndex++){
        pucks.add(new Puck(gifImages[0], 0, maxVelocity, edges, this));
```

```
    try {
        Thread.sleep(20);
    }
    catch (Exception exp) {
        System.out.println(exp.getMessage());
    }
}
```

```
    pucks.add(new Puck(gifImages[1], 1, maxVelocity, edges, this));
```

```
    pucks.add(new Puck(gifImages[1], 2, maxVelocity, edges, this));
}
```

This initializes all the sprites the application needs—12 pucks, the user's blocker, and the computer's blocker. After this initialization, the stop flag is set to false so the new thread can start animating these sprites.

In the run method, everything is enclosed in an if statement, waiting until stop is set to false (and like Aquarium, everything is enclosed inside a while loop that ends the whole application when the user closes the window or, in this case, selects the Exit item in the File menu):

```
public void run()
{
    Puck puck;
```

```
    while (runOK) {
        if(!stop){
            .
            .
            .
        }
    }
}
```

Moving Those Pucks

Handling the sprites here is a little different than in the Aquarium application, because when a puck slides into a goal, the user's score or the computer's score should be incremented and the puck should be taken out of action—which doesn't happen to fish. To make this happen, the code passes the position of both blockers to the method that moves each puck around, slide, and that method will return a value of 0 if the puck is still in play, -1 if it went into the computer's goal, and 1 if it went into the user's goal. Each Puck object also has a method named gone, which will return true if the puck is out of play (and therefore should not be moved or drawn).

The run method uses each puck's slide method to move the pucks and check to see if either the user's score or the computer's score needs to be incremented. When you call slide, you pass the rectangles specifying the location of both blockers (Pucks.elementAt(12) is the computer's blocker and Pucks.elementAt(13) is the user's) so that the method can see if a puck has hit a blocker. The slide method returns a value of 0 if the puck is still in play, -1 if it went into the computer's goal, and 1 if it went into the user's goal:

```
public void run()
{
    Puck puck;

    while (runOK) {
        if(!stop){

            int numberLeft;
            for (int loopIndex = 0; loopIndex < 12; loopIndex++){
                puck = (Puck)pucks.elementAt(loopIndex);

                if(puck.gone()){
                    continue;
                }

                retVal = puck.slide(pucks.elementAt
                    (13).rectangle, pucks.elementAt
                    (12).rectangle);

                numberLeft = 0;
                for (int loopIndex2 = 0; loopIndex2 < 12;
                    loopIndex2++){
                    if(!((Puck)pucks.elementAt(loopIndex2))
                        .gone()){
                        numberLeft++;
                    }
                }

                if(retVal < 0){
                    if(yourScore + theirScore + numberLeft == 11){
                        label1.setText(String.valueOf
                        (++yourScore));
                    }
                }

                if(retVal > 0){
                    if(yourScore + theirScore + numberLeft == 11){
                        label2.setText(String.valueOf
```

```
                    (++theirScore));
            }
        }
```

.
.
.

Getting the Pucks to Bounce Off Each Other

In the Aquarium application, one fish could swim behind another, but that doesn't work for multiple pucks on the same surface; instead, they're going to bounce off each other. Now that the pucks have all been moved, the run method works through them all to see if any pucks have hit each other. If so, it bounces them (and after the pucks have bounced, the run method checks again to see if they've hit a goal). Here's how the code checks whether one puck has struck another, taking special care not to move a blocker (that is, a Puck object whose immovable method returns true) if it was hit:

```
int struckPuck = -1;

for (int loopIndex3 = 0; loopIndex3 < 13;
    loopIndex3++){
    Puck testPuck = (Puck)pucks.elementAt
        (loopIndex3);

    if (puck == testPuck ¦¦ testPuck.gone()){
        continue;
    }

    if(puck.rectangle.intersects
        (testPuck.rectangle)){
        struckPuck = loopIndex3;
    }
}

if (struckPuck >= 0){
    Puck puck1 = (Puck)pucks.elementAt(struckPuck);
    Puck puck2 = (Puck)pucks.elementAt(loopIndex);

    if(puck2.immovable()){
        puck1.velocity.x = -puck1.velocity.x;
```

```
    retVal = puck1.slide(pucks.elementAt
        (13).rectangle, pucks.elementAt
        (12).rectangle);

    numberLeft = 0;
    for (int loopIndex4 = 0; loopIndex4 < 12;
        loopIndex4++){
        if(!((Puck)pucks.elementAt
            (loopIndex4)).gone()){
            numberLeft++;
        }
    }

    if(retVal < 0){
        if(yourScore + theirScore + numberLeft
            == 11){
            label1.setText(String.valueOf
                (++yourScore));
        }
    }

    if(retVal > 0){
        if(yourScore + theirScore + numberLeft
            == 11){
            label2.setText(String.valueOf
                (++theirScore));
        }
    }

} else if(puck1.immovable()){
    puck2.velocity.x = -puck2.velocity.x;

    retVal = puck2.slide(pucks.elementAt(13).
        rectangle, pucks.elementAt
        (12).rectangle);

    numberLeft = 0;
    for (int loopIndex5 = 0; loopIndex5 < 12;
        loopIndex5++){
        if(!((Puck)pucks.elementAt
            (loopIndex5)).gone()){
            numberLeft++;
        }
    }
```

```
        if(retVal < 0){
            if(yourScore + theirScore + numberLeft
                == 11){
                label1.setText(String.valueOf
                    (++yourScore));
            }
        }

        if(retVal > 0){
            if(yourScore + theirScore + numberLeft
                == 11){
                label2.setText(String.valueOf
                    (++theirScore));
            }
        }
    }
    else {
        retVal = puck1.slide(pucks.elementAt
            (13).rectangle, pucks.elementAt
            (12).rectangle);

        numberLeft = 0;

        for (int loopIndex6 = 0; loopIndex6 < 12;
            loopIndex6++){
            if(!((Puck)pucks.elementAt(loopIndex6))
                .gone()){
                numberLeft++;
            }
        }

        if(retVal < 0){
            if(yourScore + theirScore + numberLeft
                == 11){
                label1.setText(String.valueOf
                    (++yourScore));
            }
        }

        if(retVal > 0){
            if(yourScore + theirScore + numberLeft
                == 11){
            label2.setText(String.valueOf
                (++theirScore));
```

```
            }
        }

    retVal = puck2.slide(pucks.elementAt
        (13).rectangle, pucks.elementAt
        (12).rectangle);

    numberLeft = 0;
    for (int loopIndex7 = 0; loopIndex7 < 12;
        loopIndex7++){
        if(!((Puck)pucks.elementAt
            (loopIndex7)).gone()){
            numberLeft++;
        }
    }

    if(retVal < 0){
        if(yourScore + theirScore + numberLeft
            == 11){
            label1.setText(String.valueOf
                (++yourScore));
        }
    }

    if(retVal > 0){
        if(yourScore + theirScore + numberLeft
            == 11){
            label2.setText(String.valueOf
                (++theirScore));
        }
    }
        }
    }
```

This code moves all the pucks around each time the all-encompassing while loop iterates. But what about the blockers? How do they move? To start, the computer moves its own blocker around by itself.

How the Computer Blocks Pucks

The computer is supposed to move its blocker to intercept as many of the pucks as it can before they hit its goal. Here's how that works—if any puck is on track to hit the computer's goal, it calculates how long the puck will take to get there. It then moves to intercept the one that will hit the goal first. This is how the code calculates the next Y coordinate, impactY, at which a puck will hit the computer's goal:

```
int lowestTime = 10000;
int impactY = -1;

for (int loopIndex3 = 0; loopIndex3 < 12;
    loopIndex3++){
    Puck movingPuck = (Puck)pucks.elementAt
        (loopIndex3);
    Rectangle r = movingPuck.rectangle;
    Point mPosition = new Point(r.x, r.y);
    Point mVelocity = movingPuck.velocity;

    if(mVelocity.x > 0 && !movingPuck.gone()){
        int yHit = (mVelocity.y / mVelocity.x) *
        (backGroundImage.getWidth(this) -
            mPosition.x) + mPosition.y;

        if(yHit > 115 && yHit < 223){
            int time = (backGroundImage.getWidth
                (this) - mPosition.x)
                / mVelocity.x;
            if(time <= lowestTime){
                impactY = yHit;
            }
        }
    }
}
```

If the variable impactY is greater than zero, it holds the location where the next puck impact will be on the computer's goal. You use the slide method to move objects around in this game, but you wouldn't want the blockers to be moved around at random, like the pucks. Instead, there's a special version of the slide method built into the Puck class that lets you simply pass a new Y location, and it'll move the Puck object to that position. This is the version you'll use to move the blockers with. To make sure the computer's blocker doesn't have an unfair advantage, the code restricts its movements to 40 pixels at a time, like this:

```
if(impactY > 0){
    Puck block = pucks.elementAt(12);
    int blockPosition = block.rectangle.y;

    if(blockPosition < impactY){
        block.slide(Math.min(blockPosition +
            40, impactY));
    } else {
```

```
                block.slide(Math.max(blockPosition -
                    40, impactY));
            }
            repaint();
        }
        label2.setText(String.valueOf(theirScore));
    }
}
```

After all the pucks and the computer's blocker have been moved, and after the scores have been updated, the run method calls the repaint method to update the screen and then sleeps for a number of milliseconds until the next iteration. The speed variable, set to a value from 1 to 100, determines how long the code sleeps between iterations. When the application starts, the speed is set to 50, but the user can change that as he likes using the File menu's Set Speed... item—the game is very hard to beat at 95, for example. Here's what the repainting and sleeping code looks like at the very end of the run method:

```
repaint();
try {
    Thread.sleep(speed);
}
catch (InterruptedException e) {
    System.out.println(e.getMessage());
}
        }
    }
}
```

The repaint method calls the update method, and there you simply need to draw the background image and the pucks in the memory image—you draw the pucks with their drawPuckImage method—and then copy the result to the screen:

```
public void update(Graphics g)
{
    memoryGraphics.drawImage(backGroundImage, 0, 0, this);

    for (int loopIndex = 0; loopIndex < pucks.size(); loopIndex++){
        if(!stop){
            ((Puck)pucks.elementAt(loopIndex)).drawPuckImage
                (memoryGraphics);
        }
    }

    g.drawImage(memoryImage, 0, 0, this);
}
```

How the User Blocks Pucks

The computer moves its own blocker around, but the user is responsible for moving his blocker using the mouse. To handle the mouse, you'll need to catch mouse press, mouse drag, and mouse release events, which are handled by implementing the methods of the MouseListener and MouseMotionListener interfaces, as you've already seen.

When the user presses the mouse, Slapshot! checks to see if the mouse is over his blocker, and if so, sets a Boolean flag named dragging to true, which means that from then on the user can drag his blocker simply by moving the mouse.

When the user presses the mouse, the mousePressed method is passed a MouseEvent object, and you can use the getX and getY methods of that object to determine where the mouse was when it was pressed. The code also stores the offset at which the user clicked the blocker so that when he starts dragging the blocker, it doesn't simply assume that the mouse pointer is at location (0, 0) in the blocker, which would make the blocker's image jump when the user started dragging:

```
public class Slapshot extends Frame implements ActionListener,
➡MouseListener, MouseMotionListener, Runnable
{
    .
    .
    .

public void mousePressed(MouseEvent e)
{
    Rectangle r1 = pucks.elementAt(13).rectangle;
    if(r1.contains(new Point(e.getX(), e.getY()))){
```

REAL-WORLD SCENARIO

Worker Threads and User-Interface Threads

The Aquarium project used multithreaded sprites, but the Slapshot! game is where multi-threading really shines. In the early days of window-oriented programming, you didn't have access to threads, which made programming the user interface and the main program logic separately nearly impossible to do.

In an application such as Slapshot!, that would be a real problem, because this game needs to watch what you're doing with the mouse at the same time as it moves the pucks around. Programmers were often supremely frustrated trying to write visually intensive applications like this because as they were handling the mouse and intercepting mouse events, the rest of the application was on hold, and if things were supposed to be happening—such as pucks zinging around—a lot of flicker was caused.

continues

```
        offsetX = e.getX() - r1.x;
        offsetY = e.getY() - r1.y;
        dragging = true;
    }
}
```

You can see the methods of the `MouseEvent` class in Table 2.4.

TABLE 2.4   The Significant Methods of the `java.awt.event.MouseEvent` **Class**

Method	Does This
`int getButton()`	Returns which mouse button was pressed or released
`int getClickCount()`	Returns the number of mouse clicks that happened
`Point getPoint()`	Returns a `Point` object that holds the X and Y coordinates of the mouse event
`int getX()`	Returns the X coordinate of the mouse event
`int getY()`	Returns the Y coordinate of the mouse event

When the user releases the mouse, the `dragging` flag is set to `false`:

```
public void mouseReleased(MouseEvent e)
{
        dragging = false;
}
```

When the user drags the mouse, Java calls the `mouseDragged` method with the new mouse location. In this method, all you have to do is to pass the new Y location of the blocker to its `slide` method and repaint the game to update that blocker's location:

REAL-WORLD SCENARIO   *continued*

That's obviously a bad problem. Programmers found that while their applications were supposed to be doing some real work behind the scenes, the user interface suffered—or, if the user interface got the time it needed, the crucial background work was neglected.

This is one of the reasons Java was popular from the very beginning—since the JDK 1.0, it has offered programmers the ability to work with threads. You can launch a new thread to handle background work, such as moving pucks around, while letting the main thread deal with the user interface (or the other way around). And programmers soon found that the way threads were implemented in Java made them a lot easier to work with than in other window-oriented languages, where access to the user interface from a background thread was problematic and often caused the entire application to freeze.

Slapshot! is a good example of the need for threads in window-oriented applications. While you're moving around your blocker with the mouse, the application should still be able to move the pucks around and be able to draw them on the screen. That works just as you'd expect in Java.

```
public void mouseDragged(MouseEvent e)
{
    if(dragging){
        int newY = e.getY() - offsetY;

        pucks.elementAt(13).slide(newY);
        repaint();
    }
}
```

That's it. This gets all the blockers and all the pucks moving. How fast the pucks actually move depends on the `speed` variable, which the user can set. But how can you read the user's new setting? For that, the application uses a dialog box.

Setting the Speed

To let the user set the value in the `speed` variable, Slapshot! uses the dialog box shown in Figure 2.2; the user can even open and use this dialog box when the game is playing.

FIGURE 2.2   The Slapshot! application's dialog box.

This dialog box is opened when the user selects the Set Speed... menu item, `menuitem2`. In the `actionPerformed` method, this item simply displays the dialog box `textDialog`, an object of the `OkCancelDialog` class that was created in Slapshot!'s constructor. The user enters the new speed in the text field in the dialog box, which Slapshot! can recover using the dialog box's data member, converting the text the user enters to an integer using the `Integer.parseInt` method:

```
public class Slapshot extends Frame implements ActionListener,
➡MouseListener, MouseMotionListener, Runnable
{
        .
        .
        .
    OkCancelDialog textDialog;

public void actionPerformed(ActionEvent e)
{
```

```
        .
        .
        .
        if(e.getSource() == menuitem2){
            textDialog.setVisible(true);
            if(!textDialog.data.equals("")){
                int newSpeed = Integer.parseInt(textDialog.data);
                newSpeed = 101 - newSpeed;
                if(newSpeed >= 1 && newSpeed <= 100){
                    speed = newSpeed;
                }
            }
        }
        .
        .
        .
}
```

So how do you create the OkCancelDialog dialog class? You can do that by extending the Java Dialog class when you create the OkCancelDialog class and by implementing the ActionListener interface so you can use clickable OK and Cancel buttons in the dialog box:

```
class OkCancelDialog extends Dialog implements ActionListener
{
    .
    .
    .
}
```

The AWT dialog boxes are based on the Dialog class, and you can see the significant methods of the Dialog class in Table 2.5.

TABLE 2.5   The Significant Methods of the *java.awt.Dialog* **Class**

Method	Does This
String getTitle()	Gets the title of the dialog
void hide()	**Deprecated. Use the** Component.setVisible (boolean) **method instead**
boolean isModal()	**Returns** true **if this dialog is modal; returns** false **otherwise**
boolean isResizable()	**Returns** true **if this dialog may be resized by the user**
void setModal(boolean b)	**Specifies whether this dialog is modal**
void setResizable(boolean resizable)	**Specifies whether this dialog may be resized by the user**
void setTitle(String title)	**Specifies the title of this dialog**
void show()	**Deprecated. Use the** Component.setVisible (boolean) **method instead**

This dialog box sports an OK button, a Cancel button, and a text field where the user can enter the new game speed. Here's how those controls are set up:

```
class OkCancelDialog extends Dialog implements ActionListener
{
    Button ok, cancel;
    TextField text;
    public String data;

    OkCancelDialog(Frame hostFrame, String title, boolean dModal)
    {
        super(hostFrame, title, dModal);
        setSize(280, 100);
        setLayout(new FlowLayout());
        text = new TextField(30);
        add(text);
        ok = new Button("OK");
        add(ok);
        ok.addActionListener((ActionListener)this);
        cancel = new Button("Cancel");
        add(cancel);
        cancel.addActionListener(this);
        data = new String("");
    }
        .
        .
        .
```

You can see the significant methods of the Button class in Table 2.6 and the significant methods of the TextField class in Table 2.7.

TABLE 2.6   The Significant Methods of the *java.awt.Button* Class

Method	Does This
void addActionListener(ActionListener l)	**Adds the given action listener to the button so the listener will be notified of button events**
ActionListener[] getActionListeners()	**Returns an array of all action listeners that listen to this button**
String getLabel()	**Returns the text in the label of this button**
void removeActionListener(ActionListener l)	**Removes the given action listener, which means that it will not get events from this button**
void setLabel(String label)	**Sets the button's label to the string you pass this method**

TABLE 2.7   The Significant Methods of the *java.awt.TextField* Class

Method	Does This
`void addActionListener(ActionListener l)`	**Adds the given action listener to the text field so the listener will be notified of text field events**
`ActionListener[] getActionListeners()`	**Returns an array of all action listeners that listen to this text field**
`int getColumns()`	**Returns the number of columns currently in this text field**
`Dimension getMinimumSize()`	**Returns the minimum size allowed for this text field**
`Dimension getMinimumSize(int columns)`	**Returns the minimum size of a text field that has the number of columns you pass to this method**
`Dimension getPreferredSize()`	**Returns the text field's preferred size**
`Dimension getPreferredSize(int columns)`	**Returns the text field's preferred size, given the number of columns you pass to this method**
`Dimension minimumSize()`	**Deprecated. Use the** getMinimumSize **method instead**
`Dimension minimumSize(int columns)`	**Deprecated. Use the** getMinimumSize(int) **method instead**
`Dimension preferredSize()`	**Deprecated. Use the** getPreferredSize **method instead.**
`Dimension preferredSize(int columns)`	**Deprecated. Use the** getPreferredSize(int) **method instead.**
`void removeActionListener(ActionListener l)`	**Removes the given action listener, which means that it will not get events from this text field**
`void setColumns(int columns)`	**Sets the text field's number of columns**
`void setText(String t)`	**Sets the text that this text field will display**

When the user clicks the OK button, the dialog box stores the text from the text field in the member named data, or it stores an empty string in data if the user clicks the Cancel button:

```
public void actionPerformed(ActionEvent event)
{
    if(event.getSource() == ok){
        data = text.getText();
    } else {
        data = "";
    }
    setVisible(false);
}
}
```

Okay, you've gotten everything working now—except the pucks themselves, with their slide and drawPuckImage methods. And that's coming up next.

Creating the Pucks

The pucks are represented by the sprite class Puck. The constructor of this class is responsible for storing all the information passed to it—the image for the puck, the type of puck (0 for a standard puck, 1 for the computer's blocker, and 2 for the user's blocker), the rectangle named edges corresponding to the dimensions of the rink, and so on. The constructor also sets up the puck's (random) initial position and velocity. Here's what the Puck constructor looks like:

```
public Puck(Image image1, int type, int maxVelocity,
    Rectangle edges, Component rink)
{
    this.rink = rink;
    this.image1 = image1;
    if (type > 0){
        doNotMove = true;
    }
    this.maxVelocity = maxVelocity;
    this.edges = edges;

    random = new Random(System.currentTimeMillis());

    if(type == 0){
        location = new Point(100 + (Math.abs(random.nextInt())
            % 300), 100 + (Math.abs(100 + random.nextInt()) %
            100));

        this.velocity = new Point(random.nextInt() % maxVelocity,
            random.nextInt() % maxVelocity);

        while(velocity.x == 0){
            velocity.x = random.nextInt(maxVelocity / 2)
                - maxVelocity / 2;
        }
    }

    if(type == 1){
        location = new Point(((Slapshot)rink).backGroundImage
            .getWidth(rink) - 18, ((Slapshot)rink).backGroundImage.getHeight
            (rink)/2);
        this.velocity = new Point(0, 0);
```

```
    }

    if(type == 2){
        location = new Point(10,
            ((Slapshot)rink).backGroundImage.getHeight(rink)/2);
        this.velocity = new Point(0, 0);
    }

    this.rectangle = new Rectangle(location.x, location.y,
        image1.getWidth(rink), image1.getHeight(rink));
}
```

The major method of the Puck class is slide, which moves the puck around. Every so often, the puck should change direction as well. The slide method is also responsible for checking whether this puck has made it to a goal, and if so, setting the appropriate return value and taking the puck out of action by setting its outOfAction member variable to true. Here's how the slide method works; first, it might change the puck's current velocity:

```
public int slide(Rectangle blocker, Rectangle blocker2)
{
    Point position = new Point(rectangle.x, rectangle.y);
    int returnValue = 0;

    if (doNotMove){
        return returnValue;
    }

    if(random.nextInt(100) <= 1){
        velocity.x += random.nextInt() % maxVelocity;

        velocity.x = Math.min(velocity.x, maxVelocity);
        velocity.x = Math.max(velocity.x, -maxVelocity);

        while(velocity.x == 0){
            velocity.x = random.nextInt(maxVelocity / 2)
            - maxVelocity / 2;
        }

        velocity.y += random.nextInt() % maxVelocity / 2;

        velocity.y = Math.min(velocity.y, maxVelocity / 2);
        velocity.y = Math.max(velocity.y, -(maxVelocity / 2));
    }
    .
    .
    .
```

Then this method updates the puck's position by adding the velocity to it:

```
position.x += velocity.x;
position.y += velocity.y;
.
.
.
```

The next step is to see if the puck has hit a goal, in which case the puck should be taken out of action and the user's score or the computer's score incremented:

```
if (position.x < edges.x + 5) {

    if(position.y > 120 && position.y < 225){
        if(!rectangle.intersects(blocker)){
            returnValue = 1;
            outOfAction = true;
            return returnValue;
        }
    }
    position.x = edges.x;

    if(velocity.x > 0){
        velocity.x = -6;
    }else{
        velocity.x = 6;
    }
}else if ((position.x + rectangle.width)
    > (edges.x + edges.width - 5)){
    if(position.y > 120 && position.y < 225){
        if(!rectangle.intersects(blocker2)){
            returnValue = -1;
            outOfAction = true;
            return returnValue;
        }
    }
    position.x = edges.x + edges.width - rectangle.width;

    if(velocity.x > 0){
        velocity.x = -6;
    }else{
        velocity.x = 6;
    }
}
```

```
    if (position.y < edges.y){
        position.y = edges.y;
        velocity.y = -velocity.y;

    }else if ((position.y + rectangle.height)
        > (edges.y + edges.height)){
        position.y = edges.y + edges.height -
            rectangle.height;
        velocity.y = -velocity.y;
    }

    this.rectangle = new Rectangle(position.x, position.y,
        image1.getWidth(rink), image1.getHeight(rink));
    return returnValue;
}
```

There's also a slide method in the Puck class for use with the blockers that lets you set their Y position directly, no futzing around with random numbers needed. Here's what that method looks like, short and sweet:

```
public void slide(int y)
{
    rectangle.y = y;
}
```

There are also two short convenience methods that return information about the puck—gone, which returns true if the puck is out of action, and immovable, which indicates that the puck is actually a blocker that should not be moved like other pucks:

```
public boolean gone()
{
    return outOfAction;
}

public boolean immovable()
{
    return doNotMove;
}
```

All that's left is the drawPuckImage method, which draws the puck in the Graphics object passed to this method—unless that puck is out of action:

```
public void drawPuckImage(Graphics g)
{
    if(!outOfAction){
        g.drawImage(image1, rectangle.x,
```

```
            rectangle.y, rink);
    }
}
```

That's it. This completes the entire Slapshot! application, and it's ready to go.

NOTE

Download the complete source code for the Slapshot! project, Slapshot.java, and the associated image files at the Sams website. All you need to do is to compile it as discussed next and run it to get it going.

If you're using Java 1.5, compile Slapshot! this way (note that if javac isn't in your path, you'll have to preface it with the correct path, something like c:\jdk1.5\bin\javac in Windows):

```
%javac Slapshot.java
```

Then make sure the needed image files (rink.gif, puck.gif, and blocker.gif) are in the same directory as Slapshot.class and run the application this way (preface the java command with the correct path, if needed):

```
%java Slapshot
```

The results appear in Figure 2.1, shown earlier in the chapter.

If you're using Java 1.4, follow the same steps, but make sure you've changed the line

```
Vector<Puck> pucks = new Vector<Puck>();
```

at the beginning of the code, to this:

```
Vector pucks = new Vector();
```

Also, change the line

```
Pucks = new Vector<Puck>();
```

at the beginning of the init method, to this:

```
Pucks = new Vector();
```

Now you're ready to hit the ice.

Conclusion

This chapter presented Slapshot!, a fast-paced hockey game where the computer plays against you, the user. Slapshot! sends a dozen pucks whizzing around a hockey rink, and it's your job to keep them out of your goal while the computer tries to do the same with its goal. The pucks bounce off the walls of the rink, each other, and the blockers in front of the two goals. The computer player is not infallible by any means, but when those speeds get up there, it's a hard player to beat.

This game built on the Aquarium project of the previous chapter, adding a lot of interactive power. It uses many of the techniques you saw in the Aquarium project, such as starting a worker thread, using double buffering to avoid flickering, handing images with media trackers, and so on.

Slapshot! has a menu system to let the user start and stop a game, as well as to exit the game, using Boolean flags to communicate with the worker thread. In the old days, you could use the suspend, resume, and stop methods to handle threads, but these days, the Java people want you to interact with the thread using flags.

The user can also use a menu item, Set Speed..., to set the speed (1 to 100) at which the pucks move. When the user selects that item, the application displays a dialog box with a text field and OK and Cancel buttons. The user can enter the new speed, and if the value entered is between 1 and 100, inclusive, the application uses that new speed.

Slapshot! also intercepts mouse events—mouse pressed, released, and dragged events—in order to let the user move his blocker at will (as long it's in the Y direction). There's a lot of Java power here; all in all, Slapshot! is a cool game that'll keep users on their toes, fending off those pucks.

CHAPTER 3
The Graphicizer Image-Editing and Conversion Tool

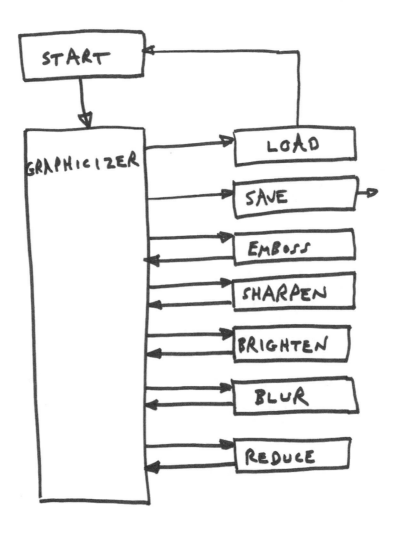

The Graphicizer application.

The Graphicizer is a very cool image-handling tool that lets you load in images, manipulate them, and save them back to disk. It'll convert image formats too—you can use the Graphicizer to load in JPEG, PNG, or GIF images and then store them in either JPEG or PNG format. When an image is loaded, you can convert it to an embossed image with the click of a button, or you can sharpen it, brighten it, blur it, or reduce its size—all using Java. You can even undo the most recent change.

Not bad.

You can see the Graphicizer at work in Figure 3.1, where it has loaded in a sample image that comes with the book's code, image.gif. To emboss this image, sharpen it, or perform other actions, all you've got to do is click a button.

FIGURE 3.1   **The Graphicizer tool at work.**

Here are some of the things this application does:

- Reads in JPG, PNG, or GIF files
- Saves images in JPG or PNG format
- Lets you work with images, pixel by pixel
- Embosses images
- Sharpens images
- Brighten images
- Blurs images
- Changes image size
- Undoes the most recent change on request

How do you create this application and get it running? As you'd expect, the first step is to create the main Graphicizer window, which acts as a canvas to display the image under design, as you see in Figure 3.1.

Creating the Graphicizer Window

As with the previous windowed application in this book, the window the application draws is created in the application's constructor. And like the previous applications so far, this one is based on the Frame class.

Here's what Graphicizer's main method and constructor looks like; the constructor creates the window:

```
public class Graphicizer extends Frame implements ActionListener
{
    BufferedImage bufferedImage, bufferedImageBackup;
    Image image;
    Menu menu;
    MenuBar menubar;
    MenuItem menuitem1, menuitem2, menuitem3, menuitem4;
    Button button1, button2, button3, button4, button5;
    FileDialog dialog;

    public static void main(String[] args)
    {
        new Graphicizer();
    }

    public Graphicizer()
    {
        setSize(400, 360);

        setTitle("The Graphicizer");

        setVisible(true);

        this.addWindowListener(new WindowAdapter(){
            public void windowClosing(
                WindowEvent e){
                    System.exit(0);
                }
            }
        );
        .
        .
        .
```

It adds the buttons the applications uses as drawing tools, which you can see in Figure 3.1:

```
button1 = new Button("Emboss");
button1.setBounds(30, getHeight() - 50, 60, 20);
add(button1);
button1.addActionListener(this);

button2 = new Button("Sharpen");
button2.setBounds(100, getHeight() - 50, 60, 20);
add(button2);
button2.addActionListener(this);

button3 = new Button("Brighten");
button3.setBounds(170, getHeight() - 50, 60, 20);
add(button3);
button3.addActionListener(this);

button4 = new Button("Blur");
button4.setBounds(240, getHeight() - 50, 60, 20);
add(button4);
button4.addActionListener(this);

button5 = new Button("Reduce");
button5.setBounds(310, getHeight() - 50, 60, 20);
add(button5);
button5.addActionListener(this);
    .
    .
    .
```

It also adds a File menu with the items Open..., Save As..., Undo, and Exit:

```
menubar = new MenuBar();

menu = new Menu("File");

menuitem1 = new MenuItem("Open...");
menu.add(menuitem1);
menuitem1.addActionListener(this);

menuitem2 = new MenuItem("Save As...");
menu.add(menuitem2);
menuitem2.addActionListener(this);
```

```
menuitem3 = new MenuItem("Undo");
menu.add(menuitem3);
menuitem3.addActionListener(this);

menuitem4 = new MenuItem("Exit");
menu.add(menuitem4);
menuitem4.addActionListener(this);

menubar.add(menu);

setMenuBar(menubar);
    .
    .
    .
```

Besides the menu and button system, the constructor also creates a `FileDialog` object, which will be used to display a File dialog box when the user wants to open or save files:

```
dialog = new FileDialog(this, "File Dialog");
}
```

And that's exactly how the user starts—by opening a file and displaying it in the Graphicizer.

Opening an Image File

All the user needs to do to open an image file is to use the File menu's Open... item. When the user selects that item, the `actionPerformed` method is called. Then, after making sure the Open... item was selected, the code sets the dialog object's mode to `FileDialog.LOAD` and makes the dialog box visible with the `dialog.setVisible(true)` call:

```
public void actionPerformed(ActionEvent event)
{
    if(event.getSource() == menuitem1){

        dialog.setMode(FileDialog.LOAD);

        dialog.setVisible(true);
        .
        .
        .
```

Setting the File dialog box's mode to `FileDialog.LOAD` (the only other option is `FileDialog.SAVE`) makes the dialog box display the File Open dialog box you see in Figure 3.2.

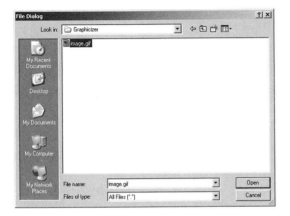

FIGURE 3.2   Opening a file.

You can see the significant methods of the FileDialog class in Table 3.1.

TABLE 3.1   The Significant Methods of the *java.awt.FileDialog* **Class**

Method	Does This
String getDirectory()	Returns the directory selected by the user
String getFile()	Returns the file selected by the user
FilenameFilter getFilenameFilter()	Returns the filename filter used by this File dialog box
int getMode()	Returns the dialog box's mode, which sets whether this File dialog box is to be used in reading a file or saving a file
void setDirectory(String dir)	Sets the directory used by this File dialog box when it starts to the given directory
void setFile(String file)	Sets the selected file used by this File dialog box to the given file
void setFilenameFilter(FilenameFilter filter)	Sets the filename filter for the dialog box to the given filter
void setMode(int mode)	Specifies the mode of the File dialog box, either reading or writing

If the user selects a file to open, the dialog box's getFile method will return the filename, and the getDirectory method will return the directory the file is in. Opening a file is a sensitive operation, so everything's enclosed in a try/catch block here. The code creates a File object corresponding to the image file the user wants to open as the first stage in actually opening that file:

```
public void actionPerformed(ActionEvent event)
{
```

```
if(event.getSource() == menuitem1){

    dialog.setMode(FileDialog.LOAD);

    dialog.setVisible(true);

    try{
        if(!dialog.getFile().equals("")){
            File input = new File(dialog.getDirectory()
                + dialog.getFile());
            .
            .
            .
        }
    catch(Exception e){
        System.out.println(e.getMessage());
    }
    .
    .
    .
}
```

You can see the significant methods of the `File` class in Table 3.2.

TABLE 3.2   The Significant Methods of the *`java.io.File`* Class

Method	Does This
boolean canRead()	Returns `true` if you can read the file specified by this `File` object
boolean canWrite()	Returns `true` if you can modify the file specified by this `File` object
boolean createNewFile()	Creates a new, empty file corresponding to this file and path—if (and only if) that file does not already exist
boolean delete()	Deletes the file or directory specified by this `File` object
boolean exists()	Returns `true` if the file or directory specified by this `File` object exists
File getAbsoluteFile()	Returns the absolute form of this file's path and name
String getAbsolutePath()	Returns the absolute form of this file's path
String getName()	Returns the name of the file (or directory) specified by this File object
String getPath()	Returns the path of the file (or directory) specified by this `File` object
boolean isAbsolute()	Returns `true` if the file's pathname, as stored in this `File` object, is absolute

TABLE 3.2   Continued

Method	Does This
boolean isDirectory()	Returns true if the file referred to by this File object is a directory
boolean isFile()	Returns true if the file referred to by this File object is a standard file
boolean isHidden()	Returns true if the file referred to by this File object is a hidden file
long lastModified()	Returns the time at which the file was last modified
long length()	Returns the length of the file
boolean mkdir()	Makes a directory corresponding to the name and path given in this File object
boolean renameTo(File dest)	Renames the file to the name and path given by the File object you pass
boolean setLastModified(long time)	Sets the last-modified time of this file or directory
boolean setReadOnly()	Makes the file (or directory) given by this File object read-only
URI toURI()	Returns a URI that represents the file given by this File object
URL toURL()	Returns a URL that represents the file given by this File object

To read in the image file, the application uses the relatively new Java ImageIO class. All you have to do is to pass the File object to the ImageIO class's read method, which reads in the file (unless there's an error, which will be caught in the catch block) and returns a BufferedImage object:

```
public void actionPerformed(ActionEvent event)
{
    if(event.getSource() == menuitem1){

        dialog.setMode(FileDialog.LOAD);

        dialog.setVisible(true);

        try{
            if(!dialog.getFile().equals("")){
                File input = new File(dialog.getDirectory()
                    + dialog.getFile());
                bufferedImage = ImageIO.read(input);
                .
                .
                .

        }
```

```
        catch(Exception e){
            System.out.println(e.getMessage());
        }
            .
            .
            .
    }
```

You can see the significant methods of the ImageIO class in Table 3.3.

TABLE 3.3   **The Significant Methods of the** *javax.imageio.ImageIO* **Class**

Method	Does This
static String[] getReaderFormatNames()	Returns an array holding all the format names the current readers can read
static String[] getReaderMIMETypes()	Returns an array holding all the MIME types the current readers can read
static String[] getWriterFormatNames()	Returns an array holding all the format names the current writers can write
static String[] getWriterMIMETypes()	Returns an array holding all the MIME types the current writers can write
static BufferedImage read(File input)	Reads in a file as specified by the File object and returns a BufferedImage object
static BufferedImage read(ImageInputStream stream)	Reads in a file as specified by the ImageInputStream object and returns a BufferedImage object
static BufferedImage read(InputStream input)	Reads in a file as specified by the InputStream object and returns a BufferedImage object
static BufferedImage read(URL input)	Reads in a file as specified by the URL object and returns a BufferedImage object
static boolean write(RenderedImage im, String formatName, File output)	Writes an image using a RenderedImage object, a format name string, and a File object
static boolean write(RenderedImage im, String formatName, ImageOutputStream output)	Writes an image using a RenderedImage object, a format name string, and an ImageOutputStream object
static boolean write(RenderedImage im, String formatName, OutputStream output)	Writes an image using a RenderedImage object, a format name string, and an OutputStream object

Why does the Graphicizer use `BufferedImage` objects instead of `Image` objects? Primarily because the `ImageIO` class uses them instead of `Image` objects—and the `ImageIO` class gives you the functionality you need in an application such as Graphicizer. Using that class, you can read in files in various formats (GIF, PNG, and JPEG) and save them in various formats (PNG and JPEG).

Using the `Toolkit` class's image-handling methods you saw in the Aquarium and Slapshot! applications, you can only read in files; not only can you *not* change their format when you save them, you can't even save them in the first place. You can see the significant methods of the `BufferedImage` class in Table 3.4.

TABLE 3.4   The Significant Methods of the *java.awt.image.BufferedImage* Class

Method	Does This
`WritableRaster copyData(WritableRaster outRaster)`	Copies a rectangular region of the `BufferedImage` to the given `WritableRaster`
`Graphics2D createGraphics()`	Returns a new `Graphics2D` object, which you can use to draw in this `BufferedImage`
`ImageCapabilities getCapabilities` `(GraphicsConfiguration gc)`	Returns the imaging capabilities of this `BufferedImage` object
`ColorModel getColorModel()`	Returns the color model used by this `BufferedImage` object
`Raster getData(Rectangle rect)`	Returns a region of the `BufferedImage` object
`Graphics getGraphics()`	Returns a `Graphics2D` object, which you can use to draw in this `BufferedImage`

REAL-WORLD SCENARIO

Why Can't You Write GIF Files?

The `ImageIO` class is all about reading in images and writing them out again. You can read in GIF, PNG, and JPEG files, and write out PNG and JPEG files. What's missing from this equation?

By default, you can't use the `ImageIO` class to write GIF files. Why is that? It turns out that the people responsible for the GIF format began requiring software that uses some patented aspects of GIF formatting to have a license, and that's quite probably the reason.

Entering widespread use in about 1987, the GIF (Graphics Interchange Format) image format became very popular. At the end of 1994, however, CompuServe Inc. and Unisys Corporation said that developers would have to pay a license fee to be able to use technology that had been patented by Unisys supporting the GIF format.

Among developers, this caused quite a controversy. Programmers whose software could use GIF files were unsure of their legal standing (note, incidentally, that this sidebar is not intended as a substitute for legal advice!), and loud discussions among developers ensued.

continues

TABLE 3.4 Continued

Method	Does This
`int getHeight()`	Returns the height of the `BufferedImage`
`int getHeight(ImageObserver observer)`	Returns the height of the image in this `BufferedImage` object
`int getMinX()`	Returns the minimum X coordinate of the image in this `BufferedImage` object
`int getMinY()`	Returns the minimum Y coordinate of the image in this `BufferedImage` object
`WritableRaster getRaster()`	Returns the `WritableRaster` object used by this `BufferedImage` object
`int getRGB(int x, int y)`	Returns a pixel specified by the X and Y coordinates using the default RGB color model (`TYPE_INT_ARGB`) and default sRGB colorspace
`int[] getRGB(int startX, int startY, int w, int h, int[] rgbArray, int offset, int scansize)`	Returns an array of pixels using the default RGB color model (`TYPE_INT_ARGB`) and default sRGB colorspace
`BufferedImage getSubimage(int x, int y, int w, int h)`	Returns a section of the image specified by the given rectangular region
`int getTransparency()`	Returns the transparency setting of this `BufferedImage` object

REAL-WORLD SCENARIO *continued*

People whose software relied on GIF formatting had to deal with this issue, and in time, some developers began to move away from that format.

Some of the patents have begun to expire now (see http://www.unisys.com/about_unisys/lzw), but a number of developers are still wary. Although Sun hasn't said so, this is probably the reason why you can't write GIF format files with the `ImageIO` class by default (various third parties have provided plug-ins that let you do so). You can determine which readable and writeable formats can be used by calling the `ImageIO.getReaderFormatNames` and `ImageIO.getWriterFormatNames` methods.

Alternatives, such as Portable Network Graphics (PNG) format, appeared in the web community and are becoming increasingly popular. Personally, I like the PNG format and use it extensively. It's readable by all the major browsers, and it doesn't suffer from the image quality losses that most JPEG files do. If you want a high-quality way to store images, my advice is to use PNG format; you're going to see more and more of it in the coming years.

TABLE 3.4   Continued

Method	Does This
`int getType()`	Returns the type of the image
`int getWidth()`	Returns the width of the image contained in this `BufferedImage` object
`int getWidth(ImageObserver observer)`	Returns the width of the image contained in this `BufferedImage` object using an `ImageObserver`
`boolean isAlphaPremultiplied()`	Returns `true` if the alpha values for this image have been premultiplied
`void setData(Raster r)`	Sets a rectangular region of the image using the given `Raster` object
`void setRGB(int x, int y, int rgb)`	Sets a pixel in this `BufferedImage` to the given RGB value
`void setRGB(int startX, int startY, int w, int h, int[] rgbArray, int offset, int scansize)`	Sets a pixel array in this `BufferedImage` to the given RGB value

After the image has been read in and is stored in the `BufferedImage` object, the code resizes its window in order to display the new image, while still maintaining a minimum size. You can determine the size of the image with the `BufferedImage` class's `getWidth` and `getHeight` methods, so here's what resizing the window to match the image looks like:

```
public void actionPerformed(ActionEvent event)
{
    if(event.getSource() == menuitem1){

        dialog.setMode(FileDialog.LOAD);

        dialog.setVisible(true);

        try{
            if(!dialog.getFile().equals("")){
                File input = new File(dialog.getDirectory()
                    + dialog.getFile());
                bufferedImage = ImageIO.read(input);

                setSize(getInsets().left + getInsets().right +
                    Math.max(400, bufferedImage.getWidth() + 60),
                    getInsets().top + getInsets().bottom +
                    Math.max(340, bufferedImage.getHeight() + 60));

                    .
                    .
                    .

}
```

You also have to move the buttons to match and then repaint the entire window so the loaded image will appear; here's what that looks like in the code:

```
public void actionPerformed(ActionEvent event)
{
    if(event.getSource() == menuitem1){
        .
        .
        .
        try{
            if(!dialog.getFile().equals("")){
                File input = new File(dialog.getDirectory()
                    + dialog.getFile());
                bufferedImage = ImageIO.read(input);

                setSize(getInsets().left + getInsets().right +
                    Math.max(400, bufferedImage.getWidth() + 60),
                    getInsets().top + getInsets().bottom +
                    Math.max(340, bufferedImage.getHeight() + 60));

                button1.setBounds(30, getHeight() - 30, 60, 20);
                button2.setBounds(100, getHeight() - 30, 60, 20);
                button3.setBounds(170, getHeight() - 30, 60, 20);
                button4.setBounds(240, getHeight() - 30, 60, 20);
                button5.setBounds(310, getHeight() - 30, 60, 20);
            }
        }
        catch(Exception e){
            System.out.println(e.getMessage());
        }

        repaint();
    }
}
```

To actually paint the image, Graphicizer will overload the Frame's paint method, coming up next.

Painting the Image

Now that the user has loaded a new image, you have to make sure that it appears when the window is redrawn. You can do that in the paint method. There's not going to be a lot of fancy animation in this application, so it doesn't use any double buffering. All it does is draw the current image when required in the paint method.

The paint method first makes sure there actually is a `BufferedImage` object to draw:

```
public void paint(Graphics g)
{
    if(bufferedImage != null){
        .
        .
        .
    }
}
```

If there is an image to draw, you can use the `Graphics` object passed to the paint method to paint that image, using the Graphics object's `drawImage` method. Even though that method is usually passed an `Image` object, you can also pass it a `BufferedImage` object and it'll be automatically cast to an `Image` object.

Here's how you can draw the loaded image centered in the window (the last parameter passed to the `drawImage` method here corresponds to an `ImageObserver` object if you want to use one to monitor the image—this application doesn't use an `ImageObserver` object, so it simply passes a pointer to the current object for this parameter):

```
public void paint(Graphics g)
{
    if(bufferedImage != null){
        g.drawImage(bufferedImage, getSize().width / 2
            - bufferedImage.getWidth() / 2,
            getInsets().top + 20, this);
    }
}
```

This draws the newly loaded image, and the results appear in Figure 3.1, where, as you can see, the figure is centered in the client area and above the buttons.

Not bad.

So what about saving images?

Saving an Image File

After the user has worked on a file, the Graphicizer would certainly let him down if he couldn't save his changes back to a file. Imagine doing a lot of work on an image and not being able to store the results.

That's why this application has a Save As... menu item, which, when selected, displays a File Save dialog box, created by setting the dialog object's mode to `FileDialog.SAVE`:

```
public void actionPerformed(ActionEvent event)
{
```

```
        .
        .
        .
        if(event.getSource() == menuitem2){

            dialog.setMode(FileDialog.SAVE);

            dialog.setVisible(true);
        .
        .
        .

}
```

This displays the File Save dialog you see in Figure 3.3.

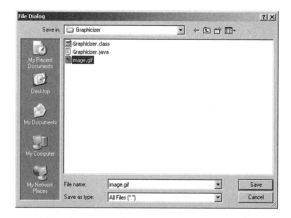

FIGURE 3.3   Saving an image file.

This dialog box's job is to get the name of the file the user wants to store the image file to. When you have that name, you can use the ImageIO class's write method to actually write the file.

If the user doesn't specify a file, or if he clicks the Cancel button, you'll get an empty string back from the dialog box's getFile method. Otherwise, you should try to create a File object using the name and path the user has given you. Just be sure to enclose everything in a try/catch block, as shown here:

```
    public void actionPerformed(ActionEvent event)
    {
        .

        .

        .

        if(event.getSource() == menuitem2){
```

```
        dialog.setMode(FileDialog.SAVE);

        dialog.setVisible(true);

        try{
            if(!dialog.getFile().equals("")){

                String outfile = dialog.getFile();

                File outputFile = new File(dialog.getDirectory()
                    + outfile);
                    .
                    .
                    .
            }
        }
        catch(Exception e){
            System.out.println(e.getMessage());
        }
    }
```

If you've been able to create the `File` object corresponding to the output file, you can use the `ImageIO` class's `write` method to write the `bufferedImage` object to the file. You pass the `BufferedImage` object you want to write to the `write` method, followed by the type of image you want to write ("JPG" or "PNG") and the output `File` object.

How do you determine the three-letter type of image file to write? You can pass a value such as "PNG" or "JPG" to the `write` method, and in the Graphicizer, the code will simply take the type of the file to write from the extension of the filename (for example, "image.png" would yield "png").

NOTE

If you want to be more careful, you can add code to check the format type and make sure it's "JPG" or "PNG". If it's not, you can then display a warning dialog box asking the user to select again.

Here's how the output image file is written to disk, using the `ImageIO` class's `write` method:

```
File outputFile = new File(dialog.getDirectory()
    + outfile);

ImageIO.write(bufferedImage,
    outfile.substring(outfile.length() - 3,
    outfile.length()), outputFile);
```

.
.
.

Okay, at this point, Graphicizer can now load and save images. Very cool; that means it can function as an image converter, converting between various formats.

But what about actually *doing* something with an image when it has been loaded? That's coming up next.

Embossing an Image

The first button in Graphicizer is Emboss, which converts an image into an "embossed" image, making it look as though it were embossed on paper in a three-dimensional way. For example, you can see the results when the sample image (image.gif) that comes with the application is embossed in Figure 3.4.

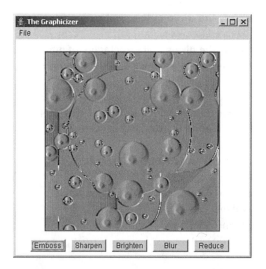

FIGURE 3.4   Embossing an image.

To create an embossed image, Graphicizer has to get access to the individual pixels in the image. You can load these pixels into an array using the Java `PixelGrabber` class, which is what Graphicizer does. You can see the significant methods of the `PixelGrabber` class in Table 3.5.

NOTE

You can also access the pixels in an image with the `BufferedImage` class's `getRGB` and `setRGB` methods. So why doesn't the Graphicizer do things that way? It turns out that these methods take a significant amount of time to execute, and when you multiply that by the millions of pixels you can have in an image, you wind up with a problem. It's a heck of a lot faster to load all the pixels from the image into an array using a `PixelGrabber` object, work on the array in Java code, and then simply fill the image from the array again.

TABLE 3.5 The Significant Methods of the `java.awt.image.PixelGrabber` Class

Method	Does This
`ColorModel getColorModel()`	Returns the color model used by the data stored in the array
`int getHeight()`	Returns the height of the pixel buffer, as measured in pixels
`Object getPixels()`	Returns the pixel buffer used by the `PixelGrabber` object
`int getWidth()`	Returns the width of the pixel buffer, as measured in pixels
`boolean grabPixels()`	Gets all the pixels in the rectangle of interest and transfers them individually to the pixel buffer
`boolean grabPixels(long ms)`	Gets all the pixels in the rectangle of interest and transfers them individually to the pixel buffer, subject to the timeout time, ms (in milliseconds)
`void setColorModel(ColorModel model)`	Sets the color model used by this `PixelGrabber` object
`void setDimensions(int width, int height)`	Sets the dimensions of the image to be grabbed
`void setPixels(int srcX, int srcY, int srcW, int srcH, ColorModel model, byte[] pixels, int srcOff, int srcScan)`	Sets the actual pixels in the image
`void startGrabbing()`	Makes the `PixelGrabber` object start getting the pixels and transferring them to the pixel buffer

How do you go about embossing the image, now that you have it stored in an array? You can emboss an image by finding the difference between each pixel and its neighbor and then adding that difference to the color gray.

To start each drawing operation, Graphicizer stores the present image in a backup object, `bufferedImageBackup`, in case the user selects the Undo menu item:

```
public void actionPerformed(ActionEvent event)
{
       .
       .
       .
    if(event.getSource() == button1){

        bufferedImageBackup = bufferedImage;
       .
       .
       .

}
```

If the user selects the File menu's Undo item, Graphicizer can use the backed-up version of the image, bufferedImageBackup, to restore the original image.

After creating a backup buffered image, the code uses a PixelGrabber object, pg, to load the actual pixels from the image into an array.

To create that pixel grabber, you pass the PixelGrabber constructor the image you want to grab and the offset at which to start in the image—in this case, (0, 0). You also pass the width and height of the image, the array to store the image in (named pixels in this example), the offset into the array at which you want to start storing data (that's 0 here), and the "scansize," which is the distance from one row of pixels to the next in the array (that'll be width here). Here's what this looks like in code:

```
public void actionPerformed(ActionEvent event)
{
       .
       .
       .
    if(event.getSource() == button1){

        bufferedImageBackup = bufferedImage;

        int width = bufferedImage.getWidth();
        int height = bufferedImage.getHeight();
        int pixels[] = new int[width * height];

        PixelGrabber pg = new PixelGrabber(bufferedImage, 0, 0,
            width, height, pixels, 0, width);

        try {
            pg.grabPixels();
        }
        catch(InterruptedException e){
            System.out.println(e.getMessage());
```

```
        }
        .
        .
        .
}
```

If this operation is successful, the image has been stored in the int array `pixels`. That's perfect, because now you can work with each individual pixel as an integer in an array, without having to go to the trouble of fetching it from the image itself, which can take a good deal of time.

The image data is ready to work on, but first, you need to pay some attention to the border of the image. Because the embossing algorithm compares each pixel to its neighbor and draws the resulting difference, that leaves some untouched space at the edges of the image, so the code first fills in a two-pixel border around the image with gray:

```
public void actionPerformed(ActionEvent event)
{
        .
        .
        .
    if(event.getSource() == button1){
        .
        .
        .
        for (int x = 0; x <= 1; x++){
            for (int y = 0; y < height - 1; y++){
                pixels[x + y * width] = 0x88888888 ;
            }
        }

        for (int x = width - 2; x <= width - 1; x++){
            for (int y = 0; y < height - 1; y++){
                pixels[x + y * width] = 0x88888888 ;
            }
        }

        for (int x = 0; x <= width - 1; x++){
            for (int y = 0; y <= 1; y++){
                pixels[x + y * width] = 0x88888888 ;
            }
        }
        .
        .
        .
}
```

Now you're ready to emboss the image. You can do that by looping over every pixel in the image, first looping over rows (the X direction in the array), then with an inner loop looping over each column (the Y direction in the array):

```
public void actionPerformed(ActionEvent event)
{
    .
    .
    .

        for (int x = 2; x < width - 1; x++){
            for (int y = 2; y < height - 1; y++){
                .
                .
                .
            }
        }
    }
    .
    .
    .

}
```

Inside these loops, you can compare the red, green, and blue component of each pixel to its neighbor, add that difference to a neutral gray, and store the results in the pixel array. That's the operation you perform to emboss the image.

Here's what the actual byte-by-byte manipulation looks like—the color components of each pixel are extracted, compared to their neighbor, and then repacked into the integer for that pixel in the `pixels` array:

```
public void actionPerformed(ActionEvent event)
{
    .
    .
    .

    if(event.getSource() == button1){
        .
        .
        .
        for (int x = 2; x < width - 1; x++){
            for (int y = 2; y < height - 1; y++){

                int red = ((pixels[(x + 1) + y * width + 1] & 0xFF)
                    - (pixels[x + y * width] & 0xFF)) + 128;

                int green = (((pixels[(x + 1) + y * width + 1]
                    & 0xFF00) / 0x100) % 0x100 - ((pixels[x + y * width]
```

```
                   & 0xFF00) / 0x100) % 0x100) + 128;

             int blue = (((pixels[(x + 1) + y * width + 1]
                 & 0xFF0000) / 0x10000)
                 % 0x100 - ((pixels[x + y * width] & 0xFF0000) / 0x10000)
                 % 0x100) + 128;

             int avg = (red + green + blue) / 3;

             pixels[x + y * width] = (0xff000000 | avg << 16
                 | avg << 8 | avg);
          }
       }
     }
     .
     .
     .
}
```

That stores the new image in the `pixels` array. How do you get it into the `bufferedImage` object for display? There's no easy way to do that, because no `BufferedImage` constructor takes an array of pixels.

You have to get this done by first creating an `Image` object using the `Component` class's `createImage` method, then creating a new `BufferedImage` object, and finally using the `BufferedImage` object's `createGraphics` and `drawImage` methods to draw the `Image` object in the `BufferedImage` object (which is the way you convert from `Image` objects to `BufferedImage` objects—there is no `BufferedImage` constructor that will do the job for you).

Here's how the code loads the `pixels` array into the `bufferedImage` object and then paints it on the screen:

```
public void actionPerformed(ActionEvent event)
{
        .
        .
        .

        image = createImage(new MemoryImageSource(width,
            height, pixels, 0 , width));

        bufferedImage = new BufferedImage (width, height,
            BufferedImage.TYPE_INT_BGR );

        bufferedImage.createGraphics().drawImage(image, 0, 0, this );

        repaint();
```

```
    }
        .
        .
        .
}
```

And that's all you need; now you've embossed the image by getting into the pixels in the image and working with them one by one.

Sharpening an Image

The next button is the Sharpen button, which sharpens an image by accenting the borders between colors. You can see image.gif after it has been sharpened in Figure 3.5 (the sharpening may not be totally evident with the limited-resolution image in the figure, but it's very clear when you run the Graphicizer and click the Sharpen button).

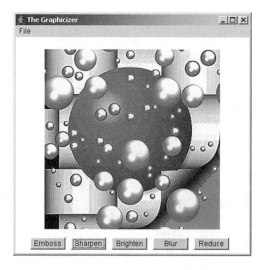

FIGURE 3.5   **Sharpening an image.**

As with embossing an image, you have to work pixel by pixel to sharpen an image. That could mean a lot of work, as you just saw when embossing. However, if you don't want to do anything too fancy, there's an easier way to work pixel by pixel and combine a pixel with its surrounding neighbors—you can use the Kernel class and the ConvolveOp class to do the work for you.

The Kernel class lets you define a matrix that specifies how a pixel should be combined with the other pixels around it to produce a new result, and the ConvolveOp class lets you apply a kernel to a BufferedImage object, pixel by pixel.

You can see the significant methods of the `Kernel` object in Table 3.6 and the significant methods of the `ConvolveOp` class in Table 3.7.

TABLE 3.6   The Significant Methods of the `java.awt.image.Kernel` **Class**

Method	Does This
`int getHeight()`	Returns the height of the matrix specified by this `Kernel` object
`float[] getKernelData(float[] data)`	Returns the kernel data as an array
`int getWidth()`	Returns the width of the matrix specified by this `Kernel` object
`int getXOrigin()`	Returns the X origin of the data in this `Kernel` object
`int getYOrigin()`	Returns the Y origin of the data in this `Kernel` object

TABLE 3.7   The Significant Methods of the `java.awt.image.ConvolveOp` **Class**

Method	Does This
`BufferedImage createCompatibleDestImage (BufferedImage src, ColorModel destCM)`	Creates a compatible destination image
`BufferedImage filter(BufferedImage src, BufferedImage dst)`	Performs a convolution operation on `BufferedImage` objects
`WritableRaster filter(Raster src, WritableRaster dst)`	Performs a convolution operation on `Raster` objects
`Rectangle2D getBounds2D(BufferedImage src)`	Returns the rectangle specifying the bounds of the destination image
`Rectangle2D getBounds2D(Raster src)`	Returns the rectangle specifying the bounds of the destination raster
`int getEdgeCondition()`	Returns the edge condition, which specifies how you want to handle the edges of the image
`Kernel getKernel()`	Returns the `Kernel` object used by this `ConvolveOp` object

Here's how this all works for sharpening an image when the Sharpen button is clicked. After storing the present buffered image in the image backup, `bufferedImageBackup` (in case the user wants to undo the sharpening operation), the code creates a new kernel for the operation.

A kernel is really a matrix that will multiply a pixel and its neighbors. Here is the kernel you can use to sharpen the image; you pass the `Kernel` constructor thee dimensions of the matrix and then the matrix itself:

```
public void actionPerformed(ActionEvent event)
{
    .
    .
    .
```

```
if(event.getSource() == button2){

    bufferedImageBackup = bufferedImage;

    Kernel kernel =
        new Kernel(3, 3, new float[] {
            0.0f, -1.0f,  0.0f,
            -1.0f,  5.0f, -1.0f,
            0.0f, -1.0f,  0.0f
        });
        .
        .
        .
```

Now you've got to apply the new kernel to the image, which you do with the ConvolveOp
class's filter method. As you'll recall, there were problems when embossing the image with
the pixels at the edge of the image, because what we did involved combining pixels with
their neighbors. To handle that situation when filtering with ConvolveOp, you can pass the
filter method the constant ConvolveOp.EDGE_NO_OP, which means that pixels at the edge of
the image will be copied to the destination image without modification. (The other option is
ConvolveOp.EDGE_ZERO_FILL, which means that pixels at the edge of the destination image
will be set to zero.)

You also can pass an object to the ConvolveOp constructor that will give ConvolveOp some
hints on how to draw the image, but that's not needed here. Therefore, the code just passes
null as the third parameter to the ConvolveOp constructor:

```
public void actionPerformed(ActionEvent event)
{
    .
    .
    .

    if(event.getSource() == button2){

        bufferedImageBackup = bufferedImage;

        Kernel kernel =
            new Kernel(3, 3, new float[] {
                0.0f, -1.0f,  0.0f,
                -1.0f,  5.0f, -1.0f,
                0.0f, -1.0f,  0.0f
            });

        ConvolveOp convolveOp =
            new ConvolveOp(
                kernel, ConvolveOp.EDGE_NO_OP, null);
```

.
.
.

Now you're ready to sharpen the image with the `filter` method. You pass this method a source image and a destination image, and after the filtering is done, the code will copy the new image over into the image displayed by Graphicizer, `bufferedImage`, and repaint that image this way:

```
public void actionPerformed(ActionEvent event)
{
    .
    .
    .

        if(event.getSource() == button2){

            bufferedImageBackup = bufferedImage;

            Kernel kernel =
                new Kernel(3, 3, new float[] {
                    0.0f, -1.0f,  0.0f,
                    -1.0f,  5.0f, -1.0f,
                    0.0f, -1.0f,  0.0f
                });

            ConvolveOp convolveOp =
                new ConvolveOp(
                    kernel, ConvolveOp.EDGE_NO_OP, null);

            BufferedImage temp = new BufferedImage(
                bufferedImage.getWidth(), bufferedImage.getHeight(),
                BufferedImage.TYPE_INT_ARGB);

            convolveOp.filter(bufferedImage, temp);

            bufferedImage = temp;

            repaint();
        }
```

That's all it takes; the results appear in Figure 3.5.

Brightening an Image

If the user clicks the Brighten button, Graphicizer brightens the image, as you can see in Figure 3.6.

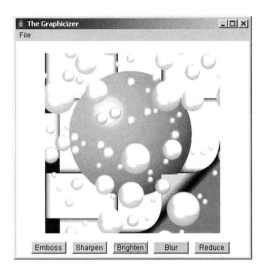

FIGURE 3.6   **Brightening an image.**

To brighten an image, you simply multiply the intensity of each pixel. In this case, all you need is a one-dimensional kernel. Here's what the code looks like, complete with `Kernel` and `ConvolveOp` objects:

```
if(event.getSource() == button3){

    bufferedImageBackup = bufferedImage;

    Kernel kernel = new Kernel(1, 1, new float[] {3});

    ConvolveOp convolveOp = new ConvolveOp(kernel);

    BufferedImage temp = new BufferedImage(
        bufferedImage.getWidth(), bufferedImage.getHeight(),
        BufferedImage.TYPE_INT_ARGB);

    convolveOp.filter(bufferedImage, temp);

    bufferedImage = temp;

    repaint();
}
```

That completes the brightening operation—now you can lighten any image with just the click of a button.

Blurring an Image

You can also use Graphicizer to blur an image by clicking the Blur button. You can see the results in Figure 3.7, where the image has an out-of-focus look.

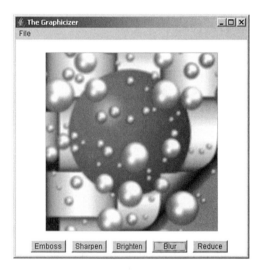

FIGURE 3.7   Blurring an image.

To blur an image, the code will simply combine the pixels surrounding a particular pixel. Here's what this looks like using a `Kernel` object and a `ConvolveOp` object:

```
if(event.getSource() == button4){

    bufferedImageBackup = bufferedImage;

    Kernel kernel = new Kernel(3, 3, new float[]
        {.25f, 0,  .25f,
          0,   0,  0,
         .25f, 0,  .25f});

    ConvolveOp convolveOp = new ConvolveOp(kernel);

    BufferedImage temp = new BufferedImage(
        bufferedImage.getWidth(), bufferedImage.getHeight(),
        BufferedImage.TYPE_INT_ARGB);

    convolveOp.filter(bufferedImage, temp);
```

```
            bufferedImage = temp;

            repaint();
        }
```

And that's all it takes—now you can blur images just by clicking the Blur button.

Reducing an Image

If the user clicks the Reduce button, the image is reduced by a factor of two in each dimension, as you can see in Figure 3.8.

FIGURE 3.8   Reducing an image.

This one works by using the BufferedImage class's getScaledInstance method, which it inherits from the Image class. This method changes the size of an image, but it returns an Image object, so it takes a little work to get back to a BufferedImage object:

```
        if(event.getSource() == button5){

            bufferedImageBackup = bufferedImage;

            image = bufferedImage.getScaledInstance
                (bufferedImage.getWidth()/2, bufferedImage.getHeight()/2, 0);

            bufferedImage = new BufferedImage (
                bufferedImage.getWidth()/2,
                bufferedImage.getHeight()/2,
                BufferedImage.TYPE_INT_BGR );
```

```
        bufferedImage.createGraphics().drawImage(image, 0, 0, this );
            .
            .
            .
    }
```

After you convert from an Image object back to a BufferedImage object, you need to resize the window, subject to a certain minimum size, to correspond to the new image:

```
    if(event.getSource() == button5){
        .
        .
        .
        bufferedImage = new BufferedImage (
            bufferedImage.getWidth()/2,
            bufferedImage.getHeight()/2,
            BufferedImage.TYPE_INT_BGR );

        bufferedImage.createGraphics().drawImage(image, 0, 0, this );

        setSize(getInsets().left + getInsets().right + Math.max(400,
            bufferedImage.getWidth() + 60),
            getInsets().top + getInsets().bottom +
            Math.max(340, bufferedImage.getHeight() + 60));

        button1.setBounds(30, getHeight() - 30, 60, 20);
        button2.setBounds(100, getHeight() - 30, 60, 20);
        button3.setBounds(170, getHeight() - 30, 60, 20);
        button4.setBounds(240, getHeight() - 30, 60, 20);
        button5.setBounds(310, getHeight() - 30, 60, 20);

        repaint();
    }
```

That completes the Resize button's operation—and that completes all the buttons. The Graphicizer tools are in place.

The last operation to take a look at isn't really an operation at all—it's the Undo action that the user can select with the File menu's Undo menu item.

Undoing a Change

When the user selects the File menu's Undo menu item, Graphicizer is supposed to undo the most recent operation. For example, if you blurred an image and then selected Undo, the original version of the image would appear.

In order to undo an operation, Graphicizer makes a backup copy of each image before performing an operation, as shown here, where the backup copy, `bufferedImageBackup`, is made when the user clicks a button:

```
if(event.getSource() == button1){

    bufferedImageBackup = bufferedImage;

    .
    .
    .
```

Later, if the user selects the Undo menu item, all you need to do is to copy the backup image to `bufferedImage` and then display the newly restored image, resizing the main window if needed:

```
if(event.getSource() == menuitem3){

    if (bufferedImageBackup != null){

        bufferedImage = bufferedImageBackup;

        setSize(getInsets().left + getInsets().right + Math.max
            (400, bufferedImage.getWidth() + 60),
            getInsets().top + getInsets().bottom +
            Math.max(340, bufferedImage.getHeight() + 60));

        button1.setBounds(30, getHeight() - 30, 60, 20);
        button2.setBounds(100, getHeight() - 30, 60, 20);
        button3.setBounds(170, getHeight() - 30, 60, 20);
        button4.setBounds(240, getHeight() - 30, 60, 20);
        button5.setBounds(310, getHeight() - 30, 60, 20);

        repaint();
}
```

And that's it—that completes the Graphicizer application. Now you can load in images, convert them to other formats, write them out, emboss them, sharpen them up, blur them out, and more. You can run this project just as you ran the two previous projects—just compile them with the javac tool and run them with the java tool.

NOTE

You can download the complete source code for the Graphicizer application—Graphicizer.java—at the Sams website. Also included is a sample image, image.gif.

Conclusion

This chapter was all about the Graphicizer, an image-editing and conversion tool. Using the Graphicizer, you can read in image files, work on them, and save them back to disk.

The Graphicizer supports a number of menu items to load in image files, to write them back to disk, to undo the most recent change, and to quit the program. In addition, this application displays a set of buttons that function as image-handling tools to emboss, sharpen, brighten, blur, and reduce images.

There are several new technologies here, starting with the ImageIO class, which you use to read in images and write them back to disk. This class proves to be very handy for the Graphicizer, except that it only deals with BufferedImage objects instead of standard Image objects. By converting between BufferedImage and standard Image objects, however, the code is able to do what it is supposed to do. Graphicizer also uses a File dialog box to get the name of the file the user wants to open or save.

To work with the pixels in an image, Graphicizer uses two techniques—working with a pixel grabber to actually grab all the pixels in the image, and working with a ConvolveOp object to apply a Kernel object to all the pixels without having to work pixel by pixel.

Using a PixelGrabber object, Graphicizer is able to extract every pixel from the image being worked on and store them in an array. To work with each pixel, you only have to address it in the array individually, which is how the application embosses images.

Working with each pixel by addressing it individually and extracting its red, green, and blue color values is one way of handling images, but there's another way—using Kernel objects and ConvolveOp objects. These two objects will do the dirty work for you; the Kernel object lets you specify a matrix whose values will multiply a pixel and its neighboring pixels. And a ConvolveOp object's filter method lets you apply your kernel to each pixel automatically. The Graphicizer uses Kernel and ConvolveOp objects to sharpen, brighten, and blur images, all without a lot of programming.

It's possible to reduce an image's size by using the Image class's getScaledInstance method, and the Graphicizer lets the user reduce an image by a factor of two in both dimensions (if you prefer, you could implement a dialog box asking the user for a reduction factor instead of automatically using two).

Finally, Graphicize includes an Undo feature that's pretty easy to implement. Each time a new operation, such as sharpening or blurring, is started by the user, Graphicizer stores the current buffered image in a backup buffered image object. If the user selects the Undo menu item, Graphicizer simply takes the backup image and makes it the main image again. That provides one level of "undo" capability—if you want to provide more, you could implement an entire stack of backup buffered images and then pop them as required by the user.

All in all, Graphicizer is a useful and fun application, providing a lot more image-handling power than most developers know exists in Java. Give it a try! (There's more such power coming up later in the book, incidentally, when an online application creates JPEG files from scratch and sends them back to web browsers.)

CHAPTER 4
Creating Stunning Graphics with Painter

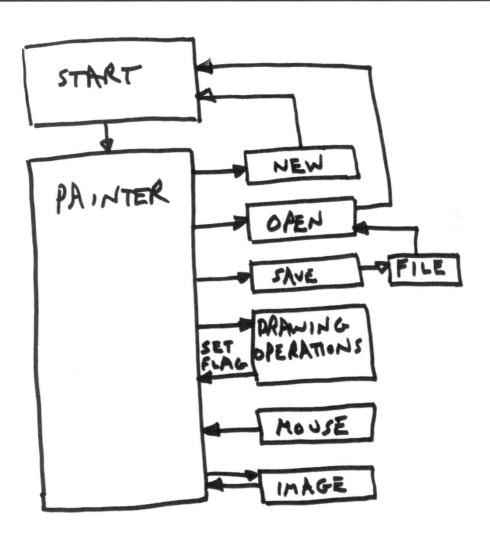

The Painter application.

In the previous chapter, the Graphicizer let you manipulate an existing image, with the click of a button: You can sharpen it, brighten it, blur it, reduce its size, save it to disk, and so on. But what about creating your own images from scratch?

That's where the Painter application comes in. This application lets you go wild drawing your own images: You can draw ellipses, rectangles, lines, or rounded rectangles—in fact, you can even draw freehand with the mouse. You can draw each shape open or you can fill it using a texture fill (you can supply your own image to be used as the fill), a solid color fill, or a gradient fill. You can draw text as well. You can give shapes a drop shadow if you want, or make them transparent, which means you'll be able to see the underlying graphics as well. You can draw using thin lines or thick lines. You can also set the drawing color. And not only can you save your work when you're done, you can read in images and work on them, annotating them with text or adding your own graphics.

All in all, Painter is a fun piece of technology to have around, and you can use it to produce some truly remarkable images. You can see this application at work in Figure 4.1.

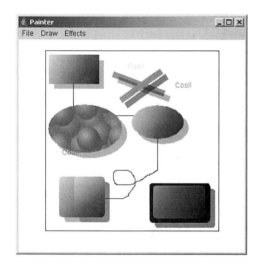

FIGURE 4.1   Painter in action.

To create this application, you start as you'd expect—by creating the main window and its menu system.

Creating the Painter Window

Painter has three menus: File, Draw, and Effects. As you'd expect, the File menu is used to create a new image, load an existing image, and save an image; here are the items in the File menu:

- New

- Open

- Save As

- Exit

The Draw and Effects menus work together; you select a drawing tool from the Draw menu (such as the line-drawing tool), and you can also select various effects from the Effects menu (such as drop shadows, texture fill, and so on). The items you select in these menus will have a check mark displayed in front of them, and they will stay checked until you select another item that is incompatible (such as selecting the ellipse-drawing tool). Here are the items in the Draw menu:

- Draw lines

- Draw rectangles

- Draw rounded rectangles

- Draw freehand

- Draw text

And here are the possible effects you can use with the drawing tools from the Effects menu:

- Plain

- Solid fill

- Gradient fill

- Texture fill

- Transparent

- Draw thick lines

- Drop shadow

- Select color...

As before, the window the application draws is created in the application's constructor. And like the previous applications so far, this one is based on the Frame class. Here's what Painter's main method and constructor look like; the constructor adds the mouse listeners the application needs for drawing operations, and it constructs the menu system:

```
public static void main(String[] args)
{
    new Painter();
}
```

```
public Painter()
{
    setLayout(null);

    addMouseListener(this);
    addMouseMotionListener(this);

    menubar = new MenuBar();

    menu1 = new Menu("File");
    menu2 = new Menu("Draw");
    menu3 = new Menu("Effects");

    newMenuItem = new MenuItem("New");
    menu1.add(newMenuItem);
    newMenuItem.addActionListener(this);

    openMenuItem = new MenuItem("Open...");
    menu1.add(openMenuItem);
    openMenuItem.addActionListener(this);

    saveMenuItem = new MenuItem("Save As...");
    menu1.add(saveMenuItem);
    saveMenuItem.addActionListener(this);

    colorMenuItem = new MenuItem("Select color...");
    menu3.add(colorMenuItem);
    colorMenuItem.addActionListener(this);

    exitMenuItem = new MenuItem("Exit");
    menu1.add(exitMenuItem);
    exitMenuItem.addActionListener(this);
    .
    .
    .
```

The Painter application has many check box menu items, where a menu item stays checked until it's unchecked by the user or the code. Here is how those items are created in the constructor:

```
    linesMenuItem = new CheckboxMenuItem("Draw lines");
    menu2.add(linesMenuItem);
    linesMenuItem.addItemListener(this);
```

```java
ellipsesMenuItem = new CheckboxMenuItem("Draw ellipses");
menu2.add(ellipsesMenuItem);
ellipsesMenuItem.addItemListener(this);

rectanglesMenuItem = new CheckboxMenuItem("Draw rectangles");
menu2.add(rectanglesMenuItem);
rectanglesMenuItem.addItemListener(this);

roundedMenuItem = new CheckboxMenuItem(
    "Draw rounded rectangles");
menu2.add(roundedMenuItem);
roundedMenuItem.addItemListener(this);

freehandMenuItem = new CheckboxMenuItem("Draw freehand");
menu2.add(freehandMenuItem);
freehandMenuItem.addItemListener(this);

plainMenuItem = new CheckboxMenuItem("Plain");
menu3.add(plainMenuItem);
plainMenuItem.addItemListener(this);

solidMenuItem = new CheckboxMenuItem("Solid fill");
menu3.add(solidMenuItem);
solidMenuItem.addItemListener(this);

gradientMenuItem = new CheckboxMenuItem("Gradient fill");
menu3.add(gradientMenuItem);
gradientMenuItem.addItemListener(this);

textureMenuItem = new CheckboxMenuItem("Texture fill");
menu3.add(textureMenuItem);
textureMenuItem.addItemListener(this);

transparentMenuItem = new CheckboxMenuItem("Transparent");
menu3.add(transparentMenuItem);
transparentMenuItem.addItemListener(this);

textMenuItem = new CheckboxMenuItem("Draw text");
menu2.add(textMenuItem);
textMenuItem.addItemListener(this);

thickMenuItem = new CheckboxMenuItem("Draw thick lines");
menu3.add(thickMenuItem);
thickMenuItem.addItemListener(this);
```

```
shadowMenuItem = new CheckboxMenuItem("Drop shadow");
menu3.add(shadowMenuItem);
shadowMenuItem.addItemListener(this);

menubar.add(menu1);
menubar.add(menu2);
menubar.add(menu3);

setMenuBar(menubar);
    .
    .
    .
```

Check box menu items are supported by the CheckboxMenuItem class, and you can see the significant methods of this class in Table 4.1.

TABLE 4.1   The Significant Methods of the *java.awt.CheckboxMenuItem* **Class**

Method	Does This
void addItemListener(ItemListener l)	Adds an item listener, which will get events from this check box menu item
ItemListener[] getItemListeners()	Returns an array containing all the item listeners connected to this check box menu item
Object[] getSelectedObjects()	Returns an array that contains the check box menu item label if the check box is selected, or returns null if the check box is not selected
boolean getState()	Returns true if this check box menu item is selected; returns false otherwise

REAL-WORLD SCENARIO

Centralizing the Code

As you can see, there are plenty of drawing tools and effects in the Painter program, and combining them in different ways gives the user many different options. Spreading the drawing logic throughout the entire program would quickly become unwieldy. When applications start to get bigger (Painter.java is about 16 pages of single-spaced code, for example), it gets harder to maintain and debug applications that have related functionality spread throughout.

For that reason, and as you may already know, developers usually try to centralize their code by function as much as possible when that code gets longer. For example, you could implement drawing operations and graphics effects throughout the code, including in the code that handles the menu items the user chooses to select a drawing tool or a graphics effect. Developers usually find, however, that it really pays to give some thought to what's going on beforehand and to concentrate related code in the same place as much as possible. This helps to avoid "spaghetti" code spread here and there throughout the application.

continues

TABLE 4.1   Continued

Method	Does This
void removeItemListener(ItemListener l)	**Removes the given item listener, which means it will no longer get item events from this check box menu item**
void setState(boolean b)	**Sets the state of the check box menu item to the given state**

Painter will also need a File dialog box for loading and saving images, so the constructor creates a new `FileDialog` object. Because the `ImageIO` class works with `BufferedImage` objects, the constructor also creates a buffered image and then displays the main window. Internally, the Painter application uses an `Image` object, named image, to do the drawing in. And there's also a dialog box of the same class put together for the Slapshot! application, `OKCancelDialog`, that Painter will use to read the text it's supposed to draw in the image. Here's how all this is set up in the constructor:

```
dialog = new FileDialog(this, "File Dialog");

bufferedImage = new BufferedImage (imageWidth, imageHeight,
    BufferedImage.TYPE_INT_BGR );

setSize(400, 400);

setTitle("Painter");
setVisible(true);
```

REAL-WORLD SCENARIO   *continued*

Accordingly, Painter was planned from the top down to handle this problem: The items in the Draw and Effects menus only set Boolean flags, such as `ellipse` when the user wants to draw ellipses, and `shadow` when the user wants to create drop shadows. These flags are used to communicate with the rest of the application.

The drawing operations themselves are centralized in the `paint` method, which simply has to check where the mouse is, check which drawing flags are set, and take it from there.

In this way, all the drawing operations and graphics effects take place in one area of the Painter program. Handling the menu items is super easy—all you have to do is to set Boolean flags, which will be checked later when it's time to actually draw something. Now that the real action is corralled in the `paint` method, you know what code to work with when there's a problem.

```
image = createImage(imageWidth, imageHeight);
textDialog = new OkCancelDialog(this, "Enter your text", true);
    .
    .
    .
```

All that's left in the constructor is to read in the image, named tile.jpg, used for filling images with text. You can use any image file for texture fills, as long as you name it tile.jpg; this application comes with a default tile.jpg file. Finally, the constructor adds the window closer as usual:

```
try{
    File inputFile = new File("tile.jpg");
    tileImage = ImageIO.read(inputFile);
} catch (java.io.IOException ioe){
    System.out.println("Need tile.jpg.");
    System.exit(0);
}

this.addWindowListener(new WindowAdapter(){
    public void windowClosing(
        WindowEvent e){
            System.exit(0);
        }
    }
);
}
```

Painter works by setting flags corresponding to the drawing operation or graphics effect you want to use and then checking those flags when it's time to do the actual drawing.

Handling Menu Selections

The actionPerformed method handles menu selections, setting the appropriate drawing flags as needed. This method handles the File menu's Open item by using the ImageIO class to open an image file:

```
public void actionPerformed(ActionEvent e)
{
    if(e.getSource() == openMenuItem){
        try{
            dialog.setMode(FileDialog.LOAD);

            dialog.setVisible(true);
```

```
        if(dialog.getFile() != ""){
            File inputFile = new File(dialog.getDirectory() +
                dialog.getFile());
            bufferedImage = ImageIO.read(inputFile);
            if(bufferedImage != null){
                image = createImage(bufferedImage.getWidth(),
                bufferedImage.getHeight());
                Graphics2D g2d = (Graphics2D)
                    image.getGraphics();
                g2d.drawImage(bufferedImage, null, 0, 0);
                imageWidth = bufferedImage.getWidth();
                imageHeight = bufferedImage.getHeight();
                setSize(imageWidth + 100, imageHeight + 90);
                repaint();
            }
        }
    }catch(Exception exp){
        System.out.println(exp.getMessage());
    }
}
  .
  .
  .
```

If the user selects the Save As menu item, Painter displays a File Save dialog box and saves the file in the same way that the Graphicizer application did:

```
if(e.getSource() == saveMenuItem){

    dialog.setMode(FileDialog.SAVE);

    dialog.setVisible(true);

    try{
        if(dialog.getFile() != ""){
            String outfile = dialog.getFile();
            File outputFile = new File(dialog.getDirectory() +
                outfile);
            bufferedImage.createGraphics().drawImage(image,
                0, 0, this);
            ImageIO.write(bufferedImage,
                outfile.substring(outfile.length() - 3,
                outfile.length()), outputFile);
        }
    }
```

```
    catch(Exception ex){
        System.out.println(ex.getMessage());
    }
}
.
.
.
```

If the user selects the File menu's New item, the application creates new `BufferedImage` and `Image` objects as well as sets the recorded location at which the mouse button was pressed (the `Point` object `start`) and the location at which the mouse button was released (`end`) to negative values so no graphics shape will be drawn when the window is repainted:

```
if(e.getSource() == newMenuItem){
    bufferedImage = new BufferedImage (300, 300,
        BufferedImage.TYPE_INT_BGR );
    image = createImage(300, 300);
    start.x = -20;
    start.y = -20;
    end.x = -20;
    end.y = -20;
    repaint();
}
.
.
.
```

When the user selects an item in the Draw or Effects menu, Painter sets the appropriate internal Boolean flags to match. Because those menu items are `CheckboxMenuItem` objects, they will call a method named `itemStateChanged`, which is where the code is that sets the various drawing and effects flags.

If the user selects the Draw menu's Draw lines menu item, the code calls a method named `setFlagsFalse` to reset the drawing flags. It then sets the `line` Boolean flag to `true`, puts a check mark in front of the Draw lines menu item, and resets the `start` and `end` locations of the mouse to begin drawing with lines, like this:

```
public void itemStateChanged(ItemEvent e)
{
    if(e.getSource() == linesMenuItem){
        setFlagsFalse();
        line = true;
        linesMenuItem.setState(true);
        start.x = -20;
        start.y = -20;
```

```
        end.x = -20;
        end.y = -20;
    }
    .
    .
    .
```

Here's the `setFlagsFalse` method:

```
void setFlagsFalse()
{
    rounded = false;
    line = false;
    ellipse = false;
    rectangle = false;
    draw = false;
    text = false;
    linesMenuItem.setState(false);
    ellipsesMenuItem.setState(false);
    rectanglesMenuItem.setState(false);
    roundedMenuItem.setState(false);
    freehandMenuItem.setState(false);
    textMenuItem.setState(false);
}
```

And here's how the other drawing flags—`ellipse`, `rectangle`, `rounded` (for rounded rectangles) and `draw` (for freehand drawing)—are set:

```
    if(e.getSource() == ellipsesMenuItem){
        setFlagsFalse();
        ellipse = true;
        ellipsesMenuItem.setState(true);
        start.x = -20;
        start.y = -20;
        end.x = -20;
        end.y = -20;
    }

    if(e.getSource() == rectanglesMenuItem){
        setFlagsFalse();
        rectangle = true;
        rectanglesMenuItem.setState(true);
        start.x = -20;
        start.y = -20;
```

```
        end.x = -20;
        end.y = -20;
    }

    if(e.getSource() == roundedMenuItem){
        setFlagsFalse();
        rounded = true;
        roundedMenuItem.setState(true);
        start.x = -20;
        start.y = -20;
        end.x = -20;
        end.y = -20;
    }

    if(e.getSource() == freehandMenuItem){
        setFlagsFalse();
        draw = true;
        freehandMenuItem.setState(true);
        start.x = -20;
        start.y = -20;
        end.x = -20;
        end.y = -20;
    }
    .
    .
    .
```

Here's how the effects flags are set when the user selects an item from the Effects menu:

```
    if(e.getSource() == solidMenuItem){
        solid = !solid;
        if(solid){
            texture = false;
            shade = false;
        }
        solidMenuItem.setState(solid);
        gradientMenuItem.setState(shade);
        textureMenuItem.setState(texture);
        plainMenuItem.setState(false);
        start.x = -20;
        start.y = -20;
        end.x = -20;
        end.y = -20;
    }
```

```
if(e.getSource() == gradientMenuItem){
    shade = !shade;
    if(shade){
        solid = false;
        texture = false;
    }
    solidMenuItem.setState(solid);
    gradientMenuItem.setState(shade);
    textureMenuItem.setState(texture);
    plainMenuItem.setState(false);
    start.x = -20;
    start.y = -20;
    end.x = -20;
    end.y = -20;
}

if(e.getSource() == textureMenuItem){
    texture = !texture;
    if(texture){
        shade = false;
        solid = false;
    }
    solidMenuItem.setState(solid);
    gradientMenuItem.setState(shade);
    textureMenuItem.setState(texture);
    plainMenuItem.setState(false);
    start.x = -20;
    start.y = -20;
    end.x = -20;
    end.y = -20;
}

if(e.getSource() == transparentMenuItem){
    transparent = !transparent;
    transparentMenuItem.setState(transparent);
    start.x = -20;
    start.y = -20;
    end.x = -20;
    end.y = -20;
}

if(e.getSource() == textMenuItem){
    textDialog.setVisible(true);
    drawText = textDialog.data;
    setFlagsFalse();
```

```
        text = true;
        textMenuItem.setState(true);
        start.x = -20;
        start.y = -20;
        end.x = -20;
        end.y = -20;
    }

    if(e.getSource() == thickMenuItem){
        thick = thickMenuItem.getState();
        start.x = -20;
        start.y = -20;
        end.x = -20;
        end.y = -20;
    }

    if(e.getSource() == plainMenuItem){
        solidMenuItem.setState(false);
        gradientMenuItem.setState(false);
        textureMenuItem.setState(false);
        transparentMenuItem.setState(false);
        plainMenuItem.setState(true);
        shade = false;
        solid = false;
        transparent = false;
        texture = false;
        start.x = -20;
        start.y = -20;
        end.x = -20;
        end.y = -20;
    }

    if(e.getSource() == shadowMenuItem){
        shadow = shadowMenuItem.getState();
        start.x = -20;
        start.y = -20;
        end.x = -20;
        end.y = -20;
    }
}
```

That's all you really have to do in the menu items—just set the Boolean flags that the rest of the program will check. After the user selects his drawing and effects options, he can use the mouse to draw figures.

Handling the Mouse

Each figure is defined by a "mouse pressed" action, which sets a point named start, and a "mouse released" action, which sets a point named end. When the mouse is released, any figure Painter is capable of drawing can be drawn—including a line, rectangle, ellipse, and so on—because start and end define the region in which the figure should be drawn.

When the user presses the mouse, the mouse position is recorded in the start point, and a flag indicating the state of the mouse, mouseUp, is set to false. While the user drags the mouse, Painter will draw the current graphics figure, expanding or reducing it to follow the mouse movements interactively. To translate between window coordinates (used when the mouse is being dragged) and coordinates inside the drawing area (represented by the box in Figure 4.1, which is used when the user releases the mouse button and the image is finalized), the offset of the drawing area will be subtracted from the mouse location in the final figure. Because you don't want that subtraction to be performed as the mouse is dragged, but rather only when the mouse button is released, the code sets a flag named adjusted to true (that is, the image is already adjusted to use window coordinates) and repaints the image. Here's what that looks like in the mousePressed method:

```
public void mousePressed(MouseEvent e)
{
    mouseUp = false;
    start = new Point(e.getX(), e.getY());
    adjusted=true;
    repaint();
}
```

When the mouse goes up, the new position is recorded as the end point, mouseUp is set to true, the flag dragging is set to false, and adjusted is set to false (meaning that the offset of the upper left of the drawing area should be subtracted from all drawing operations now that the code will be drawing in the Image object instead of the main window). Then the window, and the image in it, is redrawn to reflect the final figure. Here's what that looks like in the mouseReleased method:

```
public void mouseReleased(MouseEvent e)
{
    if(rounded || line || ellipse || rectangle || draw || text){
        end = new Point(e.getX(), e.getY());
        mouseUp = true;
        dragging = false;
        adjusted=false;
        repaint();
    }
}
```

If the user drags the mouse, the dragging flag is set to true and the image is redrawn to reflect the new position of the mouse. You can also check to be sure that the mouse is inside the drawing area before redrawing the window; here's what that looks like in the mouseDragged method:

```
public void mouseDragged(MouseEvent e)
{
    dragging = true;
        .
        .
        .
    if(new Rectangle(offsetX, offsetY,
        imageWidth, imageHeight).contains(start.x, start.y)){
        end = new Point(e.getX(), e.getY());
        repaint();
    }
}
```

In fact, the user can also draw freehand while dragging the mouse. If he's doing that, the code should store all the mouse locations as the mouse is dragged. Painter simply stores those points in an array named dots, shown here:

```
public void mouseDragged(MouseEvent e)
{
    dragging = true;
    if(new Rectangle(offsetX, offsetY,
        imageWidth, imageHeight).contains(e.getX(), e.getY())){
        if(draw){
            dot[dots] = new Point(e.getX(), e.getY());
            dots++;
        }
    }

    if(new Rectangle(offsetX, offsetY,
        imageWidth, imageHeight).contains(start.x, start.y)){
        end = new Point(e.getX(), e.getY());
        repaint();
    }
}
```

That takes care of tracking the mouse and responding to mouse actions. Now that the start and end points have been determined, specifying the locations at which the user has pressed and released the mouse, respectively, it's time to draw some graphics.

Drawing Some Graphics

The central method in Painter is the `paint` method. This is where all the drawing operations take place—drawing lines, ellipses, rectangles, text, with a wide variety of effects. To make those effects happen, Painter uses Java 2D—that is, `Graphics2D` objects, not the `Graphics` objects used in the previous chapters.

To let the user expand and reduce figures interactively while dragging the mouse, Painter uses two different `Graphics2D` objects—one corresponding to the internal image where the final figure is stored when the user is done drawing, and one corresponding to the window while the user is dragging the mouse. To make the drawing operations easier, the current graphics context is stored in a variable named `gImage`, and all drawing operations then can simply use that object. Here's how `gImage` is set in the `paint` method, depending on whether or not the user is dragging the mouse. Note that the code backs up the `Composite` object, used in drawing operations, from `gImage` in case that object is changed later and needs to be reset (more on the `Composite` object in a few pages). Also, note that the code restricts drawing operations to the drawing area with the `clip` method. Here's the code:

```
public void paint (Graphics g)
{
    Graphics2D gImage;

    if(!dragging && !adjusted){
        if(image == null){
            image = createImage(imageWidth, imageHeight);
        }
        gImage = (Graphics2D) image.getGraphics();
    }
    else{
        gImage = (Graphics2D) g;
        g.drawImage(image, offsetX, offsetY, this);
        g.drawRect(offsetX, offsetY, imageWidth, imageHeight);
        gImage.clip(new Rectangle2D.Double(offsetX, offsetY,
            imageWidth, imageHeight));
    }

        composite = gImage.getComposite();
    .
    .
    .
```

You can see the significant methods of the `Graphics2D` class in Table 4.2. That's the class Painter uses to draw and produce graphics effects, and it's worthwhile getting to know what's available here.

TABLE 4.2   The Significant Methods of the *java.awt.Graphics2D* **Class**

Method	Does This
abstract void draw(Shape s)	Draws a shape using the current settings in the Graphics2D context
void draw3DRect(int x, int y, int width, int height, boolean raised)	Draws a 3D outline of the given rectangle
abstract void drawImage(BufferedImage img, BufferedImageOp op, int x, int y)	Draws an image that is first filtered with the BufferedImageOp object (which can be null)
abstract void drawString(String str, int x, int y)	Draws the text of the given String object, using the current text drawing settings in the Graphics2D context
abstract void fill(Shape s)	Fills in the interior of a shape using the current settings of the Graphics2D context
void fill3DRect(int x, int y, int width, int height, boolean raised)	Fills in a 3D highlighted rectangle with the current color
abstract Color getBackground()	Returns the current background color (used when clearing an area)
abstract Composite getComposite()	Returns the current Composite object used in the Graphics2D context
abstract Paint getPaint()	Returns the current Paint object used in the Graphics2D context
abstract void setBackground(Color color)	Sets the background color used in this Graphics2D context
abstract void setComposite(Composite comp)	Sets the Composite object used in the Graphics2D context
abstract void setPaint(Paint paint)	Sets the Paint attribute used in the Graphics2D context

Now that the drawing graphics context is set in the gImage object, you can configure that object according to the graphics effects the user has selected. If the user has selected a drawing color (more on how that works, using a color chooser dialog box, later), you can install that color as the drawing color in the graphics context, like this:

```
if(color != null){
    gImage.setColor(color);
} else {
    gImage.setColor(new Color(0, 0, 0));
}
    .
    .
    .
```

Also, if the user has selected the Effects menu's Draw thick lines menu item, you can use the Graphics2D object's setStroke method to set the width of lines to a thicker value (Painter uses 10 pixels):

```
    if(thick){
        gImage.setStroke(new BasicStroke(10));
    } else{
        gImage.setStroke(new BasicStroke(1));
    }
        .
        .
        .
```

Now the code can start drawing operations. If the mouse goes up, or the user is dragging the mouse, Painter is supposed to be drawing, so it checks the mouseUp and dragging flags.

Because several of the Graphics2D drawing methods require you to pass the upper-left point of the figure to draw, the code has to order the start and end points to determine the upper-left point (which can change as the user drags the mouse). Painter does this by creating two new points, tempStart and tempEnd, that are ordered as the Graphics2D drawing methods want, and it also finds the height and width of the figure:

```
    if (mouseUp || dragging) {
        Point tempStart, tempEnd;

        tempStart = new Point(Math.min(end.x, start.x),
            Math.min(end.y, start.y));
        tempEnd = new Point(Math.max(end.x, start.x),
            Math.max(end.y, start.y));

        tempStart = new Point(Math.max(tempStart.x, offsetX),
            Math.max(tempStart.y, offsetY));
        tempEnd = new Point(Math.max(tempEnd.x, offsetX),
            Math.max(tempEnd.y, offsetY));

        tempStart = new Point(Math.min(tempStart.x,
            bufferedImage.getWidth() + offsetX),
            Math.min(tempStart.y, bufferedImage.getHeight() +
            offsetY));
        tempEnd = new Point(Math.min(tempEnd.x,
            bufferedImage.getWidth() + offsetX),
            Math.min(tempEnd.y, bufferedImage.getHeight() +
            offsetY));

        if(!adjusted){
            tempEnd.x -= offsetX;
            tempEnd.y -= offsetY;
            tempStart.x -= offsetX;
            tempStart.y -= offsetY;
            end.x -= offsetX;
```

```
            end.y -= offsetY;
            start.x -= offsetX;
            start.y -= offsetY;
            adjusted=true;
        }

        int width = tempEnd.x - tempStart.x;
        int height = tempEnd.y - tempStart.y;
    }
    .
    .
    .
```

That gets the setup out of the way. Now you're ready to draw using the graphics context in gImage. The first type of figure Painter takes care of is lines.

Drawing Lines

If the line flag is true, the user is drawing lines. To draw lines, Painter uses the Line2D.Double class. Because Line2D.Double is one of those rare Graphics2D objects that doesn't need to be passed only the upper-left point at which to begin drawing, you can draw the line simply by using the start and end points:

```
        if(line){
            Line2D.Double drawLine = new Line2D.Double(start.x,
            start.y, end.x, end.y);
            .
            .
            .
```

There's a graphics effect you have to take care of here as well: If the user has selected the Drop shadow graphics effect, you also have to draw the shadow. Shadows should not completely obscure what's underneath them; they should only be slightly darker. You can draw lines that work excellently as shadows using the Java2D Composite class. To draw a shadow, you can create a new Composite object and install it in the gImage graphics context.

First, you save the current Composite object as well as the current Paint object (which specifies things such as drawing color and stroke thickness):

```
            if(shadow){
                paint = gImage.getPaint();
                composite = gImage.getComposite();
                .
                .
                .
```

Now you can change the drawing color temporarily to black and set the opacity with which the shadow will be drawn, using the `AlphaComposite` class:

```
if(shadow){
    paint = gImage.getPaint();
    composite = gImage.getComposite();

    gImage.setPaint(Color.black);
    gImage.setComposite(AlphaComposite.getInstance
        (AlphaComposite.SRC_OVER, 0.3f));
        .
        .
        .
```

In this case, the shadow is draw over any underlying image, with an opacity of .3 (if you want darker shadows, increase that value to .4 or .5). Using Java2D, you can create all kinds of drawing effects using the `AlphaComposite` class; you can see the significant fields, such as SRC_OVER, of this class in Table 4.3.

TABLE 4.3   **The Significant Fields of the** *java.awt.AlphaComposite* **Class**

Method	Does This
static int CLEAR	Clears both the color and the alpha of the destination
static int DST	Does not change the destination
static int DST_IN	Only the part of the destination inside of the source replaces the destination
static int DST_OUT	Only the part of the destination outside of the source replaces the destination
static int DST_OVER	Composites the destination with the source, and the result is drawn as the destination
static int SRC	Copies the source to the destination
static int SRC_IN	Replaces the destination with that part of the source that is inside the destination
static int SRC_OUT	Replaces the destination with that part of the source that is outside the destination
static int SRC_OVER	The source is composited over the destination
static int XOR	That part of the source that is outside of the destination is combined with the part of the destination that is outside of the source

After the graphics object `gImage` has been primed for drawing shadows, all you have to do is to draw the line to the left and lower than the original line, restore the `gImage` context to its original settings, and then draw the original line itself (which will then lie on top of any shadow):

```
Line2D.Double line2 =
    new Line2D.Double(start.x + 9, start.y + 9,
```

```
                        end.x + 9, end.y + 9);

             gImage.draw(line2);

               gImage.setPaint(paint);
               gImage.setComposite(composite);
         }
            gImage.draw(drawLine);
     }
     .
     .
     .
```

You can see an example in Figure 4.2, where the user is drawing some thick lines with drop shadows.

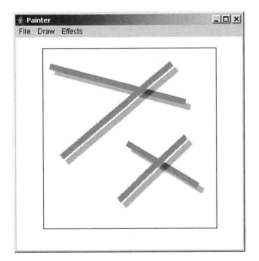

FIGURE 4.2   **Drawing some lines.**

That completes how Painter draws lines. What about ellipses?

Drawing Ellipses

If the ellipse flag is true, the user is drawing ellipses. Ellipses are a little more complex, because they can be filled in with color, texture, gradients, and so on. You can start by defining the ellipse the user wants to draw:

```
    if(ellipse && width != 0 && height != 0){
```

```
Ellipse2D.Double ellipse =
    new Ellipse2D.Double(tempStart.x, tempStart.y,
    width, height);
```

                    .
                    .
                    .

If the shadow flag is set to true, the user wants to draw drop shadows, which you can do like this (note that if the ellipse is filled in, which means one of the solid, shade, transparent, or texture flags will be set to true, you should draw the shadow to match, which you do with the gImage context's fill method, not the draw method):

```
if(shadow){
    paint = gImage.getPaint();
    composite = gImage.getComposite();

    gImage.setPaint(Color.black);
    gImage.setComposite(AlphaComposite.getInstance
        (AlphaComposite.SRC_OVER, 0.3f));

    Ellipse2D.Double ellipse2 =
        new Ellipse2D.Double(tempStart.x + 9,
        tempStart.y + 9, width, height);

    if(solid || shade || transparent || texture){
        gImage.fill(ellipse2);
    }
    else{
        gImage.draw(ellipse2);
    }

    gImage.setPaint(paint);
    gImage.setComposite(composite);
}
```

                    .
                    .
                    .

That draws the drop shadow first, if one is needed. But what about other graphics effects? For example, the user may have selected the Solid fill item in the Effects menu, which means he wants to fill the ellipse with a solid color. You can set the fill color with the Graphics2D object's setColor method, setting that color to the current drawing color like this:

```
if(solid){
    gImage.setPaint(color);
}
```

.
.
.

You can see what a solid-filled ellipse looks like, with a drop shadow added, in the upper-left area of Figure 4.3.

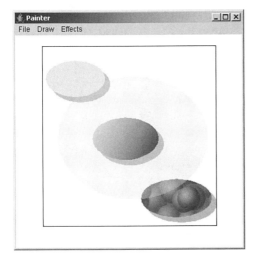

FIGURE 4.3   Various graphics effects with ellipses.

If the user wants to draw an ellipse with a gradient fill, you can use the Java2D GradientPaint class. You pass this class's constructor the location at which the gradient should start, the starting color, the location where the gradient should end, and the ending color. Painter uses the drawing color as the starting color and uses black as the ending color:

```
if(shade){
    gImage.setPaint(
    new GradientPaint(
        tempStart.x, tempStart.y, color,
        tempEnd.x, tempEnd.y, Color.black));
}
```

.
.
.

You can see what a gradient-filled ellipse looks like, also with a drop shadow, in the middle of Figure 4.3.

If the user wants to use a texture fill, you can use the Java2D TexturePaint class. You pass an image to use for the texture fill, and you pass a rectangle to anchor the image location.

Painter uses the `tileImage` object it read in from the file tile.jpg in its constructor, creating a texture fill like this:

```
if(texture){
    Rectangle2D.Double anchor =
    new Rectangle2D.Double(0, 0, tileImage.getWidth(),
    tileImage.getHeight());

    TexturePaint texturePaint =
        new TexturePaint(tileImage, anchor);

    gImage.setPaint(texturePaint);
}
      .
      .
      .
```

You can see what a gradient-filled ellipse looks like, with an added drop shadow, in the lower-right area of Figure 4.3.

Another graphics effect is to make figures "transparent" so that the underlying image comes through. If the user has selected the Effects menu's Transparent item, the transparent flag will be `true`, and the code sets the graphics context's composite to use a transparent fill:

```
if(transparent){
    gImage.setComposite(AlphaComposite.getInstance
    (AlphaComposite.SRC_OVER,0.1f));
}
      .
      .
      .
```

You can see what a transparent ellipse looks like in Figure 4.3; it's the largest ellipse shown there. It overlaps all the others (which are still visible through it).

All that work has set up the actual ellipse-drawing operation. If the ellipse is solid, you should use the `Graphics2D` fill method to draw it; otherwise, you use the `draw` method. And if the ellipse was drawn transparent, you also should restore the composite in the `Graphics2D` graphics context, like this:

```
if(solid ¦¦ shade ¦¦ transparent ¦¦ texture){
    gImage.fill(ellipse);
}
else{
    gImage.draw(ellipse);
}
if(transparent){
```

```
        gImage.setComposite(composite);
    }
}
```

And that completes the drawing operations for ellipses, complete with the various effects that Painter supports.

Drawing Rectangles

If the rectangle flag is true, the user is drawing rectangles, and the code creates a Rectangle2D.Double rectangle to correspond to the ordered starting point, tempStart, and the figure's height and width. The Rectangle2D.Double constructor takes the same arguments as the Ellipse.Double constructor, so it works like this:

```
if(rectangle && width != 0 && height != 0){

    Rectangle2D.Double rectangle =
        new Rectangle2D.Double(tempStart.x, tempStart.y,
        width, height);

    .
    .
    .
```

If the user wants a drop shadow, you should draw that first, which the code does like this:

```
    if(shadow){
        paint = gImage.getPaint();
        composite = gImage.getComposite();

        gImage.setPaint(Color.black);
        gImage.setComposite(AlphaComposite.getInstance
            (AlphaComposite.SRC_OVER, 0.3f));

        Rectangle2D.Double rectangle2 =
            new Rectangle2D.Double(tempStart.x + 9,
            tempStart.y + 9, width, height);

        if(solid || shade || transparent || texture){
            gImage.fill(rectangle2);
        }
        else{
            gImage.draw(rectangle2);
        }

        gImage.setPaint(paint);
```

```
            gImage.setComposite(composite);
        }
```
.
.
.

If the user wants a solid-filled rectangle, you can set the `Graphics2D` graphics context to use the current drawing color this way:

```
        if(solid){
            gImage.setPaint(color);
        }
```
.
.
.

If the `shade` flag is set, the user wants to fill the rectangle with a gradient fill. As before, the code will create a gradient ranging from the current drawing color to black:

```
        if(shade){
            gImage.setPaint(
                new GradientPaint(
                tempStart.x, tempStart.y, color,
                tempEnd.x, tempEnd.y, Color.black));
            }
```
.
.
.

You can also create transparent rectangles by setting the graphics context's composite to make the drawing results transparent:

```
        if(transparent){
            gImage.setComposite(AlphaComposite.getInstance
            (AlphaComposite.SRC_OVER,0.3f));
        }
```
.
.
.

And if the user wants a texture fill, you can set that up this way:

```
        if(texture){
            Rectangle2D.Double anchor =
                new Rectangle2D.Double(0,0,
                tileImage.getWidth(), tileImage.getHeight());
            TexturePaint texturePaint =
```

```
            new TexturePaint(tileImage,anchor);

        gImage.setPaint(texturePaint);
    }
    .
    .
    .
```

The final step is to actually draw the rectangle and restore the composite if need be:

```
        if(solid || shade || texture || transparent){
            gImage.fill(rectangle);
        }
        else{
            gImage.draw(rectangle);
        }

        if(transparent){
            gImage.setComposite(composite);
        }
    }
```

You can see what a variety of rectangles looks like, with some graphics effects added, in Figure 4.4.

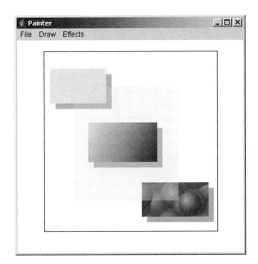

FIGURE 4.4 Various graphics effects with rectangles.

Drawing Rounded Rectangles

Another type of figure you can draw using the `Graphics2D` methods is the rounded rectangle, where the corners are rounded. If the user wants to draw rounded rectangles, you can use the `RoundRectangle2D.Double` class, whose constructor is just like the `Rectangle2D.Double` class, except that it also takes two values giving the X and Y radius you want to use for rounding the corners. Painter sets those radii to 10 pixels:

```
if(rounded && width != 0 && height != 0){

    RoundRectangle2D.Double round =
        new RoundRectangle2D.Double(tempStart.x,
        tempStart.y, width, height, 10, 10);
    .
    .
    .
```

After you've created the figure you want to draw, you can apply various effects as before, if required:

```
        if(shadow){
            paint = gImage.getPaint();
            composite = gImage.getComposite();

            gImage.setPaint(Color.black);
            gImage.setComposite(AlphaComposite.getInstance
                (AlphaComposite.SRC_OVER, 0.3f));

            RoundRectangle2D.Double round2 =
                new RoundRectangle2D.Double(tempStart.x + 9,
                tempStart.y + 9, width, height, 10, 10);

            if(solid || shade || transparent || texture){
                gImage.fill(round2);
            }
            else{
                gImage.draw(round2);
            }

            gImage.setPaint(paint);
            gImage.setComposite(composite);
        }

        if(solid){
            gImage.setPaint(color);
        }
```

```
        if(shade){
            gImage.setPaint(
                new GradientPaint(
                    tempStart.x, tempStart.y, color,
                    tempEnd.x, tempEnd.y, Color.black));
        }

        if(transparent){
            gImage.setComposite(AlphaComposite.getInstance
            (AlphaComposite.SRC_OVER,0.3f));
        }

        if(texture){
            Rectangle2D.Double anchor =
                new Rectangle2D.Double(0,0,
                tileImage.getWidth(), tileImage.getHeight());

            TexturePaint texturePaint =
                new TexturePaint(tileImage,anchor);

            gImage.setPaint(texturePaint);
        }

        if(solid || shade || texture || transparent){
            gImage.fill(round);
        }
        else{
            gImage.draw(round);
        }

        if(transparent){
            gImage.setComposite(composite);
        }
    }
```

That's all it takes; you can see what a variety of rounded rectangles looks like, with some graphics effects added, in Figure 4.5.

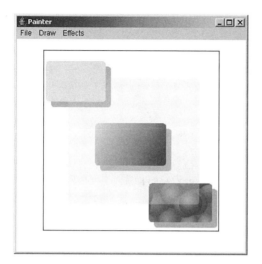

FIGURE 4.5   Various graphics effects with rounded rectangles.

Drawing Freehand

If the user has selected the Draw menu's Draw freehand item, he can use the mouse to draw freehand. As you'll recall, the successive locations of the mouse are stored in an array named dots if the user is drawing freehand, so all that's necessary is to connect those dots.

If the user wants a drop shadow, you should draw that first, then reproduce what the user has drawn with the mouse. Here's what it looks like in code:

```
if(draw){
    Line2D.Double drawLine;

    if(shadow){
        paint = gImage.getPaint();
        composite = gImage.getComposite();

        gImage.setPaint(Color.black);
        gImage.setComposite(AlphaComposite.getInstance
            (AlphaComposite.SRC_OVER, 0.3f));

        for(int loop_index = 0; loop_index < dots - 1;
            loop_index++){
            if(dragging){
```

```
                    drawLine = new Line2D.Double(
                        dot[loop_index].x + 9,
                        dot[loop_index].y + 9,
                        dot[loop_index + 1].x + 9,
                        dot[loop_index + 1].y + 9);
                }else{
                    drawLine = new Line2D.Double(
                        dot[loop_index].x - offsetX + 9,
                        dot[loop_index].y - offsetY + 9,
                        dot[loop_index + 1].x - offsetX + 9,
                        dot[loop_index + 1].y - offsetY + 9);
                }
                gImage.draw(drawLine);
            }

            gImage.setPaint(paint);
            gImage.setComposite(composite);
        }

        for(int loop_index = 0; loop_index < dots - 1;
            loop_index++){
            if(dragging){
                drawLine = new Line2D.Double(dot[loop_index].x,
                    dot[loop_index].y, dot[loop_index + 1].x,
                    dot[loop_index + 1].y);
            }else{
                drawLine = new Line2D.Double(dot[loop_index].x
                    - offsetX, dot[loop_index].y - offsetY,
                    dot[loop_index + 1].x - offsetX,
                    dot[loop_index + 1].y - offsetY);
            }
            gImage.draw(drawLine);
        }
        if(!dragging){
            dots = 0;
        }
    }
}
```

You can see an example in Figure 4.6, where the user is drawing freehand with the mouse and using a drop shadow.

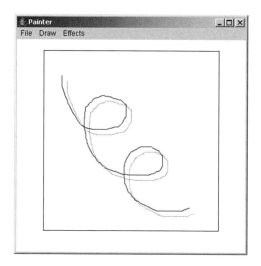

FIGURE 4.6 **Drawing freehand, with a drop shadow.**

Drawing Text

You can also draw text with the Graphics2D object's drawText method. When the user selects the Draw menu's Draw Text item, Painter displays a dialog box of the OkCancelDialog class (which you saw earlier in the Slapshot! game):

```
class OkCancelDialog extends Dialog implements ActionListener
{
    Button ok, cancel;
    TextField text;
    public String data;

    OkCancelDialog(Frame hostFrame, String title, boolean dModal)
    {
        super(hostFrame, title, dModal);
        setSize(280, 100);
        setLayout(new FlowLayout());
        text = new TextField(30);
        add(text);
        ok = new Button("OK");
        add(ok);
        ok.addActionListener((ActionListener)this);
        cancel = new Button("Cancel");
        add(cancel);
        cancel.addActionListener(this);
        data = new String("");
    }
```

```
public void actionPerformed(ActionEvent event)
{
    if(event.getSource() == ok){
        data = text.getText();
    } else {
        data = "";
    }
    setVisible(false);
}
}
```

This class displays a dialog box on request, and it stores the text the user has entered in its member named data. Here's how that text is stored in Painter's drawText variable:

```
if(e.getSource() == textMenuItem){
    textDialog.setVisible(true);
    drawText = textDialog.data;
    setFlagsFalse();
    text = true;
    textMenuItem.setState(true);
    start.x = -20;
    start.y = -20;
    end.x = -20;
    end.y = -20;
}
```

Now when the user clicks the mouse in the drawing area, that text will appear, with a shadow if required. Here's what that looks like in the paint method:

```
if(text){
    if(drawText != null && end != null && end.x !=0 &&
        end.y !=0){

        if(shadow){
            paint = gImage.getPaint();
            composite = gImage.getComposite();

            gImage.setPaint(Color.black);
            gImage.setComposite(AlphaComposite.getInstance
                (AlphaComposite.SRC_OVER, 0.3f));

            gImage.drawString(drawText, end.x + 9, end.y + 9);

            gImage.setPaint(paint);
            gImage.setComposite(composite);
        }
```

```
        gImage.drawString(drawText, end.x, end.y);
    }
}
```

You can see an example in Figure 4.7, where the user is entering text, complete with a drop shadow.

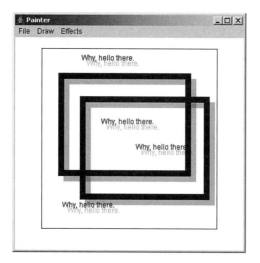

FIGURE 4.7 Drawing text, with a drop shadow.

Drawing the Final Image

At the very end of the `paint` method, the code draws the internal image on the screen, if the user is not dragging the mouse. If the user isn't dragging the mouse, the image has been finalized, which is why Painter draws the `image` object onscreen. After drawing the image, Painter also refreshes the black rectangle outlining the image in Painter's window, which you need to do in case the window was minimized and then restored or in case an overlapping window was moved:

```
    if(!dragging){
        g.drawImage(image, offsetX, offsetY, this);
    }
    g.setColor(Color.black);
    g.drawRect(offsetX, offsetY, imageWidth, imageHeight);
}
```

There's one last task to cover—letting the user select the drawing color.

Setting Colors

The user can use the Effects menu's Select Color... menu item to set the drawing color used for all drawing operations. When the user selects a drawing color, figures are drawn using that color, even if the user is drawing freehand with the mouse. Solid fills are drawn with that color, and gradient fills are drawn starting with that color and shading off to black. Even text is drawn in the color the user selects.

To let the user select a drawing color, Painter uses a Swing JColorChooser dialog box. This dialog box is easy to put to work, and it has a great deal of utility. Here's all you need to do: Use the JColorChooser class's static showDialog method and store the returned color; Painter stores that value in a Color object named color. Here's how it displays the color chooser (setting the default color to black) and stores the selected color:

```
if(e.getSource() == colorMenuItem){
    color = JColorChooser.showDialog(this, "Select your color",
        Color.black);
    start.x = -20;
    start.y = -20;
    end.x = -20;
    end.y = -20;
}
```

You can see the color chooser in Figure 4.8. As you can tell, there's a lot of functionality in that dialog box.

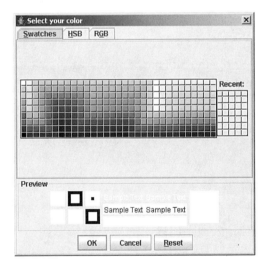

FIGURE 4.8   Selecting a color.

You can see the significant methods of the JColorChooser class in Table 4.4.

TABLE 4.4 The Significant Methods of the *javax.swing.JColorChooser* Class

Method	Does This
void addChooserPanel(AbstractColorChooserPanel panel)	**Adds a new color chooser panel to this color chooser for use in choosing colors**
AbstractColorChooserPanel[] getChooserPanels()	**Returns the color panels in the color chooser**
Color getColor()	**Returns the current color value set in the color chooser**
JComponent getPreviewPanel()	**Returns the preview panel, which displays a chosen color**
AbstractColorChooserPanel removeChooserPanel (AbstractColorChooserPanel panel)	**Removes a given color panel**
void setChooserPanels(AbstractColorChooserPanel[] panels)	**Specifies the color panels used to choose a color value**
void setColor(Color color)	**Specifies the current color in the color chooser to be the given color**
void setColor(int r, int g, int b)	**Specifies the current color in the color chooser to be the given RGB color**
void setPreviewPanel(JComponent preview)	**Sets the preview panel that will be used by this color chooser**
static Color showDialog(Component component, String title, Color initialColor)	**Displays the color chooser dialog box, letting the user select a color**

In the paint method, where the actual drawing is done, Painter installs color as the new drawing color (and uses black as a default drawing color if no other color was selected):

```
if(color != null){
    gImage.setColor(color);
} else {
    gImage.setColor(new Color(0, 0, 0));
}
```

And that completes the Painter application—everything's all packed into the code now, and it's ready to roll.

NOTE

Download the complete source code for the Painter application—Painter.java and tile.jpg—at the Sams website. You can run Painter as you have the previous projects—just compile and run it using Java. Make sure that tile.jpg (which comes in the download) is in the same directory as Painter.class when you run Painter.

Conclusion

This chapter presented the Painter application, a graphics tool that lets you draw your own images, or modify already-existing images, with a variety of Java2D effects.

Painter lets you draw different graphics figures—lines, ellipses, rectangles, rounded rectangles, text, and freehand drawing—with the mouse. You can watch your new graphics figure being stretched into place as you drag the mouse. And you can load in images from GIF, JPG, or PNG files, or you can create new images from scratch.

Painter gives you a whole palette of graphics effects as well. You can draw thick lines and select the drawing color. You can select from a variety of fill techniques: plain fill, solid fill, gradient fill, and texture fill, where you can supply your own texture in an image file named tile.jpg. You can also draw figures "transparently," where the image underneath shows through, as well as give them a drop shadow, which produces a 3D quality.

Very cool.

CHAPTER 5
Chatting on the Internet with the Chat Room

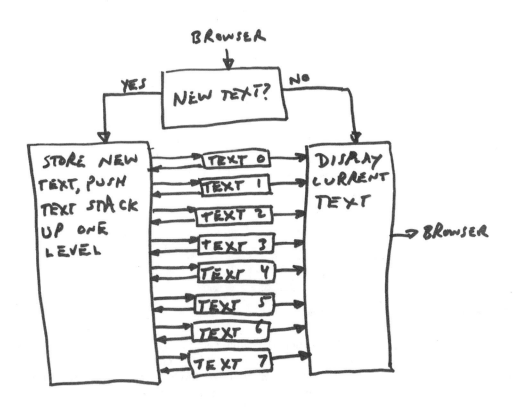

The Chat Room.

How about an Internet chat room? This project, Chat, is your own private chat room, and it'll keep you in touch with whomever you want to stay in touch with—all you need is Internet access and a Java-enabled web server. Talk all you like—all you're paying for is the local Internet connection, which is often free in hotels these days. You can also use Chat to set up your own chat rooms, dedicated to your own interests, on your own website. Among other things, you can avoid long-distance phone bills this way—I use a variant of this application to stay in touch with home when I'm on the road.

How does someone enter the chat room? It's easy. The user simply enters the URL for chat.html in the browser. You can see what it looks like in Figure 5.1—other people only need to go to the same URL, enter their name in the text field (the default is "Guest"), type their comments, and click the Submit button. Their comments will show up in the top part of the page, which is refreshed every 5 seconds (you can alter the refresh rate). And the whole conversation takes off.

Not bad.

FIGURE 5.1   The chat room at work.

That's an HTML page in Figure 5.1. So where does Java come into this? There are two files needed for this project—chat.html and chat.jsp. The second file, chat.jsp, is where the real action is. This is a JavaServer Pages (JSP) file, and you're going to see how to create it in this chapter. JSP files can contain both normal Java code and HTML, in the same file, which is perfect for working online.

NOTE

To use Java online, you're going to need a web server that supports JavaServer Pages. Many web servers do support JSP these days, so ask your ISP whether its servers do. If not, it's easy to find a web server that does—just search for "jsp host" on the Internet. You'll find hundreds.

The first file, chat.html, provides the framework that displays the output of chat.jsp.

Creating the Chat HTML Page

There are two parts to this application—the part that reads new comments from the user, and the part that displays the current comments every 5 seconds in the upper half of the screen. To keep those two parts separate, Chat uses HTML frames. The top frame, where everyone's comments appear, is given 65% of the vertical space, and the bottom frame, where the user enters his own comments, is given 35%. Also, the frames are borderless, which gives users the impression that the result is all a single, seamless page:

```
<HTML>
    <HEAD>
        <TITLE>Chat</TITLE>
    </HEAD>
    <FRAMESET ROWS="65%, 35%" FRAMEBORDER='0' FRAMESPACING='0'>
        .
        .
        .
    </FRAMESET>
</HTML>
```

Although not very likely, some users may be using older browsers that don't support frames, so it's customary to display a message, using the <NOFRAMES> HTML element, telling them they need a browser that supports frames:

```
<HTML>
    <HEAD>
        <TITLE>Chat</TITLE>
    </HEAD>

    <FRAMESET ROWS="65%, 35%" FRAMEBORDER='0' FRAMESPACING='0'>
        <NOFRAMES>Sorry, you need frames to use chat.</NOFRAMES>
        .
        .
        .
    </FRAMESET>
</HTML>
```

Because both the top and bottom frames need to share the text data sent in by the user, they're both handled by the same JSP file, chat.jsp:

```
<HTML>
    <HEAD>
```

```
        <TITLE>Chat</TITLE>
    </HEAD>

    <FRAMESET ROWS="65%, 35%" FRAMEBORDER='0' FRAMESPACING='0'>
        <NOFRAMES>Sorry, you need frames to use chat.</NOFRAMES>
        <FRAME NAME="_display" SRC="chat.jsp">
        <FRAME NAME="_data" SRC="chat.jsp">
    </FRAMESET>
</HTML>
```

However, chat.jsp should have some way of knowing which half of the display it's dealing with—the upper half (where the current comments are displayed) or the lower half (where the user enters comments). To give chat.jsp a hint about what it should be doing, chat.html passes a little extra data when it fetches the top frame from chat.jsp. It does that with a process called *URL encoding*, which is used when passing data from HTML forms to JSP files or other files on a web server. In this case, it passes a parameter named t, setting that parameter's value to "1":

```
<HTML>
    <HEAD>
        <TITLE>Chat</TITLE>
    </HEAD>

    <FRAMESET ROWS="65%, 35%" FRAMEBORDER='0' FRAMESPACING='0'>
        <NOFRAMES>Sorry, you need frames to use chat.</NOFRAMES>
        <FRAME NAME="_display" SRC="chat.jsp?t=1">
        <FRAME NAME="_data" SRC="chat.jsp">
    </FRAMESET>
</HTML>
```

This is the way data can be sent from controls such as text fields back to JSP pages. Now chat.jsp will be able to check for that parameter (t), and if it equals "1", chat.jsp knows it's dealing with the top half of the page, so it should display the current comments.

That's all you need for chat.html; now it's time to start working on chat.jsp.

Creating JSP Pages

When Java first came to the Web, you used Java *servlets* to create interactive web pages. Servlets are compiled Java code, and they take a little bit of practice to write. For example, here's a servlet that displays the text "Hello there!" in an HTML page:

```
import java.io.*;
import javax.servlet.*;
```

```
import javax.servlet.http.*;

public class Sample extends HttpServlet
{
    public void doGet(HttpServletRequest request,
        HttpServletResponse response)
        throws IOException, ServletException
    {
        response.setContentType("text/html");
        PrintWriter out = response.getWriter();

        out.println("<HTML>");
        out.println("<HEAD>");
        out.println("<TITLE>");
        out.println("A Web Page");
        out.println("</TITLE>");
        out.println("</HEAD>");
        out.println("Hello there!");
        out.println("</BODY>");
        out.println("</HTML>");
    }
}
```

If you want to use servlets like this, you need to compile them, making sure that the class support for servlets, bundled into a JAR file, is in your class path. Also, you have to edit a deployment descriptor file when you install a servlet on a web server.

It's much easier to use JSP instead of servlets for this project, and that's how Chat is written—everything revolves around chat.jsp.

Here's a sample JSP file that does the same thing as the previous servlet did—it displays the text "Hello there!" in an HTML page:

```
<HTML>
    <HEAD>
        <TITLE>A Web Page</TITLE>
    </HEAD>

    <BODY>
        <% out.println("Hello there!"); %>
    </BODY>
</HTML>
```

As you can see, this is shorter, and it's all HTML except for one line, which is enclosed in the markup <% and %>. That's a JSP *scriptlet*, and in this case, it's executing this single line of Java:

```
out.println("Hello there!");
```

This line of code uses the out object, which is set up for you by the JSP framework, in order to display text in the browser. Just as you can use System.out.println to display text in a console, you can use out.println in JSP code to display text in the browser. Here, however, the out object is a JspWriter object.

This is a lot easier than working with servlets, where you have to instantiate your own objects before working with them. For example, if you want to write to the browser in a servlet, you have to create your own out object, which you can do like this:

```
public class Sample extends HttpServlet
{
    public void doGet(HttpServletRequest request,
        HttpServletResponse response)
        throws IOException, ServletException
    {
        response.setContentType("text/html");
        PrintWriter out = response.getWriter();

        out.println("<HTML>");
        out.println("<HEAD>");
        .
        .
        .
```

Note also that when you want to send HTML back to the browser, as in the last two lines in the preceding code snippet, you have to use Java to do it. In a JSP page, on the other hand, you can mix simple HTML with Java in the same document—when you want to use Java, you just enclose your Java code with the markup <% and %>, making it a JSP scriptlet.

REAL-WORLD SCENARIO

Why JSP?

There's a fair bit of programming in writing servlets, as you can see in the previous example. If you want to use an object like the out object to send text back to the browser, you have to create that object yourself and use its println method to send text. You have to compile the servlet, using various JAR files supplied by the servlet container (that is, the web server). You have to install the servlet and, typically, edit a deployment descriptor. Sometimes, the servlet container has to be restarted before the servlet becomes visible.

All that proved to be too much for casual HTML authors, and servlets were not a big success with the homepage crowd. Java programmers were fine with them, and still are, but the average homepage writer just didn't take to them.

That was a pity, because Java had been coming to the Web in a big way before that. In the early days of web development, web page authors loved Java applets—small, embeddable segments of Java code that could display interactive graphics and controls such as buttons.

continues

NOTE

Make no mistake—even though JSP is easy to write, you can use any Java code in JSP that you could in a servlet, and almost any that you can run on your desktop (with the exception, obviously, of windowing code). However, as your code gets longer, all that HTML mixed in with your Java gets annoying, and you should consider converting to servlets.

The chat.jsp file starts with another of the built-in objects in JSP, the `request` object. This is the object that passes on the data from the web page to the server, and you can use that object's `getParameter` method to recover that data. For example, here's how chat.jsp starts, by recovering the parameter named t and testing whether it holds "1":

```
<%
if(request.getParameter("t") != null &&
    request.getParameter("t").equals("1")){
%>
    <HTML>
        <HEAD>
            .
            .
            .
```

To develop and run chat.jsp, you'll need a web server that can run JSP pages, and for this and upcoming projects, this book uses the Apache Tomcat server because it's easy to get and easy to run. Using this server, you can develop chat.jsp step by step.

REAL-WORLD SCENARIO *continued*

In time, though, applets became old hat, supplanted by newer options such as Flash and others. These days, some major browsers no longer even support applets.

So Sun turned to the server side of things. Servlets certainly worked, but proved too hard to master for many home developers. To make things easier, Sun introduced JSP.

JSP pages come with all kinds of objects ready for you to use, they don't need to be compiled, they don't need deployment descriptors, and you can mix HTML in with your Java code in the same page—no need to print everything out with Java methods.

For all these reasons, JSP has become very popular. Using JSP will also make your life easier when writing the Chat project. Internally, what happens is that the JSP page is translated into a servlet and run as a servlet. But you don't have to take care of any of the standard baggage that comes with developing servlets—it's all done for you automatically by the JSP container, including compiling that servlet and running it.

Getting the Tomcat Web Server

To develop chat.jsp on your machine, you can download the reference web server for servlets and JSP, the Apache Tomcat server, which you can get from http://jakarta.apache.org/tomcat/ for free. To follow along, download the binary EXE file for your system and run it to install Tomcat.

After installing Tomcat, just follow the directions that come with it to start Tomcat. For example, if you're using Windows, the current version (Tomcat 5.5) installs itself as a Windows service. To start Tomcat, select the Start, Programs, Apache 5.5, Configure Tomcat item and then click the Start button to start Tomcat (or the Stop button to stop it).

To test whether Tomcat is working after you start it, start a browser and navigate to http://localhost:8080, the main page for local installations of Tomcat. You can see the results in Figure 5.2.

FIGURE 5.2   The Tomcat main page.

The localhost part is the name of the web server, and "localhost" is the name reserved for web servers running on your own machine. The 8080 part is the *port number*. Each web server uses a port number to keep it separate from other web servers. Web servers usually use port 80, but Tomcat uses port 8080 so it won't interfere with other web servers.

Here's the directory structure that installing Tomcat creates:

```
Tomcat 5.5
¦__bin          Binary executable files
¦__common       Classes available to internal classes and Web applications:
¦__conf         Configuration files (such as passwords)
¦__logs         The server's log files
¦__server       Internal Tomcat classes
¦__shared       Shared files
```

```
¦__temp                 Temporary files
¦__webapps              Directory for Web applications
¦__work                 Scratch directory for holding temporary files
```

Note in particular the webapps directory, which is where you put JSPs (and servlets) to make them accessible to your browser. For instance, the files from this chapter will go into the chat directory, so add this new directory to the webapps directory now:

```
webapps
¦__chat                             Holds chat.html and chat.jsp
```

To satisfy Tomcat, any directory containing web applications must also contain a directory named WEB-INF, with two subdirectories, classes and lib. WEB-INF, classes, and lib may all be empty—as they will be here—but Tomcat will expect them to be there before running your application:

```
webapps
¦__chat                             Holds chat.html and chat.jsp
   ¦__WEB-INF                       Information about Web applications
       ¦__classes                   Java classes used Web applications
       ¦__lib                       JAR files used by Web applications
```

Create those directories, WEB-INF, classes, and lib now. They'll be empty, but Tomcat needs to see those directories before it will serve any HTML or JSP pages for you.

To get started, store this short demo JSP in a file named ch05_01.jsp in the webapps\chat directory now:

```html
<HTML>
  <HEAD>
    <TITLE>Using JSP</TITLE>
  </HEAD>

  <BODY>
    <% out.println("This was printed using JSP."); %>
  </BODY>
</HTML>
```

This JSP uses Java to send the text "This was printed using JSP." to the browser. The out object is prepared for you by the JSP framework and is ready for use, much as the System.out object is ready for use in standalone Java programs.

Make sure this file is saved as webapps\chat\ch05_01.jsp, start Tomcat, and browse to the URL http://localhost:8080/chat/ch05_01.jsp, as shown in Figure 5.3. If things work as expected, you should see in your browser what's shown in Figure 5.3.

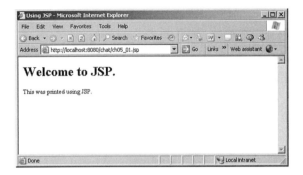

FIGURE 5.3   A first JSP page.

Using Some Java in JSP

The code you use in scriptlets is just straight Java. For example, take a look at this scriptlet, which uses a Java if statement:

```
<HTML>
    <HEAD>
        <TITLE>
            Using Java in JSP
        </TITLE>
    </HEAD>

    <BODY>
        <H1>Using Java in JSP</H1>
        <%
            int temperature = 72;

            if (temperature < 90 && temperature > 60) {
                out.println("Time for a picnic!");
            }
        %>
    </BODY>
</HTML>
```

This scriptlet should send the text "Time for a picnic!" back to the browser. To check that out, enter it into a new JSP, ch05_02.jsp, and store it as webapps\chat\ch05_02.jsp. Then navigate to the URL http://localhost:8080/chat/ch05_02.jsp. As you see in Figure 5.4, this JSP does just what you'd expect.

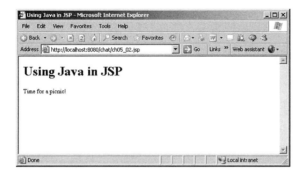

FIGURE 5.4   Using Java in JSP.

There are some restrictions on what you can do in a JSP scriptlet, however. For example, you can't declare methods or new classes in a scriptlet. For that, you need a JSP *declaration*, which is surrounded with the markup <%! and %>. Here's an example that creates a new method—and a recursive one at that—which will calculate factorials (for example, the factorial of 6, written as 6!, is 6 × 5 × 4 × 3 × 2 × 1 = 72).

The factorial method is just a typical implementation of factorials—given a number, n, it multiples that number by the result of calling itself with a value of n-1, and it continues down, stage by stage, until it reaches 1, where it simply returns through all the successive stages and you end up with the factorial:

n × (n − 1) × (n − 2) ... × 3 × 2 × 1

To use this method in JSP, you have to place it in a JSP declaration, enclosing it in the markup <%! and %>:

```
<HTML>
  <HEAD>
    <TITLE>Using Recursion in JSP</TITLE>
  </HEAD>

  <BODY>
    <H1>Using Recursion in JSP</H1>
    <%!
    int factorial(int n)
    {
        if (n == 1) {
            return n;
        }
        else {
            return n * factorial(n - 1);
        }
```

```
    }
    %>
    .
    .
    .
  </BODY>
</HTML>
```

Now you can refer to the `factorial` method in scriptlets, as here, where this example is passing a value of 6 to that method:

```
<HTML>
  <HEAD>
    <TITLE>Using Recursion in JSP</TITLE>
  </HEAD>

  <BODY>
    <H1>Using Recursion in JSP</H1>
    <%!
    int factorial(int n)
    {
        if (n == 1) {
            return n;
        }
        else {
            return n * factorial(n - 1);
        }
    }
    %>


    <%
        out.println("The factorial of 6 is " + factorial(6));
    %>
  </BODY>
</HTML>
```

To see this one running, enter the code into ch05_03.jsp and store it as webapps\chat\ch05_03.jsp. Then open that JSP in a browser, as shown in Figure 5.5. As you can see, the factorial method was declared and called, and the result is as expected.

Note, however, that Java code inside a JSP declaration does not have access to the built-in JSP objects, such as `out` and `request`. Your code can still use those objects, however, if you simply pass them to your methods.

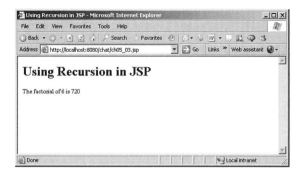

FIGURE 5.5 Calling a method in JSP.

One of the big attractions of JSP is that you can mix Java code and HTML, and that's what happens in chat.jsp. For example, you could break up the earlier script that uses an `if` statement by ending the scriptlet and then starting it again in order to display some HTML. This version will only display the HTML `<B>Time for a picnic!</B>` if the value in `temperature` is less than 90 and greater than 60 (note that the scriptlet ends just before the HTML and then starts again in order to terminate the `if` statement with the closing curly brace):

```
<HTML>
    <HEAD>
        <TITLE>
            Using Java in JSP
        </TITLE>
    </HEAD>

    <BODY>
        <H1>Using Java in JSP</H1>
        <%
            int temperature = 72;

            if (temperature < 90 && temperature > 60) {
        %>
                <B>Time for a picnic!</B>
        <%
            }
        %>
    </BODY>
</HTML>
```

Besides just displaying text, chat.jsp also has to read text from the controls in the web page. So how do you read text from HTML controls?

Reading Data from HTML Controls in JSP

Take a look at the chat room in Figure 5.1; you can see various HTML controls there, namely the text field where the users type their name, the text area where they type their comments, and the Submit button. How do those controls send data to your JSP page?

HTML controls must be enclosed in HTML forms, which you create with the <FORM> element. For example, if you want to add a text field to a web page using the <INPUT TYPE="TEXT"> element, that element must be inside a form. Here's what that looks like in an HTML example, ch05_04.html:

```
<HTML>
    <HEAD>
        <TITLE>Enter your name</TITLE>
    </HEAD>

    <BODY>
        <H1>Enter your name</H1>
        <FORM NAME="form1" ACTION="ch05_05.jsp" METHOD="POST">
            <INPUT TYPE="TEXT" NAME="text">
            <INPUT TYPE="SUBMIT" VALUE="Submit">
        </FORM>
    </BODY>
</HTML>
```

You can see this web page in Figure 5.6.

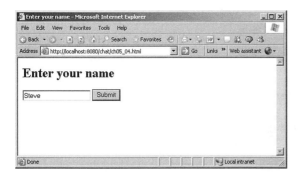

FIGURE 5.6 **Entering data to send to the server.**

You use the ACTION attribute to specify to where the data in the controls in a form should be sent when the form's Submit button is clicked. For example, to send the data in a form to http://www.edwardschat.com/jsps/chat.jsp, you'd set the ACTION attribute to that URL:

```
<FORM NAME="form1"
    ACTION="http://www.edwardschat.com/jsps/chat.jsp" METHOD="POST">
```

```
    <INPUT TYPE="TEXT" NAME="text">
    <INPUT TYPE="SUBMIT" VALUE="Submit">
</FORM>
```

You can also specify a relative URL, which means relative to the directory that the current document is in. For example, to send a form's data to chat.jsp in the same directory as the current document, you can set the ACTION attribute this way:

```
<FORM NAME="form1" ACTION="chat.jsp" METHOD="POST">
    <INPUT TYPE="TEXT" NAME="text">
    <INPUT TYPE="SUBMIT" VALUE="Submit">
</FORM>
```

You can also omit the ACTION attribute, which is how chat.jsp does it. If you do, the data in the form is simply sent back to the exact same URL as the current document.

The METHOD attribute lets you specify the way you send the form's data back to the server. There are two possible settings for this attribute—"GET" and "POST"—and JSP can handle both.

If you use the GET method, the data in the form is treated as text and appended to the URL that the browser navigates to. The server will decode that data appended to the URL and pass it on to the JSP code.

You can also use the POST method, which works just as well as GET as far as we are concerned, but encodes the data as part of the actual Hypertext Transfer Protocol (HTTP) request sent to the server. This means that the data is not visible to the user in the browser.

That sets up the form, but what about actually reading data from the HTML controls? For that, you use request objects.

Using Request Objects

When the user clicks the Submit button in ch05_04.html, the ACTION attribute in the HTML makes the browser send the data in the HTML controls to ch05_05.jsp:

```
<HTML>
    <HEAD>
        <TITLE>Enter your name</TITLE>
    </HEAD>

    <BODY>
        <H1>Enter your name</H1>
        <FORM NAME="form1" ACTION="ch05_05.jsp" METHOD="POST">
            <INPUT TYPE="TEXT" NAME="text">
            <INPUT TYPE="SUBMIT" VALUE="Submit">
        </FORM>
```

```
    </BODY>
</HTML>
```

In ch05_05.jsp, the `request` object gives you access to the data sent from the HTML form. This object is built in to the JSP framework, much like the `out` object, so it's already available to you as soon as your code starts. It's an object of the `javax.servlet.http.HttpServletRequest` class, and you can see the significant methods of `javax.servlet.http.HttpServletRequest` in Table 5.1.

TABLE 5.1   **Significant Methods of the** `javax.servlet.http.HttpServletRequest` **Class**

Method	Does This
`java.lang.Object getAttribute(java.lang.String name)`	**Returns the value of the given named attribute as a Java object**
`java.util.Enumeration getAttributeNames()`	**Returns an enumeration that holds the names of the attributes in this request**
`int getContentLength()`	**Returns the length (in bytes) of the body of the HTTP request. Returns -1 if the length is not known**
`java.lang.String getContentType()`	**Returns the MIME type of the body of the request. Returns** `null` **if the type is not known**
`ServletInputStream getInputStream()`	**Returns the body of the request as binary data using a** `ServletInputStream` **stream**
`java.util.Locale getLocale()`	**Returns the preferred locale that the client uses; for example,** `en_US` **means U.S. English**
`java.util.Enumeration getLocales()`	**Returns an enumeration of** `Locale` **objects indicating the locales that are acceptable to the browser**
`java.lang.String getParameter(java.lang.String name)`	**Returns the value of a request parameter as a** `String` **object. Returns** `null` **if the parameter does not exist**
`java.util.Enumeration getParameterNames()`	**Returns an enumeration of** `String` **objects holding the names of the parameters contained in this request**
`java.lang.String[] getParameterValues(java.lang.String name)`	**Returns an array of** `String` **objects containing the values the given request parameter has. Returns** `null` **if the parameter does not exist**
`boolean isSecure()`	**Returns** `true` **if this request was made using a secure channel, such as HTTPS. Returns** `false` **otherwise**
`void removeAttribute(java.lang.String name)`	**Removes an attribute from this request (more on request attributes later)**
`void setAttribute(java.lang.String name, java.lang.Object o)`	**Stores an attribute in this request (more on request attributes later)**

In JSP code such as chat.jsp, you use the `request` object's `getParameter` method to read data from HTML controls. For example, the text field in ch05_04.html is named `text`:

```
<HTML>
    <HEAD>
        <TITLE>Enter your name</TITLE>
    </HEAD>

    <BODY>
        <H1>Enter your name</H1>
        <FORM NAME="form1" ACTION="ch05_05.jsp" METHOD="POST">
            <INPUT TYPE="TEXT" NAME="text">
            <INPUT TYPE="SUBMIT" VALUE="Submit">
        </FORM>
    </BODY>
</HTML>
```

You can get the data the user entered in that text field on the server by passing that name to the `request.getParameter` method, as you see in ch05_05.jsp:

```
<HTML>
  <HEAD>
    <TITLE>Reading Text Using Text Fields</TITLE>
  </HEAD>

    <BODY>
        <H1>Reading Text Using Text Fields</H1>
        Your name is
        <% out.println(request.getParameter("text")); %>
    </BODY>
</HTML>
```

That's all it takes—using the Java expression `request.getParameter("text")`, you can retrieve the text in the text field named `text`. Enter ch05_05.jsp, and store it as webapps\chat\ch05_05.jsp. Now when you enter your name in ch05_04.html and click the Submit button, that name is sent to ch05_05.jsp, which displays it, as you see in Figure 5.7.

That's how it works—you can use the `request.getParameter` method to retrieve data from HTML controls, passing that method the name you've given to the control. In this case, the text field was named `text1`, and passing that name to `request.getParameter` returns the data that was in the text field (the data is returned as a Java string).

At this point, you have nearly all the technology needed to create chat.jsp; you can accept input from the user and display results. The chat.jsp application needs more power, however. Take a look at Figure 5.1, which shows Chat in action. Chat has to not only read input from the user, it has to display the current user comments, which means storing those comments on the server.

FIGURE 5.7   Reading text from a text field.

Your first thought might be to store those comments in a set of files and to treat those files as a sort of stack where the oldest comment is popped to make room as the most recent comment is pushed onto the stack. However, working with files in a multiuser web server environment is inherently prone to difficulties—in particular, what if you're writing to a file at the same time some other user tries to write to it? That's handled differently on different platforms, and you can end up in sticky situations.

If possible, it's best to steer clear of simultaneous access problems with files on a web server using Java. There's a better way to handle the users' comments—you store data in JSPs between page accesses using some built-in JSP objects.

Using the Session and Application Objects

Online programs are by default *stateless*—that is, when you load a page a number of times in succession, the data in the page is reinitialized each time. If you want to track, say, the number of times the user has accessed the page, you need to specifically store that data somewhere.

In a standard desktop program, where you're interacting with the user while the program is running, you can store data in variables. That data won't be reset to its default values the next time you look at it. Using JSP *sessions*, you actually can do the same thing in JSP—you can interact with the user as part of a "session."

While the session is active, you can store data in it, and that data will be preserved on the server in between user accesses to the page. You can set your variables in one page access, and they'll hold the same data the next time you see the page, as long as the session hasn't timed out (the default session timeout is 30 minutes).

JSP session objects are based on the `javax.servlet.http.HttpSession` interface. The data you store in a session is stored as session *attributes*. You can use the `session` object's `setAttribute` method to store data, and you can use the `getAttribute` method to recover that data as long as the session is active. You'll find the significant methods of the `javax.servlet.http.HttpSession` interface in Table 5.2.

TABLE 5.2 The Significant `javax.servlet.http.HttpSession` Methods

Method	Does this
`void addCookie(Cookie cookie)`	Adds the specified cookie to the response object
`java.lang.Object getAttribute(java.lang. String name)`	Returns the object of the given name in this session
`java.util.Enumeration getAttributeNames()`	Returns a Java Enumeration of `String` objects containing the names of all the objects in this session
`long getCreationTime()`	Returns the time when this session was created (measured in milliseconds since midnight January 1, 1970 GMT)
`long getLastAccessedTime()`	Returns the last time the client sent a request in with this session, as the number of milliseconds since midnight January 1, 1970 GMT
`int getMaxInactiveInterval()`	Returns the maximum time, in seconds, that the server will keep this session open between client accesses
`void invalidate()`	Invalidates this session
`boolean isNew()`	Returns a value of `true` if the client does not yet know about the session
`void removeAttribute(java.lang.String name)`	Removes the object with the specified name from this session
`void setAttribute(java.lang.String name, java.lang.Object value)`	Connects an object to this session, using the given name
`void setMaxInactiveInterval(int interval)`	Specifies the time, in seconds, between client requests before the server will invalidate this session

This is all best seen in an example. For instance, say you were trying to create a hit counter and therefore needed to store the number of times a page has been viewed. You're not going to get very far doing something like this, where you simply increment a variable each time a page is accessed, as shown in ch05_06.jsp:

```
<HTML>
    <HEAD>
        <TITLE>A non-working hit counter</TITLE>
    </HEAD>

    <BODY>
        <H1>A non-working hit counter</H1>
        <%
            int counter = 0;
            counter++;
```

```
        %>
        Number of times you've been here: <%=counter%>
    </BODY>
</HTML>
```

The problem is that each time the JSP is displayed, all the data in it is reinitialized, which means that the counter variable will never hold more than 1, no matter how many times you view the page, as shown in Figure 5.8.

FIGURE 5.8   A non-working hit counter.

Creating a Hit Counter Using Sessions

You need some way of storing data between page accesses, and one way of doing that is to use the session object, which comes built in to the JSP environment, ready for you to use. To use this object, you start with the JSP page directive at the top of the JSP page, setting this directive's session attribute to true to indicate that you want to use sessions:

```
<%@page import = "java.util.*" session="true"%>
```

This makes sure that opening this page starts a new session if such a session doesn't already exist.

> **NOTE**
>
> The page directive is not really necessary here, because the default for the session attribute is true, but it's included here just for completeness; you can omit it in your own code. More on this directive in Chapter 10, "Getting a Graphical Weather Forecast: The Forecaster Project."

You can keep track of the number of times the user has viewed the page in a session *attribute* named, say, counter. You store data in sessions using attributes, and you can store and retrieve data in sessions using the setAttribute and getAttribute methods.

You can't store the basic data types such as int in session attributes—you can only store Java objects, based on the java.lang.Object class. String objects are fine to store as attributes, but what about int values such as the counter value? In this case, you should use the formal Integer class, not just try to store an int value. You can create a Integer object with that class's constructor, and you can recover the data in the object with the intValue method of the Integer class.

Okay, this is ready to go. First, the code will check if the counter attribute has already been set in a former page access. The counter variable will be stored as an Integer object, so here's how you can read its current value from the session object using the getAttribute method:

```
<%@page import = "java.util.*" session="true"%>
<HTML>
    <HEAD>
        <TITLE>A hit counter using sessions</TITLE>
    </HEAD>

    <BODY>
        <H1>A hit counter using sessions</H1>
        <%
        Integer counter =
            (Integer)session.getAttribute("counter");

            .
            .
            .
```

If counter has not been set before, getAttribute will return a value of null. In that case, you should create the counter value. On the other hand, if it already exists, you should increment the value stored in it and store the new value in the session object, like this:

```
<%@page import = "java.util.*" session="true"%>
<HTML>
    <HEAD>
        <TITLE>A hit counter using sessions</TITLE>
    </HEAD>

    <BODY>
        <%
        <H1>A hit counter using sessions</H1>
        Integer counter =
            (Integer)session.getAttribute("counter");
        if (counter == null) {
            counter = new Integer(1);
        } else {
            counter = new Integer(counter.intValue() + 1);
        }
```

```
        session.setAttribute("counter", counter);
        .
        .
        .
```

That's how you can store and retrieve data in the session object. Here's what it looks like in a new, working hit counter, ch05_07.jsp:

```
<%@page import = "java.util.*" session="true"%>
<HTML>
    <HEAD>
        <TITLE>A hit counter using sessions</TITLE>
    </HEAD>

    <BODY>
        <H1>A hit counter using sessions</H1>
        <%
        Integer counter =
            (Integer)session.getAttribute("counter");
        if (counter == null) {
            counter = new Integer(1);
        } else {
            counter = new Integer(counter.intValue() + 1);
        }

        session.setAttribute("counter", counter);
        %>
        Number of times you've been here: <%=counter%>
    </BODY>
</HTML>
```

The results are shown in Figure 5.9, where the user has opened this page and reloaded it a number of times, as you can see, because the page says the user has been here three times.

FIGURE 5.9   Using a session-based hit counter.

Using sessions like this is great for storing and recovering data, as you can see—it provides you with an environment much like a standard program, where you interact with the user without having to worry about having your data reset.

That's fine, except for one thing—how do you share data between users? What if 12 users are accessing chat.jsp at once? Every time a new user loads chat.jsp, a new `session` object would be created, which means you can't share data between users this way.

But there is a new object, similar to the `session` object, that you can use and will do the trick—the `application` object.

Creating a Hit Counter Using Applications

A session lets you track one user at a time—an application lets you share data between many users. To access the current application, you can use the built-in JSP `application` object. Like the `session` object, the `application` object is based on the `javax.servlet.http.HttpSession` interface.

In the previous example, you saw how to create a `session` attribute named `counter` that stores the number of times the user has visited the page in the current session. In the same way, you can create an `application` attribute named `counter` that holds the total number of times anyone in the same application has viewed a JSP page:

```
Integer counter = (Integer)application.getAttribute("counter");
if (counter == null) {
    counter = new Integer(1);
} else {
    counter = new Integer(counter.intValue() + 1);
}

application.setAttribute("counter", counter);
```

You can see this at work in ch05_08, where the code supports an application counter (not a session counter) that stores the number of visits in the current application:

```
<HTML>
    <HEAD>
        <TITLE>A hit counter using applications</TITLE>
    </HEAD>

    <BODY>
        <H1>A hit counter using applications</H1>
        <%
        Integer counter =
            (Integer)application.getAttribute("counter");
        if (counter == null) {
```

```
            counter = new Integer(1);
        } else {
            counter = new Integer(counter.intValue() + 1);
        }

        application.setAttribute("counter", counter);
        %>
        Number of times you've been here: <%=counter%>
    </BODY>
</HTML>
```

You can see what this JSP looks like in Figure 5.10. When the user refreshes this page, the
number of hits automatically increments, as shown in the figure. And when other users
open the same page, the count also increments, because the data in the application object
is shared among those users.

FIGURE 5.10   Using an application-based hit counter.

That's exactly what Chat needs—some way of sharing stored data between multiple users of
the same JSP.

Displaying the Current User Comments

When chat.html wants to display the current user comments in its top frame, it sends
chat.jsp the parameter t, set to "1". Here's how the code at the beginning of chat.jsp checks
that parameter:

```
<%
if(request.getParameter("t") != null &&
    request.getParameter("t").equals("1")){
%>
            .
            .
            .
```

If it's time to display the current user comments, they need to be fetched from the applica-tion object. Chat keeps track of eight user comments at a time, named "text0" through "text7", as stored in the application object, and they can be retrieved using application.getAttribute("text0") and so forth. Besides simply displaying this text, chat.jsp must also tell the browser to come back in 5 seconds and get the user comments again to keep them current. It does that with an HTML tag <META> tag in the <HEAD> section of this HTML page, setting the HTTP header HTTP-EQUIV to "Refresh" and the CONTENT attribute to "5" (for 5 seconds). Note that you can set this time yourself to shorten or lengthen the time between refreshes. Here's how chat.jsp retrieves the user data from the application object and sets up the refresh rate:

```
<%
if(request.getParameter("t") != null &&
    request.getParameter("t").equals("1")){
%>
    <HTML>
        <HEAD>
            <meta HTTP-EQUIV="Refresh" CONTENT="5">
        </HEAD>
        <BODY>
<%
    String text0 = (String) application.getAttribute("text0");
    String text1 = (String) application.getAttribute("text1");
    String text2 = (String) application.getAttribute("text2");
    String text3 = (String) application.getAttribute("text3");
    String text4 = (String) application.getAttribute("text4");
    String text5 = (String) application.getAttribute("text5");
    String text6 = (String) application.getAttribute("text6");
    String text7 = (String) application.getAttribute("text7");
        .
        .
        .
```

Now you've got the text that's to be displayed; to actually display that text, chat.jsp uses an HTML table this way:

```
<%
if(request.getParameter("t") != null &&
    request.getParameter("t").equals("1")){
%>
    <HTML>
        <HEAD>
            <meta HTTP-EQUIV="Refresh" CONTENT="5">
        </HEAD>
        <BODY>
<%
```

```
String text0 = (String) application.getAttribute("text0");
String text1 = (String) application.getAttribute("text1");
String text2 = (String) application.getAttribute("text2");
String text3 = (String) application.getAttribute("text3");
String text4 = (String) application.getAttribute("text4");
String text5 = (String) application.getAttribute("text5");
String text6 = (String) application.getAttribute("text6");
String text7 = (String) application.getAttribute("text7");

out.println("<center><h1>Chat Room</h1></center>");

out.println("<center><table width='90%'>");

out.println("<tr><td><font size=2>");

if(text0 != null){
    out.println(text0);
}

out.println("</font></td></tr>");

out.println("<tr><td><font size=2>");

if(text1 != null){
    out.println(text1);
}

out.println("</font></td></tr>");

out.println("<tr><td><font size=2>");

if(text2 != null){
    out.println(text2);
}

out.println("</font></td></tr>");

out.println("<tr><td><font size=2>");

if(text3 != null){
    out.println(text3);
}

out.println("</font></td></tr>");
```

```
out.println("<tr><td><font size=2>");

if(text4 != null){
    out.println(text4);
}
out.println("</font></td></tr>");

out.println("<tr><td><font size=2>");

if(text5 != null){
    out.println(text5);
}

out.println("</font></td></tr>");

out.println("<tr><td><font size=2>");

if(text6 != null){
    out.println(text6);
}

out.println("</font></td></tr>");

out.println("<tr><td><font size=2>");

if(text7 != null){
    out.println(text7);
}

out.println("</font></td></tr>");

out.println("</table></center>");
%>
        </BODY>
    </HTML>
        .
        .
        .
```

That takes care of the upper frame in chat.html, which displays the current user comments, if there are any. What about accepting new comments when a user types something and clicks the Submit button?

Storing New Comments

If the t parameter is not set to "1", chat.html may be trying to tell you that the user is sending you new comments. The text field you see in Figure 5.1 is named text1, and the text area is named textarea1. If there is already text in those two controls, you should store the user's new comments from the text area in the text0 through text7 strings. You can start by recovering all the current user comments:

```
<%
}
else{
    if(request.getParameter("textarea1") != null){
        String name = request.getParameter("text1");

    String text0 = (String) application.getAttribute("text0");
    String text1 = (String) application.getAttribute("text1");
    String text2 = (String) application.getAttribute("text2");
    String text3 = (String) application.getAttribute("text3");
    String text4 = (String) application.getAttribute("text4");
    String text5 = (String) application.getAttribute("text5");
    String text6 = (String) application.getAttribute("text6");
    String text7 = (String) application.getAttribute("text7");

        .
        .
        .
```

Now you've got to push the new user comments onto the text0 through text7 "stack." You do that by getting rid of the current text in text7 and moving all the other comments up by one place (text6 becomes text7, text5 becomes text6, and so on). The text in the text area that the user is submitting to chat.jsp is then stored in text0 (note that the code also adds the user's name in bold in front of his comments to make it clear who said what):

```
<%
}
else{
    if(request.getParameter("textarea1") != null){
        String name = request.getParameter("text1");

    String text0 = (String) application.getAttribute("text0");
    String text1 = (String) application.getAttribute("text1");
    String text2 = (String) application.getAttribute("text2");
    String text3 = (String) application.getAttribute("text3");
    String text4 = (String) application.getAttribute("text4");
    String text5 = (String) application.getAttribute("text5");
    String text6 = (String) application.getAttribute("text6");
    String text7 = (String) application.getAttribute("text7");
```

```
    application.setAttribute("text7", text6);
    application.setAttribute("text6", text5);
    application.setAttribute("text5", text4);
    application.setAttribute("text4", text3);
    application.setAttribute("text3", text2);
    application.setAttribute("text2", text1);
    application.setAttribute("text1", text0);

    application.setAttribute("text0", "<B>" + name + ":</B> " +
        request.getParameter("textarea1"));
    }
        .
        .
        .
```

That stores the user's new comments, which will be displayed the next time any user's chat.html asks chat.jsp for the current comments.

Next, you've got to re-create the contents of the bottom frame in chat.html—namely, the text area for the user's comments and the text field containing the user's name, or "Guest" if the user hasn't entered a name. Here's how you create the text field that holds the user's name if he has supplied one (or "Guest" otherwise):

```
%>
    <HTML>
        <HEAD>
        </HEAD>
        <BODY>
            <FORM NAME="form1" METHOD="POST">
                <CENTER>
                    Your name:
<%
    if(request.getParameter("text1") != null){
%>
                    <INPUT TYPE="TEXT" NAME="text1"
                    VALUE=<%
                    out.println(request.getParameter("text1")); %>
                    ></INPUT>
<%
    }
    else{
%>
                    <INPUT TYPE="TEXT" NAME="text1" VALUE="Guest">
                    </INPUT>
<%
    }
```

```
%>
    .
    .
    .
```

What about creating the text area that you see at the bottom of Figure 5.1, which lets the users enter their comments? That's an HTML text area control, four rows high, 60 columns wide. After adding that to the form in the bottom frame, you also add the Submit button (note that there's no space between the opening and closing <TEXTAREA> tag to make sure that the text area doesn't have anything in it when it appears):

```
            <BR>
            <TEXTAREA NAME="textarea1"
            ROWS="4" COLS="60"></TEXTAREA>
            <BR>
            <INPUT TYPE="SUBMIT" VALUE="Submit">
        </CENTER>
    </FORM>
    .
    .
    .
```

Here's one more detail—after the user types his comment and clicks the Submit button to send it to the server, the page reappears with the cleared text area. But the text area no longer has the focus (that is, it's no longer the target of keyboard events), so the user has to click the text area to enter more comments. To spare the user the trouble, you can add a little JavaScript to the page in the bottom frame that gives the focus to the text area automatically when the page appears:

```
            <BR>
            <TEXTAREA NAME="textarea1"
            ROWS="4" COLS="60"></TEXTAREA>
            <BR>
            <INPUT TYPE="SUBMIT" VALUE="Submit">
        </CENTER>
    </FORM>
    <script language="javascript">
        document.form1.textarea1.focus()
    </script>
    </BODY>
    </HTML>
<%
    }
%>
```

And that's it—that completes the Chat application. After installing chat.jsp and chat.html in the chat directory of a JSP-enabled web server, you can navigate to chat.html (that's http://localhost:8080/chat/chat.html if you're using Tomcat on your own machine, as detailed in this chapter), and you'll see the page shown in Figure 5.11.

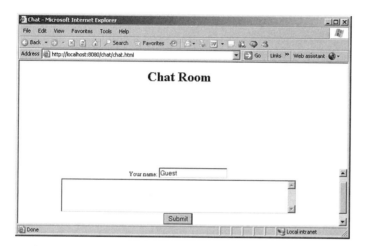

FIGURE 5.11   Starting the Chat project.

You can enter your name and type comments in the text area. After clicking the Submit button, those comments will appear in the main page, as you see in Figure 5.12.

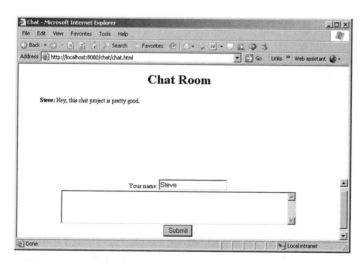

FIGURE 5.12   Entering text in the chat project.

If other users navigate to the same URL, they can also enter the chat, as you see in Figure 5.13.

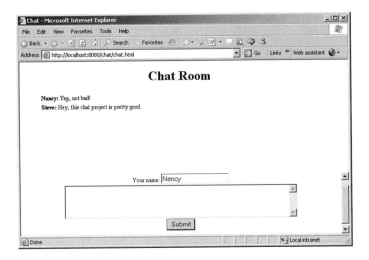

FIGURE 5.13   Others users can also enter text in the Chat project.

___
NOTE
___

You can download the complete source code for the Chat project—chat.html and chat.jsp—at the Sams website. After placing these files in the chat directory on your web server, as detailed in the beginning of the chapter, navigate to chat.html to start the Chat project.

Conclusion

This chapter presented the Chat project, a fun online application that creates an Internet-based chat room using web browsers. Using Chat, you can talk with friends on the Internet using nothing more than browsers and a JSP-enabled server.

To create the chat room, Chat uses HTML, Java, JavaScript, and JSP. The HTML part presents the frames that the rest of the application displays itself in—a bottom frame with HTML controls that lets the user enter comments, and an upper frame that displays the current comments and refreshes itself ever 5 seconds (and that time can be easily altered).

JSP did most of the work in the Chat project. Using JSP, you can display the current text as well as the HTML controls—a text area for comments, a text field for the user's name, and a Submit button—that the application needs.

The most essential item here is the JSP application object, which holds data shared among all users accessing chat.jsp. Using this object, Chat can store all the current comments, and the Java code in chat.jsp can both retrieve those comments and store them.

CHAPTER 6

Who's There? Logging Access to Your Website with WebLogger

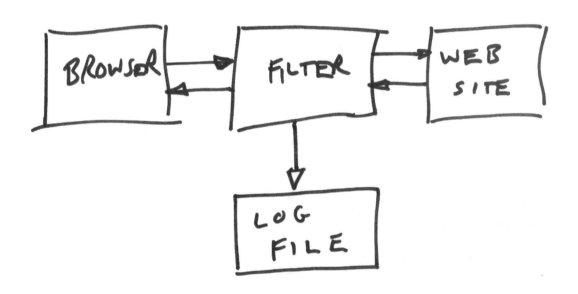

WebLogger.

Want to know who's been accessing your website? Want to track them by IP address, browser type, even username? WebLogger lets you log information about the people who come to a website, without their knowledge. Unless you tell them, they have no way of knowing that they've been tracked as you log their time of access, where on your site they went, what their username is (if they logged in to your website, as you're going to see how to do), what their IP address is (and if they have cable access, they have a fixed IP address), how long they worked with the web page they accessed, and what type of browser they have.

Want to get a handle on who comes to your site and how long they stay? Then WebLogger's for you.

Using WebLogger, you can track users as they move around your site. In fact, you can even block access if you want. What does the user see? Nothing at all, as shown in Figure 6.1, where the user is accessing a page called target.jsp—except for the text WebLogger has added to the bottom of the page. Unless that added text informed the user that he was being tracked (and, of course, you can remove that text from WebLogger), he would have no way of knowing it.

FIGURE 6.1   WebLogger at work.

Here's the information that's logged for each user:

- Access time
- Authentication type
- Username
- User IP address
- URL accessed
- Browser
- Milliseconds used

Here's what the report will look like. You can have this logged in the web server's logs or in a separate log file of your own creation—WebLogger lets you do either:

```
User access at Mon Mar 07 15:47:53 EST 2006
Authentication type: BASIC
User name: steve
User IP: 127.0.0.1
Accessing: /logger/target.jsp
Host: 127.0.0.1
Browser: Internet Explorer
Milliseconds used: 109
```

To make what it does possible, WebLogger uses a *filter*. You can get your hands on the data sent to JSPs and servlets, and on the data they return, using filters. All you have to do is to write your filter, compile it, and install it so that the web server only grants access to the web resource you're filtering through that filter. And that gives you complete control.

All About Filters

You don't have to change a web resource, such as a JSP page, HTML page, or a servlet, to log users who come to that resource, to restrict access to it, to alter the data sent to it, or to alter the data that comes back from it. All you need is a filter.

Creating a new filter isn't hard; it's just a Java class that implements the `javax.servlet.Filter` interface. You can see all the methods of this interface in Table 6.1.

TABLE 6.1 The Methods of the `javax.servlet.Filter` **Interface**

Method	Does This
`void destroy()`	Called to indicate that a filter is being destroyed
`void doFilter(ServletRequest request, ServletResponse response, FilterChain chain)`	Called when control is being passed to the filter
`void init(FilterConfig filterConfig)`	Called to indicate that a filter is being initialized

Creating a Simple Filter

A lot of filter technology is needed to build WebLogger, so to get familiar with that, let's take a look at an example. WebLogger works with both the `request` object holding the data sent from the browser and the `response` object sending data back to the browser. So how do you work with, for example, the `response` object to send data back to the browser? Say that you want to filter access to a JSP page named simple.jsp and that you want a filter to add some text to the output of this JSP sent back to the browser. Here's what that JSP page looks like—as it stands, all this page does is to display the text "Using a filter" in an <H1> HTML header:

```
<HTML>
    <HEAD>
        <TITLE>Using a filter</TITLE>
    </HEAD>
    <BODY>
        <H1>Using a filter</H1>
        <BR>
    </BODY>
</HTML>
```

Because you have access to the data sent to and from this JSP page in a filter, you can display your own text in the web page, as you can see in Figure 6.2. In this figure, a filter attached to simple.jsp wrote the text "The filter wrote this," just as WebLogger added the warning about logging user access shown at the bottom of Figure 6.1. Note that the URL still points to simple.jsp; there's nothing to indicate that the page is being filtered. Very cool.

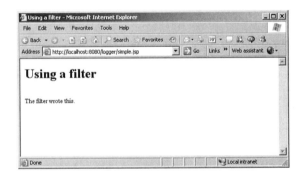

FIGURE 6.2   Adding text to a web page with a filter.

Writing the Code

So how do you create the filter to make this work? The filter here will be called Simple.java, and it will implement the `Filter` interface:

```
import java.io.*;
import javax.servlet.*;
import javax.servlet.http.*;


public class Simple implements Filter
{
```

```
        .
        .
        .
}
```

To implement this interface, you need the doFilter, init, and destroy methods:

```
import java.io.*;
import javax.servlet.*;
import javax.servlet.http.*;

public class Simple implements Filter
{

    public void doFilter(ServletRequest request, ServletResponse response,
      FilterChain chain)
      throws IOException, ServletException
    {
        .
        .
        .
    }

    public void destroy()
    {
        .
        .
        .
    }

    public void init(FilterConfig filterConfig)
    {
        .
        .
        .
    }
}
```

The init method is called when the filter is first initialized, and the destroy method is called when it's destroyed. The doFilter method is where the real action is; when the user is trying to access the web resource you're filtering, this is the method that will be called.

The doFilter method is passed the request and response objects that Java uses to work with web resources; the request object holds the data sent to the web resource by the browser, and the response object holds the data the web resource sends back to the browser.

These objects are of the ServletRequest class (not the HttpServletRequest class you saw in Chapter 5, "Chatting on the Internet with the Chat Room") and the ServletResponse class, respectively, and you can see the significant methods of these classes in Table 6.2 and 6.3.

TABLE 6.2   Significant Methods of the *javax.servlet.http.ServletRequest* **Class**

Method	Does This
java.lang.Object getAttribute(java.lang. String name)	Returns the value of the named attribute
java.util.Enumeration getAttributeNames()	Returns a Java Enumeration holding the names of the attributes in the request
java.lang.String getCharacterEncoding()	Returns the character encoding used in the request's body
int getContentLength()	Returns the length of the request body. Returns -1 if the length is not known
java.lang.String getContentType()	Returns the MIME type of the body of the request
java.util.Locale getLocale()	Returns the locale of the client browser
java.util.Enumeration getLocales()	Returns a Java Enumeration of Locale objects giving the preferred locales of the client
int getLocalPort()	Returns the IP port number where the request was received
java.lang.String getParameter(java.lang. String name)	Returns the value of a request parameter, such as the contents of an HTML control
java.util.Enumeration getParameterNames()	Returns a Java Enumeration holding the names of the parameters contained in this request.
java.lang.String[] getParameterValues (java.lang.String name)	Returns an array of strings holding the values in the specified request parameter
java.io.BufferedReader getReader()	Returns the body of the request using a BufferedReader
java.lang.String getRemoteAddr()	Returns the IP address of the client that sent the request
java.lang.String getRemoteHost()	Returns the name of the client that sent the request
int getRemotePort()	Returns the IP port of the client that sent the request
java.lang.String getScheme()	Returns the name of the Internet scheme of this request, such as HTTP, HTTPS, or FTP
java.lang.String getServerName()	Returns the name of the server where the request was sent
int getServerPort()	Returns the port number where the request was sent

TABLE 6.2 Continued

Method	Does This
`boolean isSecure()`	Returns `true` if this request was made using a secure channel, such as HTTPS
`void removeAttribute(java.lang.String name)`	Removes an attribute from this request
`void setAttribute(java.lang.String name, java.lang.Object o)`	Stores an attribute in this request

TABLE 6.3 Significant Methods of the *javax.servlet.http.ServletResponse* Class

Method	Does This
`void flushBuffer()`	Flushes any content in the buffer so it is written to the client browser
`int getBufferSize()`	Returns the buffer size used for the response, in bytes
`java.lang.String getCharacterEncoding()`	Returns the name of the encoding used in the body of this response
`java.lang.String getContentType()`	Returns the content type used for the MIME body sent in this response
`java.util.Locale getLocale()`	Returns the locale given for this response
`ServletOutputStream getOutputStream()`	Returns a `ServletOutputStream` you can use for writing binary data to the client
`java.io.PrintWriter getWriter()`	Returns a `PrintWriter` object you can use to send text to the client
`void reset()`	Resets any data in the buffer, including the status code and headers
`void resetBuffer()`	Resets the data in the buffer, without resetting the status code and headers
`void setBufferSize(int size)`	Sets the preferred buffer size for the response
`void setCharacterEncoding(java.lang. String charset)`	Sets the character encoding of the response, such as UTF-8
`void setContentLength(int len)`	Sets the length of the content in the response
`void setContentType(java.lang.String type)`	Sets the content type
`void setLocale(java.util.Locale loc)`	Sets the locale of the response

Besides the request and response objects, you're also passed a `FilterChain` object in doFilter. This object provides you with access to the filtered resource—or to other filters that have been added between the current filter and the filtered resource.

In Java-enabled web servers, you can stack filters in a *filter chain*, where control goes to the first filter, then the next, and the next, and so on, all the way to the filtered resource, such as a JSP page, servlet, or an HTML page. You don't have to know about any other possible filters, though; you can simply call the doFilter method of the FilterChain object passed to you. You pass this method both the request and response objects that were passed to you, as shown here:

```java
import java.io.*;
import javax.servlet.*;
import javax.servlet.http.*;

public class Simple implements Filter
{

  public void doFilter(ServletRequest request, ServletResponse response,
    FilterChain chain)
    throws IOException, ServletException
  {
        chain.doFilter(request, response);
      .
      .
      .
  }

  public void destroy()
  {
  }

  public void init(FilterConfig filterConfig)
  {
  }
}
```

When you call the FilterChain object's doFilter method, the next filter, if there is one, is called, followed by any other filters, and then the filtered resource itself. Control returns in the reverse order back to your filter, where you get your hands on the response object again. And that lets you write text in the response sent back to the browser, as WebLogger does. To start, you configure the MIME type of text you're going to send to the browser, setting it to "text/html":

```java
import java.io.*;
import javax.servlet.*;
import javax.servlet.http.*;

public class Simple implements Filter
{
```

```
    public void doFilter(ServletRequest request, ServletResponse response,
      FilterChain chain)
      throws IOException, ServletException
    {

       chain.doFilter(request, response);
       response.setContentType("text/html");
          .
          .
          .


    }

    public void destroy()
    {
    }

    public void init(FilterConfig filterConfig)
    {
    }
}
```

Now you can add your own text to the web page being sent back to the browser, using the response object. In particular, you use the getWriter method to get a PrintWriter object, and then you can use the println method of that object to send the message "The filter wrote this.":

```
import java.io.*;
import javax.servlet.*;
import javax.servlet.http.*;

public class Simple implements Filter
{

  public void doFilter(ServletRequest request, ServletResponse response,
    FilterChain chain)
    throws IOException, ServletException
  {

     chain.doFilter(request, response);
     response.setContentType("text/html");
     PrintWriter out = response.getWriter();
     out.println("The filter wrote this.");
  }

  public void destroy()
  {
  }
```

```
public void init(FilterConfig filterConfig)
{
}
}
```

Configuring the Web Server

That completes the code for this filter. To compile this file, add a new directory named logger for this chapter's project to Tomcat's webapps directory, then add a directory named WEB-INF under logger, and two empty directories, classes and lib, under WEB-INF:

```
webapps
¦
¦ — -logger
    ¦
    ¦ — -WEB-INF
        ¦
        ¦ — -classes
        ¦ — -lib
```

Place simple.jsp (the resource to be filtered) in the logger directory, and place Simple.java (the filter) in the classes directory. Next, copy jsp-api.jar and servlet-api.jar, the needed JAR files for this project, from the Tomcat common\lib directory to the classes directory and add them to the classpath:

```
%set classpath=jsp-api.jar;servlet-api.jar;.
```

Then compile Simple.java (add the necessary path to javac.exe if needed):

```
%javac Simple.java
```

This creates Simple.class, the compiled filter, ready to be used.

Next, you have to connect the filter to the resource you want to filter, which you do with the *deployment descriptor* file, web.xml. This file connects the filtered resource to the filter you want to use, and you store this file in the WEB-INF directory.

Because it's an XML document, web.xml starts with an XML declaration, followed by a <!DOCTYPE> element that indicates where software can find the syntax used in web.xml files to check what you've written. This part is standard, and it starts all web.xml files:

```
<?xml version="1.0" encoding="ISO-8859-1"?>
```

```
<!DOCTYPE web-app
    PUBLIC "-//Sun Microsystems, Inc.//DTD Web Application 2.3//EN"
    "http://java.sun.com/j2ee/dtds/web-app_2_3.dtd">
```

.
.
.

To group the filter together with the resource it filters, you use a `<web-app>` element in
web.xml:

```
<?xml version="1.0" encoding="ISO-8859-1"?>

<!DOCTYPE web-app
    PUBLIC "-//Sun Microsystems, Inc.//DTD Web Application 2.3//EN"
    "http://java.sun.com/j2ee/dtds/web-app_2_3.dtd">

<web-app>
    .
    .
    .
</web-app>
```

In the `<web-app>` element, you install a filter with the `<filter>` element, which encloses two
other elements, `<filter-name>` and `<filter-class>`:

```
<filter>
  <filter-name>
  <filter-class>
</filter>
```

The `<filter-name>` element holds the name you want to give to the filter ("Simple Filter" in
this example) and connects that name to the Java .class file for the filter, Simple.class, in the
`<filter-class>` element. It all looks like this in web.xml:

```
<?xml version="1.0" encoding="ISO-8859-1"?>

<!DOCTYPE web-app
    PUBLIC "-//Sun Microsystems, Inc.//DTD Web Application 2.3//EN"
    "http://java.sun.com/j2ee/dtds/web-app_2_3.dtd">

<web-app>

  <filter>
    <filter-name>Simple Filter</filter-name>
    <filter-class>Simple</filter-class>
  </filter>

    .
    .
    .

</web-app>
```

Having told the web server which Java class to use for the filter, you have to tell it which web resource you want to filter access to. That's simple.jsp here, and you connect this newly declared filter, "Simple Filter," to simple.jps using a `<filter-mapping>` element, which encloses these elements:

```
<filter-mapping>
  <filter-name>
  <url-pattern>
</filter-mapping>
```

Here, `<filter-name>` is the name of a filter you've declared in a `<filter>` element (the `<filter>` element must come before the `<filter-mapping>` element), and `<url-pattern>` is the URL of the resource you want to filter:

```
<?xml version="1.0" encoding="ISO-8859-1"?>

<!DOCTYPE web-app
    PUBLIC "-//Sun Microsystems, Inc.//DTD Web Application 2.3//EN"
    "http://java.sun.com/j2ee/dtds/web-app_2_3.dtd">

<web-app>

  <filter>
    <filter-name>Simple Filter</filter-name>
    <filter-class>Simple</filter-class>
  </filter>

  <filter-mapping>
    <filter-name>Simple Filter</filter-name>
    <url-pattern>/simple.jsp</url-pattern>
  </filter-mapping>

</web-app>
```

Note especially that the URL in `<url-pattern>` can use the * wildcard, so you can filter multiple pages with the same filter. For example, `<url-pattern>/*</url-pattern>` will filter all the web resources in the logger directory.

That's all you need. Because you've changed web.xml and created a new .class file in the webapps directory, you need to restart Tomcat before it'll be able to use simple.jsp and apply your new filter. After you restart Tomcat, navigate to http://localhost:8080/logger/simple.jsp. You should see the results displayed in Figure 6.2. After testing a filter like this, you can install it on any Java-enabled web server, ready for use by users around the world.

Restricting Access Based on Time of Day

The list of things you can do with filters is endless. You can convert, for example, the data sent to a servlet from XML to HTML, or even from French to English. You can add a common header or footer to all web pages in your site. You can use a single filter as a gateway to your entire site. You can restrict access to a JSP or servlet in case multithreading issues become a problem (on most web servers, multiple threads from multiple users can execute the same servlet or JSP code at the same time).

You can even restrict access to a resource based on the time of day. Say you have a company full of employees and don't want them to access a game on your site during the day. Here's what the restricted starting page of the game, game.jsp, might look like:

```
<HTML>
    <HEAD>
        <TITLE>Welcome to the time-wasting game</TITLE>
    </HEAD>
    <BODY>
        <H1>Welcome to the time-wasting game</H1>
        Congratulations, you're in!
        <BR>
    </BODY>
</HTML>
```

Slapping a filter on game.jsp will make it inaccessible during working hours, as you can see in Figure 6.3.

FIGURE 6.3   Restricting access based on time of day with a filter.

Writing a filter like this one isn't difficult. This one will be called Restrict.java, and it starts with the three `Filter` interface methods you need to implement, `init`, `destroy`, and `doFilter`:

```
import java.io.*;
import java.util.*;
```

```
import javax.servlet.*;
import javax.servlet.http.*;

public final class Restrict implements Filter
{
  public void doFilter(ServletRequest request, ServletResponse response,
    FilterChain chain)
    throws IOException, ServletException
  {

        .

        .

        .

  }

  public void destroy()
  {

        .

        .

        .

  }

  public void init(FilterConfig filterConfig)
  {

        .

        .

        .

  }
}
```

In the doFilter method, you can use the Java GregorianCalendar class to get an object that can act as a calendar, and a Date object to get the current time. If the current time is outside working hours—say 9 to 5—you can pass on access to the filtered resource, game.jsp, simply by calling the FilterChain object's doFilter method:

```
import java.io.*;
import java.util.*;
import javax.servlet.*;
import javax.servlet.http.*;

public final class Restrict implements Filter
{
  public void doFilter(ServletRequest request, ServletResponse response,
    FilterChain chain)
    throws IOException, ServletException
  {
```

```
    GregorianCalendar calendar = new GregorianCalendar();
    Date date1 = new Date();
    calendar.setTime(date1);
    int hour = calendar.get(Calendar.HOUR_OF_DAY);
    if(hour < 9 || hour > 17) {
        chain.doFilter(request, response);
            .
            .
            .
    }
  }

  public void destroy()
  {
  }

  public void init(FilterConfig filterConfig)
  {
  }
}
```

Otherwise, if it's during working hours, you can display the error message you see in Figure 6.3 by returning this HTML yourself:

```
import java.io.*;
import java.util.*;
import javax.servlet.*;
import javax.servlet.http.*;

public final class Restrict implements Filter
{
  public void doFilter(ServletRequest request, ServletResponse response,
    FilterChain chain)
    throws IOException, ServletException
  {

    GregorianCalendar calendar = new GregorianCalendar();
    Date date1 = new Date();
    calendar.setTime(date1);
    int hour = calendar.get(Calendar.HOUR_OF_DAY);
    if(hour < 9 || hour > 17) {
        chain.doFilter(request, response);
    } else {
        response.setContentType("text/html");
        PrintWriter out = response.getWriter();
```

```
        out.println("<HTML>");
        out.println("<HEAD>");
        out.println("<TITLE>");
        out.println("The game is not available");
        out.println("</TITLE>");
        out.println("</HEAD>");
        out.println("<BODY>");
        out.println("<H1>The game is not available</H1>");
        out.println("Sorry, that resource may not be accessed now.");
        out.println("</BODY>");
        out.println("</HTML>");
    }
  }

  public void destroy()
  {
  }

  public void init(FilterConfig filterConfig)
  {
  }
}
```

That's all you need for Restrict.java. Store game.jsp in the logger directory, and after compiling Restrict.java, store Restrict.class in the logger classes directory.

As before, you have to connect this new filter to the resource it filters in logger's web.xml file. Start by connecting the filter (named, say, "Restricting Filter") to its Java class in a `<filter>` element:

```
<?xml version="1.0" encoding="ISO-8859-1"?>

<!DOCTYPE web-app
    PUBLIC "-//Sun Microsystems, Inc.//DTD Web Application 2.3//EN"
    "http://java.sun.com/j2ee/dtds/web-app_2_3.dtd">

<web-app>

  <filter>
    <filter-name>Simple Filter</filter-name>
    <filter-class>Simple</filter-class>
  </filter>

  <filter>
    <filter-name>Restricting Filter</filter-name>
    <filter-class>Restrict</filter-class>
```

```
    </filter>

  <filter-mapping>
    <filter-name>Simple Filter</filter-name>
    <url-pattern>/simple.jsp</url-pattern>
  </filter-mapping>

</web-app>
```

Then connect this new filter to *game.jsp* in a `<filter-mapping>` element, like this, in web.xml:

```
<?xml version="1.0" encoding="ISO-8859-1"?>

<!DOCTYPE web-app
    PUBLIC "-//Sun Microsystems, Inc.//DTD Web Application 2.3//EN"
    "http://java.sun.com/j2ee/dtds/web-app_2_3.dtd">

<web-app>

  <filter>
    <filter-name>Simple Filter</filter-name>
    <filter-class>Simple</filter-class>
  </filter>

  <filter>
    <filter-name>Restricting Filter</filter-name>
    <filter-class>Restrict</filter-class>
  </filter>

  <filter-mapping>
    <filter-name>Simple Filter</filter-name>
    <url-pattern>/simple.jsp</url-pattern>
  </filter-mapping>

  <filter-mapping>
    <filter-name>Restricting Filter</filter-name>
    <url-pattern>/game.jsp</url-pattern>
  </filter-mapping>

</web-app>
```

That's all you need. To see this one at work, navigate to http://localhost:8080/logger/game.jsp.

Restricting Access Based on Password

At this point, you've made use of the `response` object in filters, but filters can also work with the `request` object, as WebLogger does. Using the `request` object lets you handle data on its way to the filtered web resource. For instance, one of the most popular uses of filters is to restrict access to web resources based on password; take a look at Figure 6.4, where an HTML page, login.html, is asking the user for his password.

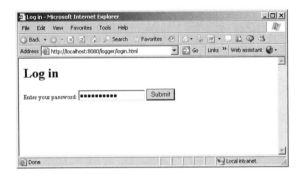

FIGURE 6.4   **Restricting access-based passwords with a filter.**

If the user enters the correct password, he's OK'd by the filter, which passes control on to a JSP named loggedin.jsp, as you see in Figure 6.5.

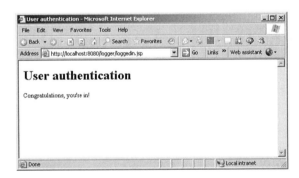

FIGURE 6.5   **Gaining access with a password.**

On the other hand, if the user enters the wrong password, the filter denies access and displays the error page you see in Figure 6.6.

FIGURE 6.6 Denying access for an incorrect password.

The interesting thing here is that you're reading data from HTML controls—a password control in this case—in the filter. The data in the password control isn't even used in the target JSP. In the first HTML page the user sees, login.html, the password control is simply named password:

```
<HTML>
    <HEAD>
        <TITLE>Log in</TITLE>
    </HEAD>

    <BODY>
        <H1>Log in</H1>
        <FORM ACTION="loggedin.jsp" METHOD="POST">
            Enter your password:
                <INPUT TYPE="PASSWORD" NAME="password">
                <INPUT TYPE="SUBMIT" VALUE="Submit">
        </FORM>
    </BODY>
<HTML>
```

When the user clicks the Submit button, the request object, including the entered password text, is sent to the JSP page given by the HTML form's action, loggedin.jsp. But the password isn't used by loggedin.jsp; instead, it's used by the filter, Authenticate.java. To recover that password, the filter uses the request object's getParameter method:

```
import java.io.*;
import javax.servlet.*;
import javax.servlet.http.*;

public final class Authenticate implements Filter
{
```

```
public void doFilter(ServletRequest request, ServletResponse response,
  FilterChain chain)
  throws IOException, ServletException
{
  String password = ((HttpServletRequest) request).getParameter("password");
      .
      .
      .

}

public void destroy()
{
}

public void init(FilterConfig filterConfig)
{
}
}
```

If the entered password matches the actual password (say, "opensesame"), the filter will pass control on to the filtered resource, loggedin.jsp:

```
import java.io.*;
import javax.servlet.*;
import javax.servlet.http.*;

public final class Authenticate implements Filter
{

  public void doFilter(ServletRequest request, ServletResponse response,
    FilterChain chain)
    throws IOException, ServletException
  {
    String password = ((HttpServletRequest) request).getParameter("password");

    if(password.equals("opensesame")) {
        chain.doFilter(request, response);
        .
        .
        .

    }
  }

  public void destroy()
  {
```

```
    }

    public void init(FilterConfig filterConfig)
    {
    }
}
```

Here's the JSP page, loggedin.jsp, that the user sees if he has entered the correct password:

```
<HTML>
    <HEAD>
        <TITLE>User authentication</TITLE>
    </HEAD>
    <BODY>
        <H1>User authentication</H1>
        Congratulations, you're in!
        <BR>
    </BODY>
</HTML>
```

On the other hand, if the password didn't match, the filter sends back an error page and denies access to the filtered resource:

```
import java.io.*;
import javax.servlet.*;
import javax.servlet.http.*;

public final class Authenticate implements Filter
{

  public void doFilter(ServletRequest request, ServletResponse response,
    FilterChain chain)
    throws IOException, ServletException
  {
    String password = ((HttpServletRequest) request).getParameter("password");

    if(password.equals("opensesame")) {
        chain.doFilter(request, response);
    } else {
        response.setContentType("text/html");
        PrintWriter out = response.getWriter();
        out.println("<HTML>");
        out.println("<HEAD>");
        out.println("<TITLE>");
        out.println("Incorrect Password");
        out.println("</TITLE>");
```

```
      out.println("</HEAD>");
      out.println("<BODY>");
      out.println("<H1>Incorrect Password</H1>");
      out.println("Sorry, that password was incorrect.");
      out.println("</BODY>");
      out.println("</HTML>");
   }
 }
     .
     .
     .
}
```

You can add this filter to web.xml, as before:

```
<?xml version="1.0" encoding="ISO-8859-1"?>
      .
      .
      .
<web-app>

  <filter>
    <filter-name>Simple Filter</filter-name>
    <filter-class>Simple</filter-class>
  </filter>

  <filter>
    <filter-name>Authentication Filter</filter-name>
```

REAL-WORLD SCENARIO

Passwords and Security

Filters are often used to enforce password access to web resources, but using a filter this way isn't the most secure way of restricting access. The problem is that sending data from password controls around the Internet means that your unencrypted text may go through as many as 20 servers to get where it's going.

Not exactly the most secure system out there, especially if you use the GET method in your HTML forms, which means that your password data will be appended to the URL, something like this: http://localhost:8080/logger/loggedin.jsp?password=opensesame.

Talk about security leaks.

If security is a serious concern, developers usually go for some other technique, such as using server-based passwords. These passwords are set on the server, and when the user logs in, the browser displays a login dialog box. How do you set up that kind of security, called HTTP authentication? See the next topic.

```
   <filter-class>Authenticate</filter-class>
 </filter>
       .
       .
       .

<filter-mapping>
  <filter-name>Authentication Filter</filter-name>
  <url-pattern>/loggedin.jsp</url-pattern>
</filter-mapping>

 <filter-mapping>
   <filter-name>Restricting Filter</filter-name>
   <url-pattern>/game.jsp</url-pattern>
 </filter-mapping>

</web-app>
```

To take a look at this filter in action, start Tomcat after installing the filter and navigate to
http://localhost:8080/logger/login.html.

Creating WebLogger

Having absorbed all the filter technology discussed so far in this chapter, it's time to build
WebLogger and start grabbing that user data when they come to your website. To let
WebLogger get even more data about users, it's set up to handle users who log in using
HTTP authentication, although that's optional—it also handles sites that don't use authenti-
cation, no problem.

Here's what this looks like. The web resource that WebLogger filters is called target.jsp, and if
the user enters the URL for target.jsp, he'll see an HTTP authentication login dialog box, as
shown in Figure 6.7.

FIGURE 6.7   Reading a password.

If the user enters the right password, he'll see target.jsp—as shown at the beginning of the chapter in Figure 6.1—and his information will be logged to both a Tomcat log and another file named log.txt. The target.jsp file just displays a message, like this:

```
<HTML>
    <HEAD>
        <TITLE>Welcome</TITLE>
    </HEAD>
    <BODY>
        <CENTER>
        <BR>
        <BR>
        <BR>
        <H1>Welcome</H1>
        <BR>
        Welcome to this web page.
        </CENTER>
    </BODY>
</HTML>
```

WebLogger will store the user's name if he has been authenticated (as mentioned, authentication is optional—if your site doesn't use it, that's no problem). How do you set up HTTP authentication in case you want to use it? You have to edit a file of users on the web server; in Tomcat, that's called tomcat-users.xml, and you can find it in the Tomcat conf directory (back up this file before working on it, because if it gets messed up, Tomcat won't start).

For example, here's how you'd add a user named steve with the password "tomcat" to the users file:

```
<?xml version='1.0' encoding='utf-8'?>
<tomcat-users>
  <role rolename="tomcat"/>
  <role rolename="role1"/>
  <role rolename="manager"/>
  <role rolename="admin"/>
  <role rolename="author"/>
  <user username="steve" password="tomcat" roles="author"/>
  <user username="tomcat" password="tomcat" roles="tomcat"/>
  <user username="both" password="tomcat" roles="tomcat,role1"/>
  <user username="role1" password="tomcat" roles="role1"/>
  <user username="admin" password="" roles="admin,manager"/>
</tomcat-users>
```

This adds the user steve to the *role* named author. A role is something you make up; it's a group of users with similar functions, and you can grant or deny them access collectively.

For example, in the web.xml file, you can tell Tomcat that you're restricting access to target.jsp to those users who are part of the author role, like this:

```xml
<?xml version="1.0" encoding="ISO-8859-1"?>
      .
      .
      .
<web-app>

  <filter>
    <filter-name>Simple Filter</filter-name>
    <filter-class>Simple</filter-class>
  </filter>
      .
      .
      .
  <filter-mapping>
    <filter-name>Simple Filter</filter-name>
    <url-pattern>/simple.jsp</url-pattern>
  </filter-mapping>
      .
      .
      .
  <security-constraint>
    <web-resource-collection>
      <web-resource-name>Secure Area</web-resource-name>
      <url-pattern>/target.jsp</url-pattern>
    </web-resource-collection>
    <auth-constraint>
      <role-name>author</role-name>
    </auth-constraint>
  </security-constraint>

  <login-config>
    <auth-method>BASIC</auth-method>
    <realm-name>Secure Area</realm-name>
  </login-config>

</web-app>
```

The `<login-config>` element in web.xml indicates that this project uses the basic authentication method, which displays the kind of password-reading dialog box you see in Figure 6.7.

That sets up the user authentication if you want to use it. How do you create the WebLogger filter itself? Keep reading.

Collecting User Data

This filter logs user accesses and times, so Logger.java starts by creating a Date object that holds the current date and getting the current system time in milliseconds:

```java
import java.io.*;
import java.util.*;
import java.security.*;
import javax.servlet.*;
import javax.servlet.http.*;

public final class Logger implements Filter
{

    public void doFilter(ServletRequest request,
        ServletResponse response, FilterChain chain)
        throws IOException, ServletException
    {

        Date date1 = new Date();
        long start = System.currentTimeMillis();
            .
            .
            .
    }

    public void destroy()
    {
    }

    public void init(FilterConfig filterConfig)
    {

    }
}
```

Next in doFilter, you can get the user's IP address with the request object's getRemoteAddr method, the URL the user is trying to reach with the request object's getRequestURI method, and the name of the user's host with the request object's getRemoteHost method:

```java
public void doFilter(ServletRequest request,
    ServletResponse response, FilterChain chain)
    throws IOException, ServletException
{
    Date date1 = new Date();
    long start = System.currentTimeMillis();
```

```
    String address =  request.getRemoteAddr();
    String file = ((HttpServletRequest) request).getRequestURI();
    String host = ((HttpServletRequest) request).getRemoteHost();
        .
        .
        .
}
```

You can also use the `request` object's `getHeader` method to read the `User-Agent` HTTP header to determine what browser the user has (after casting the `ServletRequest` object, you are passed in this method to an `HttpServletRequest` object):

```
public void doFilter(ServletRequest request,
    ServletResponse response, FilterChain chain)
    throws IOException, ServletException
{
    String browser = "";
    Date date1 = new Date();
    long start = System.currentTimeMillis();
    String address =  request.getRemoteAddr();
    String file = ((HttpServletRequest) request).getRequestURI();
    String host = ((HttpServletRequest) request).getRemoteHost();

    if(((HttpServletRequest)request).getHeader
        ("User-Agent").indexOf("MSIE") >= 0){
        browser = "Internet Explorer";
    }

    if(((HttpServletRequest)request).getHeader
        ("User-Agent").indexOf("Netscape") >= 0){
        browser = "Netscape Navigator";
    }
        .
        .
        .
}
```

If the user has logged in using HTTP authentication, you can get the type of authentication (that's "basic" here) using the `HttpServletRequest` object's `getAuthType` method, and if that's not null, you can get the user's name by getting a `Principal` object and using that object's `getName` method:

```
public void doFilter(ServletRequest request,
    ServletResponse response, FilterChain chain)
    throws IOException, ServletException
{
```

```
    String browser = "";
    String authType = "none";
    String username = "Not known";
    Date date1 = new Date();
    long start = System.currentTimeMillis();
    String address =  request.getRemoteAddr();
    String file = ((HttpServletRequest) request).getRequestURI();
    String host = ((HttpServletRequest) request).getRemoteHost();
        .
        .
        .

    String type = ((HttpServletRequest)request).getAuthType();


    if(type != null){
        Principal principal =
            ((HttpServletRequest)request).getUserPrincipal();
        authType = type;
        username = principal.getName();
    }
        .
        .
        .

}
```

Logging That Data

Now that you've gotten the data you need, how do you log it? One way is to use the
FilterConfig object sent to the filter's init method. You can use this object's
getServletContext method to get the servlet context, which is a common data space shared
by the servlets and JSPs in the web application. The servlet context supports a log method,
which can log text. Here's what that looks like in WebLogger—first, you save the
FilterConfig object, access the servlet context, and then log your data:

```
import java.io.*;
import java.util.*;
import java.security.*;
import javax.servlet.*;
import javax.servlet.http.*;

public final class Logger implements Filter
{
    private FilterConfig filterConfig = null;

    public void doFilter(ServletRequest request,
        ServletResponse response, FilterChain chain)
```

```
          throws IOException, ServletException
    {
            .

            .

            .

    filterConfig.getServletContext().log(
        "User access at " + date1.toString() +
        " Authentication type: " + authType +
        " User name: " + username +
        " User IP: " + address +
        " Accessing: " + file +
        " Host: " + host +
        " Browser: " + browser +
        " Milliseconds used: " + (System.currentTimeMillis()
        - start)
    );
            .

            .

            .

    }

    public void destroy()
    {
    }

    public void init(FilterConfig filterConfig)
    {
        this.filterConfig = filterConfig;
    }
}
```

This logs your data like so:

```
User access at Mon Mar 07 15:47:53 EST 2005
Authentication type: BASIC
User name: steve
User IP: 127.0.0.1
Accessing: /logger/target.jsp
Host: 127.0.0.1
Browser: Internet Explorer
Milliseconds used: 109
```

By default, this data goes to a file named stdout.log in the Tomcat log directory, and that's the way Logger.java works in the download for this book.

It's worth noting that you can also configure Tomcat so that your text will be sent to a log file of your choosing. For example, to store data in a Tomcat log named tomcat.log when you call the log method, you can use the popular Log4J package. Create a file called log4j.properties in the Tomcat common\classes directory and then put this text in it:

```
log4j.rootLogger=debug, R
log4j.appender.R=org.apache.log4j.RollingFileAppender
log4j.appender.R.File=${catalina.home}/logs/tomcat.log
log4j.appender.R.MaxFileSize=10MB
log4j.appender.R.MaxBackupIndex=10
log4j.appender.R.layout=org.apache.log4j.PatternLayout
log4j.appender.R.layout.ConversionPattern=%p %t %c - %m%n
log4j.logger.org.apache.catalina=DEBUG, R
```

For the Java support you'll need, download the Log4J package from http://logging.apache.org/log4j and then put Log4J JAR file in the Tomcat common\lib directory. Next, download the Commons Logging package from http://jakarta.apache.org/site/downloads/downloads_commons-logging.cgi and put commons-logging.jar in the Tomcat common\lib directory.

Doing this configures Tomcat to store your data in a file named tomcat.log when you pass text to the log method. It's a little extra work, but this way, your data isn't mixed in with a lot of Tomcat-specific messages.

Another way of logging your data is to do it yourself. For example, say that you're using Windows and want to log user data to a file named logs.txt in a directory named C:\logs. To do that, you can use a class such as Java's FileWriter class. The important methods of this class are inherited from the java.io.Writer class, which you can see in Table 6.4.

TABLE 6.4   Significant Methods of the *java.io.Writer* **Class**

Method	Does This
Writer append(char c)	**Appends the given character to this writer**
abstract void close()	**Closes the output stream after flushing it**
abstract void flush()	**Flushes the stream**
void write(char[] cbuf)	**Writes an array of characters to the writer**
abstract void write(char[] cbuf, int off, int len)	**Writes a part of an array of characters to the writer**
void write(int c)	**Writes a single character to the writer**
void write(String str)	**Writes a string to the writer**
void write(String str, int off, int len)	**Writes part of a string to the writer**

You can log the user data now by creating a new FileWriter object, then using the write method and the close method to close the FileWriter:

```
public void doFilter(ServletRequest request,
    ServletResponse response, FilterChain chain)
```

```
        throws IOException, ServletException
{
    String browser = "";
    String authType = "none";
    String username = "Not known";
    Date date1 = new Date();
    long start = System.currentTimeMillis();
    String address =  request.getRemoteAddr();
    String file = ((HttpServletRequest) request).getRequestURI();
    String host = ((HttpServletRequest) request).getRemoteHost();
            .
            .
            .
    String filename = "C:\\logs\\log.txt";
    FileWriter filewriter = new FileWriter(filename, true);
    filewriter.write("User access at " + date1.toString() +
        "User access at " + date1.toString() +
        " Authentication type: " + authType +
        " User name: " + username +
        " User IP: " + address +
        " Accessing: " + file +
        " Host: " + host +
        " Browser: " + browser +
        " Milliseconds used: " + (System.currentTimeMillis()
        - start)
    );

    filewriter.close();
            .
            .
            .

}
```

After logging the user's data, you have to call `chain.doFilter` to pass control on to target.jsp. Then you can add the message at the bottom of the results page indicating that the user's access has been logged:

```
public void doFilter(ServletRequest request,
    ServletResponse response, FilterChain chain)
    throws IOException, ServletException
{
    String browser = "";
    String authType = "none";
    String username = "Not known";
    Date date1 = new Date();
```

```
    long start = System.currentTimeMillis();
    String address =  request.getRemoteAddr();
    String file = ((HttpServletRequest) request).getRequestURI();
    String host = ((HttpServletRequest) request).getRemoteHost();
       .
       .
       .

  chain.doFilter(request, response);

    response.setContentType("text/html");
    PrintWriter out = response.getWriter();

    out.println("<BR>");
    out.println("<BR>");
    out.println("<BR>");
    out.println("<BR>");
    out.println("<BR>");
    out.println("<HR>");
    out.println("<CENTER>");
    out.println("<FONT SIZE = 2>");
    out.println("<I>");
    out.println("Your access to this page has been logged.");
    out.println("</I>");
    out.println("</FONT>");
    out.println("</CENTER>");
}
```

All that's left is to install this new filter in web.xml:

```
<?xml version="1.0" encoding="ISO-8859-1"?>
       .
       .
       .

<web-app>
       .
       .
       .

  <filter>
    <filter-name>Logging Filter</filter-name>
    <filter-class>Logger</filter-class>
  </filter>
       .
       .
       .

  <filter-mapping>
```

```
    <filter-name>Logging Filter</filter-name>
    <url-pattern>/target.jsp</url-pattern>
  </filter-mapping>
      .
      .
      .
</web-app>
```

When you run this project, the user's data will be sent to the stdout.log file as well as to the log.txt file—and you'll have the goods on him.

> **NOTE**
>
> **Download the complete source code for the WebLogger project at the Sams website. After placing the needed files (Logger.class and web.xml) in the logger directory on your web server, as detailed in the beginning of the chapter, replace the name target.jsp in web.xml with the name of the web resource whose user accesses you want to log.**

Conclusion

This chapter presented the WebLogger project, a fun online filter that grabs data about users who access your website—without their knowledge, unless you tell them they're being logged.

To log accesses to a web resource, you don't have to change that web resource; you can use a filter in Java-enabled web servers. To create a filter, you have to create a Java class that implements the Filter interface, which includes the init, doFilter, and destroy methods. When the user accesses the resource you're filtering, the doFilter method gets control, gaining access to the request object sent to the resource and the response object the resource sends back to the browser.

WebLogger uses the request object to get its information about the user, reading the URL the user is accessing, the user's IP address, hostname, and browser type. If the user is logged in using HTTP authentication, WebLogger records the type of authentication used and records the username. It also logs the time of the user's access, as well as the time he spent accessing the web resource you're filtering.

You've got options when it comes to where you want the log text sent with WebLogger. If you use Tomcat, that text is stored in stdout.log by default. But as discussed in this chapter, you can specify the log file you want to use. As also covered, you can create your own files, writing to them as you please.

WebLogger is a powerful project that lets you keep track of who's been visiting your site and log that information. Not bad.

CHAPTER 7

Running Any Program Via Remote Control with the Robot

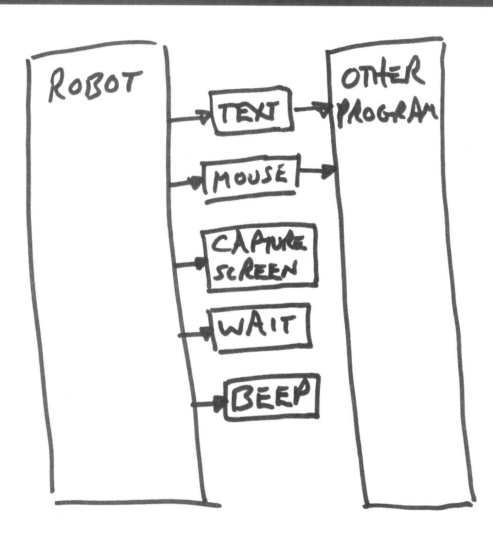

The Robot.

Ever want to run some program by remote control? Ever get into one of those cases where you're just doing the same thing over and over in a program? Ever wish you could run a program late at night—and not have to be there?

The answer is this chapter's project, the Robot. The Robot lets you run other programs by remote control, no matter what kind of programs they are. Using the Robot, you can control another program by sending keystrokes and mouse actions to it. You can even capture the screen when in the middle of some operation so you have a visual record of what happened.

Very cool.

You can see what the Robot looks like in Figure 7.1. All you have to do is to enter commands to the Robot in the text area on the left and click the Go button.

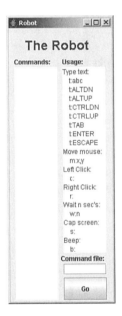

FIGURE 7.1   The Robot.

What kind of commands can you enter in Robot? You can send text to the program you're controlling by remote control. You can use the Alt and Ctrl keys. You can also send tab characters, the Enter key, or the Esc key.

NOTE

Note that you can use the Alt key in Windows to open menus and select menu items—look for the underlined character in the menu or menu item name and use that with the Alt key. For example, Alt+F will open the File menu, and Alt+X will select the Exit item in that menu.

You can also use the mouse—just enter the screen location (in pixels) where you want the mouse to move to. Then click the mouse, right-click it, or double-click it (by clicking twice).

You can also take screen captures, which is great if you've got an interim step in a process running late at night that can cause problems—you can capture the screen and look at it later.

Besides all this, you can tell the Robot to wait for a specified number of seconds before proceeding to the next step. If you want to tell the Robot to do its thing late at night, for example, this is the command to use. A companion command makes the Robot beep, informing you, even if you're not at your desk, that it's working again after one of these delays.

You don't even have to enter commands into the text area of the Robot shown in Figure 7.1—the Robot can read commands from a file, making repeated tasks that much easier to run.

What commands are available? Here's the list, from the Robot's help screen (at right in Figure 7.1):

```
Type text:
     t:abc
     t:ALTDN
     t:ALTUP
     t:CTRLDN
     t:CTRLUP
     t:TAB
     t:ENTER
     t:ESCAPE
Move mouse:
     m:x,y
Left Click:
     c:
Right Click:
     r:
Wait n sec's:
     w:n
Cap screen:
     s:
Beep:
     b:
```

Each command consists of a single letter, followed by a colon and, optionally, data for the command. For example, suppose you enter the following commands into the Robot and then click the Go button (note that there's a space at the end of the text in each line, although you can't see it here, to divide the words being sent to the target program):

```
t:Hello
t:from
t:the
t:robot.
```

The Robot would then send the text "Hello from the robot." to the program it's controlling.

Running the Robot

How does the Robot actually control a program? You first start the program you want to control, then start the Robot. After you click the Go button, the Robot disappears, which gives the focus back to the program you want to control. From then on, the Robot can send it keystrokes or control it with the mouse.

When the Robot is done with the tasks you've given it, it reappears. For example, take a look at Figure 7.2, where the Robot has entered the text "Hello from the robot." in Windows WordPad. Cool.

NOTE

Note the steps used to run the Robot. First, you start the program you want to control. Then you start the Robot.

After entering the commands you want to execute, or the name of the file that holds the commands, you click the Go button. The Robot will disappear, and the focus will revert to the program you want to control. After the Robot is done running that program, it'll reappear.

REAL-WORLD SCENARIO

A Question of Security

The Java Robot class can control other programs and even take control of your computer. Is there a security risk here?

Yes.

Is it serious?

Not really.

As any developer knows, any time a program can jump its bounds and start working with the rest of the system unasked, there's some security risk. You can imagine how upset someone would be if the mouse started moving independently, various programs started, buttons were clicked, text was entered, and so on.

However, the user would have to explicitly run the code that uses the Java Robot class in a nasty way. That makes Java Robot less of a threat, although it still might be used in email attachments that users run without thinking, or in Trojan horse programs, which contain malicious code inside a respectable-looking application.

continues

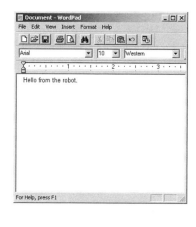

FIGURE 7.2   Using the Robot to type text.

How does the Robot do what it does? It uses a Java class called, not surprisingly, the Java Robot class. This class first appeared in Java 1.3 and has been getting better ever since.

Sun's purpose in creating this class was to "facilitate automated testing of Java platform implementations," but that's boring. It's much better to use this class to generate low-level user-interface events and control other programs by remote control, as the Robot project does.

REAL-WORLD SCENARIO   *continued*

Note that there's little you can do to the operating system with Java `Robot` that you can't do with simple system calls in code. `Robot` is good for manipulating other programs that can't be accessed so easily in code; it's not a hacker's dream-come-true. The bad things viruses and worms do involve operating system calls, not running WordPad.

The Java `Robot` class has been around since Java 1.3, and it hasn't become a security issue. Developers have been writing code using this class for a long time, and no spectacular security hole has appeared. The Java `Robot` class has become one of the trusted Java classes, and programmers make use of it without much concern for security these days.

Some operating systems take no chances, however. If the operating system you're running the Java `Robot` class on requires special privileges for low-level input control, such as that generated by this project, an `AWTException` will be thrown when you try to construct Java `Robot` objects.

In the X Window System, for example, you'll get this exception if the XTEST 2.2 standard extension is not supported by the X server.

Creating the Robot's Window

So how do you start creating the Robot? This project uses Java Swing to present the window you see in Figure 7.1. The main class, RobotProject (called that so as not to conflict with the Java Robot class), extends the Swing JFrame class and implements the ActionListener class to be able to handle events such as button clicks:

```
class RobotProject extends JFrame implements ActionListener
{
    .
    .
    .
}
```

You can find the significant methods of the JFrame class in Table 7.1.

TABLE 7.1 Significant Methods of the *javax.swing.JFrame* Class

Method	Does This
protected JRootPane createRootPane()	Called internally in order to create the default rootPane object
protected void frameInit()	Called internally to initialize the JFrame object properly
Container getContentPane()	Returns the contentPane object used in this frame
int getDefaultCloseOperation()	Returns the operation that happens when the user closes this frame
JMenuBar getJMenuBar()	Returns the menu bar used in this frame, if any
JLayeredPane getLayeredPane()	Returns the Swing LayeredPane object used in this frame
JRootPane getRootPane()	Returns the rootPane object used in this frame
static boolean isDefaultLookAndFeelDecorated()	Returns a value of true if new JFrame objects should match the current Swing look and feel
protected boolean isRootPaneCheckingEnabled()	Returns true if calls to add and setLayout are handled by the contentPane object
void remove(Component comp)	Removes the component from this container
void setContentPane(Container contentPane)	Sets the contentPane object that will be used
void setDefaultCloseOperation(int operation)	Sets the operation that will occur by default when the user closes this frame

TABLE 7.1   Continued

Method	Does This
static void setDefaultLookAndFeelDecorated (boolean defaultLookAndFeelDecorated)	**Specifies whether or not** JFrame **objects should have their borders, buttons, titles, and so on match the current look and feel**
void setGlassPane(Component glassPane)	**Sets the** glassPane **component**
void setIconImage(Image image)	**Sets the image that should be displayed as the icon for this** JFrame **object**
void setJMenuBar(JMenuBar menubar)	**Sets the menu bar for this** JFrame **object**
void setLayeredPane(JLayeredPane layeredPane)	**Sets the** LayeredPane **component**
void setLayout(LayoutManager manager)	**Sets the LayoutManager for the** JFrame **object**
protected void setRootPane(JRootPane root)	**Sets the** rootPane **property**
void update(Graphics g)	**Calls the** paint(g) **method**

When the Robot first starts, the main method creates a new RobotProject object that calls the RobotProject constructor. That constructor starts by creating a new Swing JButton object with the caption "Go" and making the current object the button's action listener:

```
class RobotProject extends JFrame implements ActionListener
{
    JButton jButton = new JButton("Go");

    public static void main(String args[])
    {
        new RobotProject();
    }

    RobotProject()
    {
        jButton.addActionListener(this);
        .
        .
        .
    }
}
```

You can see the significant methods of the JButton class in Table 7.2.

TABLE 7.2   Significant Methods of the *javax.swing.JButton* **Class**

Method	Does This
boolean isDefaultButton()	**Returns** true **if this button is the current default button**
void setDefaultCapable (boolean defaultCapable)	**Specifies whether this button can be made the default button for its Swing pane**
void updateUI()	**Resets the** UI **property to match the current look and feel**

How do you add this new button to the Robot's window? In a Swing application, you typically add controls such as buttons to the content pane, which you can get access to using the JFrame class's getContentPane method, which returns a standard Java Container object. To add a control to the content pane, making it visible, you can use the Container class's add method.

Here's how the RobotProject constructor creates the text area of the Swing JTextArea class that will accept typed commands, makes it editable, sets the font used, and adds the text area and the button to the application's content pane:

```
class RobotProject extends JFrame implements ActionListener
{
    JButton jButton = new JButton("Go");
    JTextArea jTextArea = new JTextArea("");

    public static void main(String args[])
    {
        new RobotProject();
    }

    RobotProject()
    {
        jButton.addActionListener(this);
        getContentPane().setLayout(null);
        jTextArea.setEditable(true);
        jTextArea.setFont(new Font("Times Roman", Font.BOLD, 10));
        getContentPane().add(jButton);
        getContentPane().add(jTextArea);
        .
        .
        .

    }
}
```

You can see the significant methods of the JTextArea class in Table 7.3.

TABLE 7.3   Significant Methods of the *javax.swing.JTextArea* **Class**

Method	Does This
void append(String str)	Appends the specified text to the end of the text in the text area
int getColumns()	Returns the number of columns currently in the text area control
protected int getColumnWidth()	Returns the column width of the text area control
int getLineCount()	Returns the number of lines contained in the text area control

TABLE 7.3   Continued

Method	Does This
int getLineEndOffset(int line)	Returns the offset of the end of the specified line
int getLineOfOffset(int offset)	Returns the line of an offset in the text
int getLineStartOffset(int line)	Returns the offset of the start of the specified line
boolean getLineWrap()	Returns whether or not the text area wraps lines
Dimension getPreferredSize()	Returns the preferred size of the text area control
protected int getRowHeight()	Returns the height of a row in the text area control
int getRows()	Returns the number of rows in the text area control
int getTabSize()	Returns the number of characters used to expand tabs
boolean getWrapStyleWord()	Returns the style of wrapping that will be used (if the text area control wraps lines)
void insert(String str, int pos)	Inserts text at the given position
void replaceRange(String str, int start, int end)	Replaces text in the text area control, starting from the start position and ending at the end position, using the given new text
void setColumns(int columns)	Sets the number of columns for this text area control
void setFont(Font f)	Sets the current font used in this text area control
void setLineWrap(boolean wrap)	Sets whether or not the text area control will use line wrapping
void setRows(int rows)	Sets the number of rows in this text area control
void setTabSize(int size)	Sets the number of characters used to expand tabs
void setWrapStyleWord(boolean word)	Sets the style of wrapping lines that will be used (if the text area control is wrapping lines)

The Robot also uses a set of labels to display the static text you see in Figure 7.1, such as the label that holds the title text "The Robot." That label is created with the Swing JLabel class:

```
class RobotProject extends JFrame implements ActionListener
{
    JButton jButton = new JButton("Go");
    JTextArea jTextArea = new JTextArea("");
    JTextArea helpInfo = new JTextArea("");
    JLabel jLabel = new JLabel("The Robot");

    public static void main(String args[])
    {
        new RobotProject();
    }

    RobotProject()
    {
        jButton.addActionListener(this);
        getContentPane().setLayout(null);
```

```
jTextArea.setEditable(true);
jTextArea.setFont(new Font("Times Roman", Font.BOLD, 10));
getContentPane().add(jButton);
getContentPane().add(jTextArea);
getContentPane().add(jLabel);
    .
    .
    .
  }
}
```

You can see the significant methods of the Swing JLabel class in Table 7.4.

TABLE 7.4   **Significant Methods of the** *javax.swing.JLabel* **Class**

Method	Does This
`Icon getDisabledIcon()`	Returns the icon that is used by the label when the label is disabled
`int getDisplayedMnemonic()`	Returns the keycode that specifies a mnemonic key
`int getHorizontalAlignment()`	Returns the alignment of the label's text horizontally
`int getHorizontalTextPosition()`	Returns the horizontal location of the label's text
`Icon getIcon()`	Returns the graphic icon that the label displays, if any
`int getIconTextGap()`	Returns the amount of space between the text and the icon that this label displays
`String getText()`	Returns the text that the label will display
`LabelUI getUI()`	Returns the look-and-feel object that displays this label
`int getVerticalAlignment()`	Returns the alignment of the label's text vertically
`int getVerticalTextPosition()`	Returns the vertical position of the label's text
`void setDisabledIcon(Icon disabledIcon)`	Sets the icon that should be displayed if this JLabel object is disabled
`void setDisplayedMnemonic(char aChar)`	Sets the displayed mnemonic as a char value
`void setDisplayedMnemonic(int key)`	Sets a keycode that specifies a mnemonic key
`void setHorizontalAlignment(int alignment)`	Sets the alignment of the label's text horizontally
`void setHorizontalTextPosition(int textPosition)`	Sets the horizontal position of the label's text
`void setIcon(Icon icon)`	Sets the icon this label will display when active
`void setIconTextGap(int iconTextGap)`	Sets the space between the label's text and icon

TABLE 7.4   Continued

Method	Does This
void setLabelFor(Component c)	Specifies the component this label labels
void setText(String text)	Specifies the text this label will display
void setUI(LabelUI ui)	Sets the look-and-feel object that will draw this label
void setVerticalAlignment(int alignment)	Sets the alignment of the label's text vertically
void setVerticalTextPosition(int textPosition)	Sets the vertical position of the label's text

Besides labels, the Robot uses a JTextField control to read the name of a command file, if the user enters one. Here's what that looks like in the code:

```
class RobotProject extends JFrame implements ActionListener
{
    JButton jButton = new JButton("Go");
    JTextArea jTextArea = new JTextArea("");
    JTextArea helpInfo = new JTextArea("");
    JTextField jFileName = new JTextField("");
    JLabel jLabel = new JLabel("The Robot");

    public static void main(String args[])
    {
        new RobotProject();
    }

    RobotProject()
    {
        jButton.addActionListener(this);
        getContentPane().setLayout(null);
        jTextArea.setEditable(true);
        jTextArea.setFont(new Font("Times Roman", Font.BOLD, 10));
        getContentPane().add(jButton);
        getContentPane().add(jTextArea);
        getContentPane().add(jLabel);
        getContentPane().add(jFileName);
        .
        .
        .

    }
}
```

You can see the significant methods of the JTextField class in Table 7.5.

TABLE 7.5   Significant Methods of the `javax.swing.JTextField` Class

Method	Does This
`void addActionListener(ActionListener l)`	Adds an action listener that will read action events from this text field control
`protected void fireActionPerformed()`	Notifies all listeners registered for this event of an event
`Action getAction()`	Returns the action for this text field control, or null if no action is set
`ActionListener[] getActionListeners()`	Returns an array of all the `ActionListener` objects that you added to this text field control
`Action[] getActions()`	Returns the list of actions for the text field control
`int getColumns()`	Returns the number of columns in this text field control
`protected int getColumnWidth()`	Returns the column width used in this text field control
`int getHorizontalAlignment()`	Returns the horizontal alignment of the text in the text field control
`BoundedRangeModel getHorizontalVisibility()`	Returns the horizontal visibility of the text field control
`Dimension getPreferredSize()`	Returns the preferred size for this text field control
`int getScrollOffset()`	Returns the scroll offset of the text field control (in pixels)
`void removeActionListener(ActionListener l)`	Removes a given action listener so that it will not receive action events from this text field control
`void scrollRectToVisible(Rectangle r)`	Scrolls the text field control
`void setAction(Action a)`	Sets the action for the text field control
`void setActionCommand(String command)`	Specifies the command string used for action events in this text field control
`void setColumns(int columns)`	Specifies the number of columns in this text field control
`void setFont(Font f)`	Sets the current font used in this text field control
`void setHorizontalAlignment(int alignment)`	Sets the horizontal alignment of the text in the text field control
`void setScrollOffset(int scrollOffset)`	Sets the scroll offset in this text field control (in pixels)

The constructor also adds the other controls you see in Figure 7.1 and then sizes all the controls appropriately, using their setBounds methods, and adds text that should be displayed, such as the help text:

```java
class RobotProject extends JFrame implements ActionListener
{
    JButton jButton = new JButton("Go");
    JTextArea jTextArea = new JTextArea("");
    JTextArea helpInfo = new JTextArea("");
    JTextField jFileName = new JTextField("");
    JLabel jLabel = new JLabel("The Robot");
    JLabel prompt = new JLabel("Commands:");
    JLabel usage = new JLabel("Usage:");
    JLabel jFileNameLabel = new JLabel("Command file:");

    public static void main(String args[])
    {
        new RobotProject();
    }

    RobotProject()
    {
        jButton.addActionListener(this);
        getContentPane().setLayout(null);
        jTextArea.setEditable(true);
        jTextArea.setFont(new Font("Times Roman", Font.BOLD, 10));
        getContentPane().add(jButton);
        getContentPane().add(jTextArea);
        getContentPane().add(jLabel);
        getContentPane().add(jFileName);
        getContentPane().add(prompt);
        getContentPane().add(helpInfo);
        getContentPane().add(usage);
        getContentPane().add(jFileNameLabel);
        jLabel.setBounds(30, 0, 120, 60);
        jButton.setBounds(100, 450, 80, 40);
        jLabel.setFont(new Font("Times Roman", Font.BOLD, 24));
        prompt.setBounds(10, 50, 80, 20);
        usage.setBounds(100, 50, 80, 20);
        jTextArea.setBounds(10, 70, 80, 420);
        jFileName.setBounds(100, 425, 80, 20);
        jFileNameLabel.setBounds(95, 405, 90, 20);
        helpInfo.setBounds(100, 70, 80, 335);
        helpInfo.setEditable(false);
        helpInfo.setText("Type text:\n    t:abc\n    t:ALTDN"
            + "\n    t:ALTUP"
            + "\n    t:CTRLDN"
            + "\n    t:CTRLUP"
            + "\n    t:TAB"
```

```
                + "\n    t:ENTER"
                + "\n    t:ESCAPE"
                + "\nMove mouse:\n    m:x,y\n"
                + "Left Click:\n    c:\n"
                + "Right Click:\n    r:\n"
                + "Wait n sec's:\n    w:n\n"
                + "Cap screen:\n    s:\n"
                + "Beep:\n    b:");
            .
            .
            .

    }
}
```

All that's left in the constructor is to set the title for the main window, make that window
visible, and handle window-closing events. The code handles that this way:

```
class RobotProject extends JFrame implements ActionListener
{
    JButton jButton = new JButton("Go");
    JTextArea jTextArea = new JTextArea("");
    JTextArea helpInfo = new JTextArea("");
    JTextField jFileName = new JTextField("");
    JLabel jLabel = new JLabel("The Robot");
    JLabel prompt = new JLabel("Commands:");
    JLabel usage = new JLabel("Usage:");
    JLabel jFileNameLabel = new JLabel("Command file:");
    String commands[] = new String[1024];
    int numberCommands;

    public static void main(String args[])
    {
        new RobotProject();
    }

    RobotProject()
    {
        .
        .
        .

        helpInfo.setBounds(100, 70, 80, 335);
        helpInfo.setEditable(false);
        helpInfo.setText("Type text:\n    t:abc\n    t:ALTDN"
            + "\n    t:ALTUP"
            + "\n    t:CTRLDN"
```

```
          +  "\n     t:CTRLUP"
          +  "\n     t:TAB"
          +  "\n     t:ENTER"
          +  "\n     t:ESCAPE"
          +  "\nMove mouse:\n    m:x,y\n"
          +  "Left Click:\n    c:\n"
          +  "Right Click:\n    r:\n"
          +  "Wait n sec's:\n    w:n\n"
          +  "Cap screen:\n    s:\n"
          +  "Beep:\n    b:");

        setTitle("Robot");
        setSize(200,520);
        setVisible(true);

        this.addWindowListener(
            new WindowAdapter(){
            public void windowClosing(WindowEvent e)
                {
                    System.exit(0);
                }
            }
        );
    }
}
```

At this point, then, the Robot's window has been set up, as shown in Figure 7.1. Now it's time to get the Robot working. Now what about actually executing commands when the user clicks the Go button?

Reading the Robot's Commands

When the user clicks the Go button, Java will call the actionPerformed method in the RobotProject class. That method is where all the excitement happens in this project.

Everything starts by removing the Robot from the screen, which is done simply by calling the setVisible method of JFrame with a value of false:

```
public void actionPerformed(ActionEvent e)
{
    try{

        setVisible(false);
```

.
.
.

}

When the Robot disappears from the screen, the program the user wants to control regains the focus, so all the Robot has to do is to send keystrokes and mouse events to it.

All that's done with a Java Robot object, and you can see the methods of the Robot class in Table 7.6.

TABLE 7.6   Significant Methods of the `java.awt.Robot` **Class**

Method	Does This
`BufferedImage createScreenCapture` `(Rectangle screenRect)`	Creates an image using pixels captured from the screen
`void delay(int ms)`	Makes the robot pause for the given time in milliseconds
`int getAutoDelay()`	Returns the number of milliseconds this Robot automatically pauses after generating an event
`Color getPixelColor(int x, int y)`	Returns the color of a pixel at the specified screen coordinates as a Java `Color` object
`boolean isAutoWaitForIdle()`	Returns `true` if this Robot automatically calls `waitForIdle` after generating an event
`void keyPress(int keycode)`	Presses a specified key, sending it to the target program
`void keyRelease(int keycode)`	Releases a specified key
`void mouseMove(int x, int y)`	Moves the mouse pointer to the specified screen coordinates
`void mousePress(int buttons)`	Presses one or more mouse buttons
`void mouseRelease(int buttons)`	Releases one or more mouse buttons
`void mouseWheel(int wheelAmt)`	Rotates the scroll wheel on mice that use wheels
`void setAutoDelay(int ms)`	Sets the number of milliseconds this Robot automatically sleeps after generating an event
`void setAutoWaitForIdle(boolean isOn)`	Specifies whether this Robot should automatically call `waitForIdle` after generating an event
`void waitForIdle()`	Makes the Robot wait until all the events in the event queue have been processed before proceeding

To perform its magic, the Robot project uses a Java Robot object named robot, and everything starts by creating that object and making it pause for half a second while the Robot project's window disappears from the screen:

```
public void actionPerformed(ActionEvent e)
{
```

```
        try{

            setVisible(false);

            Robot robot = new Robot();
            robot.delay(500);
                .
                .
                .

    }
```

The Robot has to parse the commands given it by the user, whether they come from a file or the text area. In either case, there is only one command to a line.

If the user specified a filename for the Robot to read commands from, the commands are read in from that file with a `BufferedReader` object, which reads text line by line:

```
public void actionPerformed(ActionEvent e)
{
    try{

        setVisible(false);

        Robot robot = new Robot();
        robot.delay(500);

            if (!jFileName.getText().equals("")){
                BufferedReader bufferedFile = new BufferedReader(
                    new FileReader(jFileName.getText()));

                int commandIndex = 0;
                String inline = "";

                while((inline = bufferedFile.readLine()) != null){
                    commands[commandIndex++] = inline;
                }
                numberCommands = commandIndex;
            }
                .
                .
                .
```

This stores the number of commands in an int variable named numberCommands and the actual commands in a String array named commands. For example, if the control file contained the text

```
t:abc
t:xyz
```

in two lines, then commands[0] would hold "t:abc" and commands[1] would hold "t:xyz".

Alternatively, if the user entered his commands in the text area that appears in Figure 7.1, you can read the text there and split it on newline characters to fill numberCommands and commands:

```
public void actionPerformed(ActionEvent e)
{
    try{

        setVisible(false);

        Robot robot = new Robot();
        robot.delay(500);

        if (!jFileName.getText().equals("")){
            BufferedReader bufferedFile = new BufferedReader(
                new FileReader(jFileName.getText()));

            int commandIndex = 0;
            String inline = "";

            while((inline = bufferedFile.readLine()) != null){
                commands[commandIndex++] = inline;
            }

            numberCommands = commandIndex;

        }
        else {
            commands = jTextArea.getText().split("\n");
            numberCommands = commands.length;
        }

        .
        .
        .
```

Executing Commands

Having read all the commands to execute, you can loop over those commands with a `for` loop. Each command, such as `t:abc`, which sends the text "abc" to the program the Robot project is controlling, is made up of an operation ("t" for text here) and data ("abc" here).

Here's how the Robot project extracts the operation and data from each command as it loops over all commands:

```
public void actionPerformed(ActionEvent e)
{
    try{
        .
        .
        .
        for (int loopIndex = 0; loopIndex < numberCommands;
            loopIndex++){

            String operation = commands[loopIndex].substring(0, 1);
            String data = commands[loopIndex].substring(2);

        .
        .
        .
```

Sending Keystrokes

Each command is a single character, so you can use a `switch` statement to handle them all. Each operation corresponds to a method of the `Robot` class—for example, to send text with the `t` operation, you can use the `keyPress` method.

If the data is "ALTDN", the user wants to press the Alt key, which you can do by calling `robot.keyPress(KeyEvent.VK_ALT)`. That's how you send text—by converting it to constants using the `KeyEvent` class's fields, such as `VK_A`, `VK_B`, `VK_ALT`, and so forth. Here's what it looks like in the code when the user wants to press the Alt key:

```
public void actionPerformed(ActionEvent e)
{
    try{
        .
        .
        .
        for (int loopIndex = 0; loopIndex < numberCommands;
            loopIndex++){

            String operation = commands[loopIndex].substring(0, 1);
```

```
        String data = commands[loopIndex].substring(2);

        switch(operation.toCharArray()[0])
        {
            case 't':
                if(data.equals("ALTDN")){
                    robot.keyPress(KeyEvent.VK_ALT);
                }
    .
    .
    .
```

Each of the commands that can be handled with a single keystroke—pressing the Alt key, releasing the Alt key, and so on—are easy to implement with the keyPress and keyRelease methods:

```
switch(operation.toCharArray()[0])
{
    case 't':
        if(data.equals("ALTDN")){
            robot.keyPress(KeyEvent.VK_ALT);
        }

        else if(data.equals("ALTUP")){
            robot.keyRelease(KeyEvent.VK_ALT);
        }

        if(data.equals("CTRLDN")){
            robot.keyPress(KeyEvent.VK_CONTROL);
        }

        else if(data.equals("CTRLUP")){
            robot.keyRelease(KeyEvent.VK_CONTROL);
        }

        else if(data.equals("ENTER")){
            robot.keyPress(KeyEvent.VK_ENTER);
            robot.keyRelease(KeyEvent.VK_ENTER);
        }

        else if(data.equals("TAB")){
            robot.keyPress(KeyEvent.VK_TAB);
            robot.keyRelease(KeyEvent.VK_TAB);
        }
```

```
else if(data.equals("ESCAPE")){
        robot.keyPress(KeyEvent.VK_ESCAPE);
        robot.keyRelease(KeyEvent.VK_ESCAPE);
}
    .
    .
    .
```

What about handling text strings such as "abc"? In that case, you need to break the text into individual characters and handle them one by one. In the Robot project, such text is placed into a character array named chars, and each character is looped over:

```
else{
    char chars[] = data.toCharArray();
    for(int charIndex = 0;
        charIndex < chars.length;
        charIndex++){
        .
        .
        .

    }
    .
    .
    .
```

You're responsible for pressing the key, releasing it, and even pressing the Shift key for capital letters. Here's what that looks like in code:

```
else{
    char chars[] = data.toCharArray();
    for(int charIndex = 0;
        charIndex < chars.length;
        charIndex++){

        if(chars[charIndex] >= 'a' &&
            chars[charIndex] <= 'z'){
            robot.keyPress((int)
                chars[charIndex]
                - ('a' -'A'));
            robot.keyRelease((int)
                chars[charIndex]
                - ('a' -'A'));
        }

        else if(chars[charIndex] >= 'A' &&
            chars[charIndex] <= 'Z'){
```

```
            robot.keyPress(KeyEvent.VK_SHIFT);
            robot.keyPress((int)
                chars[charIndex]);
            robot.keyRelease((int) chars
                [charIndex]);
            robot.keyRelease
                (KeyEvent.VK_SHIFT);
        }
        .
        .
        .
```

If the character isn't a letter or a capital letter, the code simply passes the character code to the program it's controlling:

```
            else{
            robot.keyPress((int)
                chars[charIndex]);
            robot.keyRelease((int)
                chars[charIndex]);
            robot.delay(100);
            }
        }
    }

    break;
```

You can see an example in Figure 7.2. That handles the text the user wants to send to the target program. Now what about mouse events?

Sending Mouse Events

The Java Robot class includes a number of mouse methods, such as mouseMove and mousePress, that the Robot project puts to work. For example, if the user issues a command such as "m:500,200", he wants to move the mouse pointer to (500, 200) on the screen, where (0, 0) is at upper left. To handle the "m" operation, then, you recover the x and y coordinates this way:

```
    case 'm':
        String coords[] = data.split(",");
        .
        .
        .
    break;
```

Then you convert the coordinates from text to int values, and you pass them on to the Robot class's mouseMove method:

```
case 'm':
    String coords[] = data.split(",");
    int x = Integer.parseInt(coords[0]);
    int y = Integer.parseInt(coords[1]);
    robot.mouseMove(x, y);
    robot.delay(500);

    break;
```

That moves the mouse where the user wants it. For example, you can see the mouse responding to the Robot command m:500,300 in the WordPad window shown in Figure 7.3.

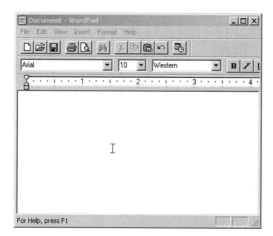

FIGURE 7.3   **The Robot moves the mouse.**

Clicking the mouse is easy—just press the mouse and release it. You can select which mouse button you want to press with the InputEvent class's button masks; for the left mouse button, you use InputEvent.BUTTON1_MASK:

```
case 'c':
    robot.mousePress(InputEvent.BUTTON1_MASK);
    robot.delay(500);
    robot.mouseRelease(InputEvent.BUTTON1_MASK);

    break;
```

If you want to double-click the mouse, just issue two "c:" commands.

What about right-clicking the mouse? Just click the right mouse button with the use of InputEvent.BUTTON3_MASK (InputEvent.BUTTON2_MASK corresponds to the middle mouse button, if the mouse has one):

```
case 'r':
      robot.mousePress(InputEvent.BUTTON3_MASK);
      robot.delay(500);
      robot.mouseRelease(InputEvent.BUTTON3_MASK);

      break;
```

You can see the Robot right-clicking WordPad in Figure 7.4.

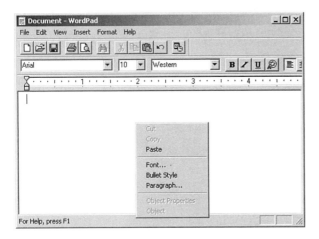

FIGURE 7.4   **The Robot right-clicking the mouse.**

Making the Robot Wait

You can make the Robot wait for as long as you like between commands, and even before running the first command at all. When the user passes a command such as w:500 to the Robot, he wants to pause for 500 seconds.

All the Robot needs to do is to parse the number of seconds to wait, multiply this by 1000 to convert to milliseconds, and then call the Java Robot class's delay method with that number:

```
case 'w':
      int numberSeconds = Integer.parseInt(data);

      robot.delay(numberSeconds * 1000);

      break;
```

If you want to schedule the Robot for late at night, this is the way to do it—just make it wait the number of seconds you want to pause before beginning the action.

Making the Robot Beep

Beeping is an easy task—you can use the Java `Toolkit` object's `beep` method. Using the default `Toolkit` object you get with the static `getDefaultToolkit` method, you can make the computer beep this way:

```
case 'b':
        Toolkit.getDefaultToolkit().beep();

        break;
```

Taking a Screenshot

When the Robot is working with your computer, especially late at night, it can be a good idea to watch what's going on. You don't even have to be present—you can have the Robot take a screenshot for you, using the `s:` command.

How do you take a screenshot? First, you need to get the size of the screen in pixels, which you can do with the default `Toolkit` object's `getScreenSize` method:

```
case 's':

        Dimension screenSize =
            Toolkit.getDefaultToolkit().
            getScreenSize();
        .
        .
        .
```

To capture the screen, you can use the Java `Robot` class's `createScreenCapture` method, passing it a rectangle corresponding to the screen dimensions. This method returns a `BufferedImage` object holding the screenshot:

```
case 's':

        Dimension screenSize =
            Toolkit.getDefaultToolkit().
            getScreenSize();

        BufferedImage bufferedImage =
            robot.createScreenCapture(new
                Rectangle(screenSize));
        .
        .
        .
    break;
```

`BufferedImage` objects are easy to store on disk, as you've already done in the Graphicizer project. You create a new `File` object—the Robot saves screen captures in a file named cap.png using the PNG format—and write that file to disk with the `ImageIO.write` method:

```
case 's':

    Dimension screenSize =
        Toolkit.getDefaultToolkit().
        getScreenSize();

    BufferedImage bufferedImage =
        robot.createScreenCapture(new
            Rectangle(screenSize));

    File outputFile = new File("cap.png");

    ImageIO.write(bufferedImage, "PNG",
        outputFile);

    break;
```

When you save a screen capture, two options are available by default: the PNG format and the JPG format. The Robot uses the PNG format because it's clearer and suffers from fewer distortions due to compression. If you want to use the JPG format, just switch the format used in the `ImageIO.write` method.

Making the Robot Reappear

There are a few last items to take care of in the Robot project. To end the `switch` statement, the code displays an error message if it can't understand an entered command. Also, the `try` statement that encloses all the `Robot` operations ends with a `catch` statement that reports any errors. And at the very end of the code, the `setVisible` method of `JFrame` brings the Robot back into view:

```
default:
    System.out.println(
        "I didn't understand that command.");
}

catch (Exception ex){System.out.println("Error: " +
    ex.getMessage());}

setVisible(true);
}
```

That completes the code—you're ready to start running other programs via remote control, sending keystrokes and mouse events, taking screen shots, and more. There's a lot of power here.

> **NOTE**
>
> Download the complete source code for the Robot project, RobotProject.java, at the Sams website. After compiling the needed file (to create RobotProject.class), you can run it and get started controlling other programs.

Conclusion

This chapter presented the Robot project, a powerful program that can run any other program by remote control. If you want to perform repetitious tasks, the Robot is for you. If you want to schedule tasks to be performed late at night, the Robot is for you, too.

You enter commands for the Robot in a text area or in a command file. Each command is of the form *operation:data*, where *operation* is one character—either t (text), m (move mouse), c (click), r (right-click), w (wait), s (screen shot), or b (beep).

You first start the program you want to control, then start the Robot. Enter the commands you want to use to control the target program and then click Go. The Robot will disappear, giving the focus back to the target program, and the Robot will send your commands to that program.

Using the t command, the Robot can send text to the program it's controlling. You can send test strings to the other program, and you can press the Alt key (good for giving you access to the menu system in Windows) or the Ctrl key and then release it. You can also send Tab, Enter, and Esc keys.

For that matter, you can also use the mouse to control the other program. You can use the m command to move the mouse to where you want it via screen coordinates. You can left-click the mouse with the c command, and you can right-click the mouse with the r command.

You can make the Robot wait using the w command, passing it the number of seconds to wait. For example, w:60 makes the Robot wait for 60 seconds.

You can also make the Robot take screenshots for you—you just have to pass it the s command. When the Robot takes a screenshot for you, it stores the result as a PNG file in cap.png.

And finally, you can make the Robot beep using the b command. Beeps serve as notifications that the Robot has woken up after a delay and is active again.

The Robot is both powerful and useful; all you have to do is to start it up, tell it what to do, and let it do its thing.

CHAPTER 8

Creating a Custom Web Browser in Java: The Browser Project

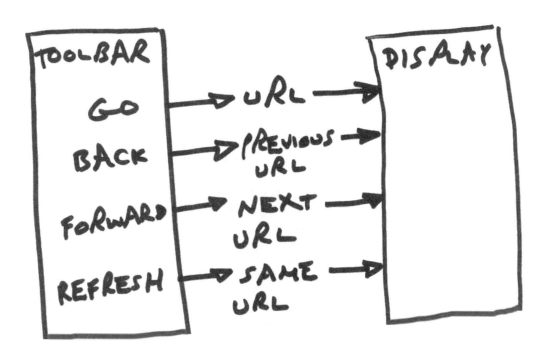

The Browser project.

The kinds of GUIs you can build in Java are extensive and have plenty of capability built in. But one of the things that isn't built in is an easy way to display a web browser. In larger projects for use by the general public, I've found including a browser can be very useful, especially for letting the user browse documentation by automatically navigating the browser to the right page, whether that page is online or local. If you've got lots of online help documentation and you want to let the user click a help topic and see that topic displayed, using a browser as a built-in control is perfect. Same goes for automatically registering the user's copy of your program online, filling out feedback forms, letting the user ask tech support questions, and much more. In fact, a built-in browser control is great for any kind of image and text handling, whether local or on the Web. It's an asset in any application that can impress the heck out of people.

How can you get a browser control that you can use in Java? Java comes with some built-in support for connecting to web servers, so you could try writing such a control yourself.

For example, say you were trying to display the home page of Sun Microsystems, the developers of Java. You could use the URLConnection class to open a URL connection to the Sun server, asking for the page you want (in this case, http://www.sun.com/index.html) in a project named, say, TextBrowser.java:

```java
import java.io.*;
import java.net.*;

class TextBrowser
{
    public static void main(String args[]) throws Exception
    {
        URL url = new URL("http://www.sun.com/index.html");
        URLConnection urlconnection = url.openConnection();

        .
        .
        .

}
```

Then you could open an InputStream from the server, reading characters one by one and displaying them:

```java
import java.io.*;
import java.net.*;

class TextBrowser
{
    public static void main(String args[]) throws Exception
    {
        int character;

        URL url = new URL("http://www.sun.com/index.html");
```

```
URLConnection urlconnection = url.openConnection();

        InputStream in = urlconnection.getInputStream();

        while ((character = in.read()) != -1) {
            System.out.print((char) character);
        }

        in.close();
    }
}
```

This actually works, and here's the output you get as of this writing:

```
<!DOCTYPE HTML PUBLIC "-//W3C//DTD HTML 4.01 Transitional//EN">

<html>
<head>
<title> Sun Microsystems </title>
<meta name="keywords" content="sun microsystems, sun, java, java computing,
solaris, sparc, unix, jini, computer systems, server, mission critical, RAS,
high availability, cluster, workgroup server, desktop, workstation, storage,
backup solutions, network computer, network computing, hardware, software,
service, consulting, support, training, compiler, jdk, technical computing,
scientific computing, high performance, enterprise computing, staroffice,
starportal, sun ray">
<meta name="description" content="Sun Microsystems, Inc. The Network Is
The Computer™.">
<meta http-equiv="pics-label" content='(pics-1.1
"http://www.icra.org/ratingsv02.html" l gen true for
"http://www.sun.com" r (cz 1 lz 1 nz 1 oz 1 vz 1)
"http://www.rsac.org/ratingsv01.html" l gen true for
"http://www.sun.com" r (n 0 s 0 v 0 l 0))'>
<meta http-equiv="content-type" content="text/html; charset=iso-8859-1">
    .
    .
    .
```

Swell, but no user is going to want to see 20 pages of untreated HTML. What about display-ing images and formatted text as you'd see in a standard browser?

No problem. Just download the Standard Widget Toolkit (SWT), which you can get for free with the Eclipse Java Integrated Development Environment (a superb tool in its own right). Using the SWT, you can create a browser control easily, and it'll give you many of the full features available in a browser in your Java programs, as you see in Figure 8.1, which shows the Browser project at work—displaying the Sun Microsystems home page, in fact.

FIGURE 8.1   The Custom Browser project.

Just as you'd expect in a real browser, the Browser project features these buttons:

- **Go**—Go to the URL in the text box.
- **Forward**—Go forward one page in the browser's history.
- **Back**—Go back one page in the browser's history.
- **Refresh**—Refresh the page.
- **Stop**—Stop all operations.

REAL-WORLD SCENARIO

Why SWT?

Developers have always had some issues with the GUI toolkits that come with Java. The Abstract Windowing Toolkit, AWT, was Sun's first version of a GUI toolkit for Java, and it was created hastily. So hastily, in fact, that it used the underlying operating system's GUI elements instead of its own. In Windows, you'd see a Windows button. On the Mac, you'd see a Mac button. This limited Sun to only those controls that were common to all operating systems that supported Java, and in consequence, the AWT was very limited.

Next came Swing, with a set of built-in Java controls. This set of Java-specific controls gave Java applications a common look across multiple platforms, but it also didn't let you develop applications that looked like they were designed for Windows, the Mac, and so on. To get around that, Sun added a "look-and-feel" emulation that lets your applications look like they

Very cool.

NOTE

The SWT doesn't actually create a browser from scratch, including full support for graphics, JavaScript, Flash, and so on built in. It uses Internet Explorer, and that's the Internet Explorer you see in Figure 8.1. You'll need IE installed on your system before you can use SWT to create your own browser controls.

Introducing the SWT

What is the SWT? The Standard Widget Toolkit was created by IBM, and it was intended as a replacement for both the Java Abstract Windowing Toolkit (AWT) and Swing.

The SWT is an extensive GUI toolkit, as you'd expect if it was intended to replace both the AWT and Java Swing. Controls are called "widgets" in the SWT. Here's the current list of the available SWT widgets:

- Button
- Canvas
- Caret
- Combo
- Composite
- CoolBar

REAL-WORLD SCENARIO *Continued*

were designed for the operating system they're running on. Unfortunately, the "look and feel" has lagged behind the new versions of many operating systems that have appeared. And Swing controls, written in Java, can be a great deal slower than the native controls in an operating system.

The SWT addresses these problems, and it makes developers happier by offering them a set of widgets that use native controls when they're available (for speed and visual compatibility with other programs). If such controls aren't available, the SWT adds them using code written and compiled for the operating system being used (not in Java).

The SWT is steadily gaining ground, especially because it comes built in to the very popular Eclipse Integrated Development Environment. Watch for the SWT to make a substantial impact in the coming years.

- CoolItem
- Group
- Label
- List
- Menu
- MenuItem
- ProgressBar
- Sash
- Scale
- ScrollBar
- Shell
- Slider
- TabFolder
- TabItem
- Table
- TableColumn
- TableItem
- Text
- ToolBar
- ToolItem
- Tracker
- Tree
- TreeItem

As you can see, the SWT is a serious GUI toolkit.

Getting the SWT

As far as we're concerned in this chapter, what's attractive about the SWT is that it includes a Browser class that lets you create Browser widgets. So how do you get the SWT for use in your applications?

The support for the SWT is in a JAR file named swt.jar, and you can get that file simply by downloading the current Eclipse zip/tar.gz file, which contains swt.jar. Navigate to http://www.eclipse.org, click the Downloads button, and select the compressed file for your operating system. As of this writing, that's eclipse-SDK-3.0.1-win32.zip for Windows, eclipse-SDK-3.0.1-linux-motif.zip for Linux x86/Motif, eclipse-SDK-3.0.1-linux-gtk.zip for Linux x86/GTK 2, and so on—they're all listed on the Downloads page. Decompress the compressed file, which will give you the swt.jar file (along with many, many other files) you'll need for this project.

You're also going to need the precompiled native support for the SWT in order to run SWT programs. This is where the SWT's fast connection to the operating system is implemented. For example, in the current Windows version of Eclipse, those files are swt-awt-win32-3063.dll and swt-win32-3063.dll, so place them in the directory you're going to run the Browser project from. How can you find which precompiled files you need for your operating system? If you expand the Eclipse zip/tar.gz file, you'll find them in the following directories. Make sure you copy the files you find there to the directory where you're creating the Browser project (replace the 3.0.1 part in these paths with the version of Eclipse you download):

- Win32: eclipse\plugins\org.eclipse.swt.win32_3.0.1\os\win32\x86
- Linux GTK: eclipse/plugins/org.eclipse.swt.gtk_3.0.1/os/linux/x86
- Linux Motif: eclipse/plugins/org.eclipse.swt.motif_3.0.1/os/linux/x86
- Solaris Motif: eclipse/plugins/org.eclipse.swt.motif_3.0.1/os/solaris/sparc
- AIX Motif: eclipse/plugins/org.eclipse.swt.motif_3.0.1/os/aix/ppc
- HPUX Motif: eclipse/plugins/org.eclipse.swt.motif_3.0.1/os/hpux/PA_RISC
- Photon QNX: eclipse/plugins/org.eclipse.swt.photon_3.0.1/os/qnx/x86
- Mac OS X: eclipse/plugins/org.eclipse.swt.carbon_3.0.1/os/macosx/ppc

That gives you the support you're going to need to run SWT applications. So how about creating one?

Creating an SWT Application

To create the Browser project, you're going to have to know how SWT applications work. Take a look at Figure 8.2, where you'll see just about the simplest such application. It just displays the text "An SWT label, very cool." in an SWT Label widget inside an SWT window.

This application, LabelProject.java, starts importing the SWT classes it needs and creating a new LabelProject object in the main method:

```
import org.eclipse.swt.*;
import org.eclipse.swt.widgets.*;
```

```
public class LabelProject
{
        public static void main(String [] args)
     {
        new LabelProject();
     }
        .
        .
        .
}
```

FIGURE 8.2   **An SWT application.**

In the constructor, you create a new GUI handler of the SWT Display class, and then you
create a new Shell object using that Display object. It's that Shell object that corresponds
to the window you see in Figure 8.2. Here's how you create these objects:

```
import org.eclipse.swt.*;
import org.eclipse.swt.widgets.*;

public class LabelProject
{
    Display display;
    Shell shell;

    public static void main(String [] args)
    {
        new LabelProject();
    }

    LabelProject()
    {
        display = new Display();
        shell = new Shell(display);
        shell.setSize(200, 200);
```

```
    .
    .
    .
}
```

You can find the significant methods of the SWT `Shell` class in Table 8.1. This class is an important one; it's the basis of the browser window you see in Figure 8.1.

TABLE 8.1   **Significant Methods of the** *org.eclipse.swt.widgets.Shell* **Class**

Method	Does This
`void addShellListener(ShellListener listener)`	Adds the given listener to the listeners that will be notified when events occur in the widget
`void close()`	Closes the widget, just as if the user clicked the close button
`void dispose()`	Disposes of the operating system resources connected to this the widget
`Rectangle getBounds()`	Returns a `Rectangle` object holding the widget's size and location
`boolean getEnabled()`	Returns `true` if the widget is enabled. Returns `false` otherwise
`Point getLocation()`	Returns a point holding the widget's location
`Region getRegion()`	Returns a `Region` object holding the widget's location
`Point getSize()`	Returns a point holding the widget's size
`boolean isEnabled()`	Returns `true` if the widget is enabled. Returns `false` otherwise
`boolean isVisible()`	Returns `true` if the widget is visible. Returns `false` otherwise
`void open()`	Opens the widget, making it visible
`void removeShellListener(ShellListener listener)`	Removes the listener from the widget
`void setEnabled(boolean enabled)`	Enables the widget if you pass a value of `true`, and disables it if you pass `false`
`void setRegion(Region region)`	Sets the shape of the shell to the region you pass this method
`void setVisible(boolean visible)`	Makes the widget visible if you pass it a value of `true`. Makes the widget invisible otherwise

Now you create an SWT label to hold the text displayed in Figure 8.2. To create the label, you pass the `shell` object to the label's constructor. Then you can use the label's `setText` method to set the displayed text, and you can use the `setBounds` method to specify where you want it (this centers text in the label with the `SWT.CENTER` style):

```java
import org.eclipse.swt.*;
import org.eclipse.swt.widgets.*;


public class LabelProject
{
    Display display;
    Shell shell;
    Label label;

    public static void main(String [] args)
    {
        new LabelProject();
    }

    LabelProject()
    {
     display = new Display();
     shell = new Shell(display);
     shell.setSize(200, 200);

        label = new Label(shell, SWT.CENTER);
        label.setText("An SWT label, very cool.");
        label.setBounds(5, 20, 180, 40);

        .
        .
        .

}
```

You can find the significant methods of the SWT `Label` class in Table 8.2.

TABLE 8.2   Significant Methods of the `org.eclipse.swt.widgets.Label` **Class**

Method	Does This
Point computeSize(int wHint, int hHint, boolean changed)	Returns the preferred size of the label
int getAlignment()	Returns a constant indicating the position of text or an image in the label
Image getImage()	Returns the label's image, if it has one, or null otherwise
String getText()	Returns the label's text, if there is any, or null otherwise
void setAlignment(int alignment)	Sets how text and images should appear in the label
void setImage(Image image)	Sets the image that will appear in the label
void setText(String string)	Sets the text that will appear in the label

All that's left is to display the shell and handle the window-closing event, which happens when the user clicks the close button, by disposing of the `display` object:

```
import org.eclipse.swt.*;
import org.eclipse.swt.widgets.*;

public class LabelProject
{
     Display display;
     Shell shell;
     Label label;

     public static void main(String [] args)
     {
         new LabelProject();
     }

     LabelProject()
     {
      display = new Display();
      shell = new Shell(display);
      shell.setSize(200, 200);
         .
         .
         .
      shell.open();

      while(!shell.isDisposed()) {
          if(!display.readAndDispatch()) display.sleep();
      }
      display.dispose();
     }
}
```

That completes LabelProject.java. To compile it, make sure swt.jar is in your classpath. For example, if swt.jar is in the same directory as LabelProject.java, set the classpath this way:

```
%set classpath=swt.jar;.
```

Then compile LabelClass.java this way (this assumes javac is in your path; otherwise, prefix it with the correct path):

```
%javac LabelClass.java
```

To run the resulting LabelClass.class file, you have to tell Java where to find the SWT native code support, such as in win32-3063.dll and swt-win32-3063.dll in Windows. Assuming you've copied the needed files to the same directory where LabelClass.class is, you can execute that class file like this:

```
%java -Djava.library.path=. LabelClass
```

Running this application should give you the results you see in Figure 8.2.

That's the basics of an SWT application—at least one that does nothing but displaying some text. The Browser project is going to have to do a lot more, however, such as handling SWT events such as button clicks.

Working with SWT Events

Take a look at the example in Figure 8.3, ButtonProject.java, which is designed to show how to handle events in SWT applications. When you click the button in this project, the application catches that event and then the message "Thanks for clicking." appears in the Text widget.

FIGURE 8.3   Handling events in SWT applications.

This application starts by creating the Button widget it needs, giving it the caption "Click here," and making it a push button (the allowed styles are SWT.ARROW, SWT.CHECK, SWT.PUSH, SWT.RADIO, SWT.TOGGLE, SWT.FLAT, SWT.UP, SWT.DOWN, SWT.LEFT, SWT.RIGHT, and SWT.CENTER):

```
import org.eclipse.swt.*;
import org.eclipse.swt.events.*;
import org.eclipse.swt.widgets.*;

public class ButtonProject
{
    Display display;
    Shell shell;
    Button button;

    public static void main(String [] args)
    {
        new ButtonProject();
    }
```

```
ButtonProject()
{
    display = new Display();
    shell = new Shell(display);
    shell.setSize(240, 150);
    shell.setText("SWT Buttons");

    button = new Button(shell, SWT.PUSH);
    button.setText("Click here");
    button.setBounds(10, 35, 60, 30);
        .
        .
        .

}
```

You can find the significant methods of the SWT `Button` class in Table 8.3.

TABLE 8.3   **Significant Methods of the** *org.eclipse.swt.widgets.Button* **Class**

Method	Does This
void addSelectionListener (SelectionListener listener)	Adds the given listener to the listeners that will be notified when an event occurs in the Text widget
Point computeSize(int wHint, int hHint, boolean changed)	Returns the preferred size of the Text widget
int getAlignment()	Returns a constant indicating the position of text or an image in the Text widget
Image getImage()	Returns the Text widget's image, if it has one, or null otherwise
boolean getSelection()	Returns true if the Text widget is selected. Returns false otherwise
String getText()	Returns the Text widget's text, if there is any, or null otherwise
void removeSelectionListener (SelectionListener listener)	Removes the listener from the listeners that will be notified when the Text widget is selected by the user
void setAlignment(int alignment)	Sets how text, images, and arrows will be displayed in the Text widget
void setImage(Image image)	Sets the image displayed in the Text widget to the given image
void setSelection(boolean selected)	Sets the selection state of the Text widget
void setText(String string)	Sets the text that will appear in the Text widget

To handle button clicks, you add a `SelectionListener` to the button, which you can do with the `addSelectionListener` method. Listeners in SWT are much like listeners in AWT; here are some of the most popular:

- **Listener**—Handles generic events

- **ControlListener**—Handles moving and resizing

- **FocusListener**—Handles the getting and losing of focus

- **KeyListener**—Handles keystrokes

- **MouseListener, MouseMoveListener, and MouseTrackListener**—Handle the mouse

- **SelectionListener**—Handles widget selections (including button clicks)

You use a `SelectionListener` object to handle button clicks. To implement a selection listener, you need to override two methods: `widgetSelected`, called when the widget is selected or clicked, and `widgetDefaultSelected`, called when the default event for the window occurs (such as when the user enters text in a Text widget and presses Enter).

Here's how to add the target Text widget and handle the button-click event in the ButtonProject application (the allowed styles are `SWT.CENTER`, `SWT.LEFT`, `SWT.MULTI`, `SWT.PASSWORD`, `SWT.SINGLE`, `SWT.RIGHT`, `SWT.READ_ONLY`, `SWT.WRAP`, `SWT.SHADOW_IN`, and `SWT.SHADOW_OUT`):

```java
import org.eclipse.swt.*;
import org.eclipse.swt.events.*;
import org.eclipse.swt.widgets.*;

public class ButtonProject
{
    Display display;
    Shell shell;
    Button button;
    Text text;

    public static void main(String [] args)
    {
        new ButtonProject();
    }

    ButtonProject()
    {
        .
        .
        .
        button = new Button(shell, SWT.PUSH);
        button.setText("Click here");
        button.setBounds(10, 35, 60, 30);
```

```
      text = new Text(shell, SWT.SHADOW_IN);
      text.setBounds(80, 40, 120, 20);

      button.addSelectionListener(new SelectionListener()
      {
        public void widgetSelected(SelectionEvent event)
        {
          text.setText("Thanks for clicking.");
        }

        public void widgetDefaultSelected(SelectionEvent event)
        {
          text.setText("No worries!");
        }
      });

      shell.open();
      while(!shell.isDisposed()) {
        if(!display.readAndDispatch()) display.sleep();
      }
      display.dispose();
    }
}
```

You can find the significant methods of the SWT Text class, such as setText to set the text in the widget, in Table 8.4.

TABLE 8.4 **Significant Methods of the** `org.eclipse.swt.widgets.Text` **Class**

Method	Does This
void addSelectionListener (SelectionListener listener)	Adds the given selection listener to the listeners that will be notified when the Text widget is selected
void addModifyListener (ModifyListener listener)	Adds the given modify listener to the listeners that will be notified when the Text widget is selected
void addVerifyListener (VerifyListener listener)	Adds the given verify listener to the listeners that will be notified when the Text widget is selected
void append(String string)	Appends a string to the text in the Text widget
void clearSelection()	Clears the current selection in the Text widget
Point computeSize(int wHint, int hHint, boolean changed)	Returns the preferred size of the Text widget
void copy()	Copies the text currently selected in the Text widget
void cut()	Cuts the text currently selected in the Text widget
int getBorderWidth()	Returns the width of the Text widget's border

TABLE 8.4   Continued

Method	Does This
`boolean getEditable()`	Returns `true` if the text in the Text widget may be edited
`int getLineCount()`	Returns the number of lines in the Text widget
`int getLineHeight()`	Returns the height of a line in the Text widget
`int getOrientation()`	Returns the current orientation of the Text widget, which can be either `SWT.LEFT_TO_RIGHT` or `SWT.RIGHT_TO_LEFT`
`Point getSelection()`	Returns the location of the selected text in the Text widget
`int getSelectionCount()`	Returns the number of characters selected in the Text widget
`String getSelectionText()`	Returns the text currently selected in the Text widget
`String getText()`	Returns the text in the Text widget
`String getText(int start, int end)`	Returns a range of text, extending from start to end
`int getTextLimit()`	Returns the maximum number of characters that the Text widget can contain
`void insert(String string)`	Inserts a text string into the Text widget
`void paste()`	Pastes text from the clipboard into the Text widget
`void removeModifyListener (ModifyListener listener)`	Removes the given modify listener from the Text widget
`void removeSelectionListener (SelectionListener listener)`	Removes the given selection listener from the Text widget
`void removeVerifyListener (VerifyListener listener)`	Removes the given verify listener from the Text widget
`void selectAll()`	Selects all the text in the Text widget, making it the current selection
`void setEditable(boolean editable)`	Sets whether the text in the Text widget may be edited
`void setFont(Font font)`	Sets the font that will be used in the Text widget for text
`void setOrientation(int orientation)`	Sets the orientation of the Text widget: `SWT.LEFT_TO_RIGHT` or `SWT.RIGHT_TO_LEFT`
`void setSelection(int start)`	Sets the current selection in the Text widget, from the start to the end of the text
`void setSelection(int start, int end)`	Sets the current selection in the Text widget, from start to end
`void setText(String string)`	Sets the text in the Text widget to the specified text

You can see the results in Figure 8.3; when you click the button, the application's message appears in the Text widget as it should. Very nice.

Using SWT Toolbars

The Browser project uses an SWT ToolBar widget to display a set of buttons, as you see in Figure 8.1. To create a toolbar in the SWT, you just connect the toolbar with the shell you're working with and set its style.

For example, take a look at the SWT ToolbarProject application, which appears in Figure 8.4. There are four buttons in the toolbar, and when the user clicks one, that button is identified in a message that appears in the Text widget.

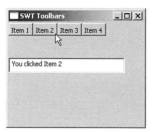

FIGURE 8.4   Using a toolbar in an SWT application.

The ToolbarProject.java application creates a new Toolbar object this way (the SWT.NONE style indicates that the toolbar won't have any special styling; the allowable styles for toolbars are SWT.FLAT, SWT.NONE, SWT.WRAP, SWT.RIGHT, SWT.HORIZONTAL, SWT.VERTICAL, SWT.SHADOW_IN, and SWT.SHADOW_OUT):

```
import org.eclipse.swt.*;
import org.eclipse.swt.widgets.*;

public class ToolbarProject
{
    Display display;
    Shell shell;
    ToolBar toolbar;
        .
        .
        .
    public static void main(String [] args)
    {
        new ToolbarProject();
    }

    ToolbarProject()
    {
        display = new Display();
        shell = new Shell(display);
```

```
shell.setText("SWT Toolbars");
shell.setSize(240, 200);

toolbar = new ToolBar(shell, SWT.NONE);
    .
    .
    .
```
}

You can find the significant methods of the SWT Toolbar class in Table 8.5. The Browser project will use one of these ToolBar widgets.

TABLE 8.5   Significant Methods of the org.eclipse.swt.widgets.Toolbar **Class**

Method	Does This
Point computeSize(int wHint, int hHint, boolean changed)	Returns the preferred size of the ToolBar widget
Rectangle computeTrim(int x, int y, int width, int height)	Passing a specific client area to this method returns the bounding rectangle for the ToolBar widget required to enclose that client area
ToolItem getItem(int index)	Returns the item at the given index in the toolbar
ToolItem getItem(Point point)	Returns the item at the given point in the toolbar, or null if there is no item at that point
int getItemCount()	Returns the number of items the toolbar contains
ToolItem[] getItems()	Returns an array of ToolItem objects that are contained in the toolbar
int getRowCount()	Returns the number of rows in the ToolBar widget
int indexOf(ToolItem item)	Returns the index of the specified item in the toolbar
void setFont(Font font)	Sets the font that the ToolBar widget will use to draw text

Each of the four toolbar buttons you see in Figure 8.4 is created using an SWT ToolItem object. They're created with the style SWT.PUSH, to make them appear as push buttons (the allowable styles are SWT.PUSH, SWT.CHECK, SWT.RADIO, SWT.SEPARATOR, and SWT.DROP_DOWN):

```
import org.eclipse.swt.*;
import org.eclipse.swt.widgets.*;

public class ToolbarProject
{
    Display display;
    Shell shell;
    ToolBar toolbar;
    ToolItem item1, item2, item3, item4;

    public static void main(String [] args)
    {
```

```
    new ToolbarProject();
}

ToolbarProject()
{
    display = new Display();
    shell = new Shell(display);
    shell.setText("SWT Toolbars");
    shell.setSize(240, 200);

    toolbar = new ToolBar(shell, SWT.NONE);
    item1 = new ToolItem(toolbar, SWT.PUSH);
    item1.setText("Item 1");
    item2 = new ToolItem(toolbar, SWT.PUSH);
    item2.setText("Item 2");
    item3 = new ToolItem(toolbar, SWT.PUSH);
    item3.setText("Item 3");
    item4 = new ToolItem(toolbar, SWT.PUSH);
    item4.setText("Item 4");
    .
    .
    .
}
```

You can find the significant methods of the SWT ToolItem class in Table 8.6.

TABLE 8.6　Significant Methods of the `org.eclipse.swt.widgets.ToolItem` Class

Method	Does This
void addSelectionListener (SelectionListener listener)	Adds the given selection listener to the listeners that will be notified when the item is selected
Rectangle getBounds()	Returns a rectangle containing the item's size and location
Image getDisabledImage()	Returns the image used to indicate the item is disabled
boolean getEnabled()	Returns true if the item is enabled. Returns false otherwise
Image getHotImage()	Returns the image the item will display as the mouse moves over it
ToolBar getParent()	Returns the item's parent toolbar
boolean getSelection()	Returns true if the item is selected. Returns false otherwise
String getToolTipText()	Returns the item's tool tip text. Returns null if it has no tool tip text
int getWidth()	Returns the width of the item, in pixels.
boolean isEnabled()	Returns true if the item is enabled. Returns false otherwise

TABLE 8.6   Continued

Method	Does This
void removeSelectionListener (SelectionListener listener)	Removes the given listener from the listeners that will be notified when the item is selected
void setDisabledImage(Image image)	Sets the image that will appear in the item when it is disabled
void setEnabled(boolean enabled)	Enables the item if you pass a value of true. Disables it otherwise
void setHotImage(Image image)	Sets the image that will appear when the mouse passes over the item
void setImage(Image image)	Sets the image that will appear in the item
void setSelection(boolean selected)	Sets the selection state of the item
void setText(String string)	Sets the text that appears in the item
void setToolTipText(String string)	Sets the item's tool tip text
void setWidth(int width)	Sets the width of the item, in pixels

There are four buttons here—how can you tell which button was clicked? You use a Listener object and override the handleEvent method. This method is passed an Event object:

```
Listener listener = new Listener() {
    public void handleEvent(Event event) {
        .
        .
        .
    }
};
```

You can determine which button was selected by recovering the ToolItem widget that was clicked—which you can do with the Event object's widget field—and by getting that item's caption text:

```
Listener listener = new Listener() {
    public void handleEvent(Event event) {
        ToolItem item =(ToolItem)event.widget;
        String string = item.getText();
        .
        .
        . {
    }
};
```

Now you can display the appropriate message in a Text widget, based on which item was clicked, which you determine by checking the caption of the item:

```java
import org.eclipse.swt.*;
import org.eclipse.swt.widgets.*;

public class ToolbarProject
{
    Display display;
    Shell shell;
    ToolBar toolbar;
    ToolItem item1, item2, item3, item4;
    Text text;

    public static void main(String [] args)
    {
        new ToolbarProject();
    }

    ToolbarProject()
    {
        display = new Display();
        shell = new Shell(display);
        shell.setText("SWT Toolbars");
        shell.setSize(240, 200);

        toolbar = new ToolBar(shell, SWT.NONE);
        item1 = new ToolItem(toolbar, SWT.PUSH);
        item1.setText("Item 1");
        item2 = new ToolItem(toolbar, SWT.PUSH);
        item2.setText("Item 2");
        item3 = new ToolItem(toolbar, SWT.PUSH);
        item3.setText("Item 3");
        item4 = new ToolItem(toolbar, SWT.PUSH);
        item4.setText("Item 4");

        toolbar.setBounds(0, 0, 200, 40);

        text = new Text(shell, SWT.BORDER);
        text.setBounds(0, 60, 200, 25);

        Listener listener = new Listener() {
            public void handleEvent(Event event) {
                ToolItem item =(ToolItem)event.widget;
                String string = item.getText();{
```

```
            if(string.equals("Item 1"))
                text.setText("You clicked Item 1");
            else if(string.equals("Item 2"))
                text.setText("You clicked Item 2");
            else if(string.equals("Item 3"))
                text.setText("You clicked Item 3");
            else if(string.equals("Item 4"))
                text.setText("You clicked Item 4");
        }
    };

    item1.addListener(SWT.Selection, listener);
    item2.addListener(SWT.Selection, listener);
    item3.addListener(SWT.Selection, listener);
    item4.addListener(SWT.Selection, listener);

    shell.open();

    while (!shell.isDisposed()) {
        if (!display.readAndDispatch()){
            display.sleep();
        }
    }
    display.dispose();
    }
}
```

That finishes ToolbarProject.java; you can see it at work in Figure 8.4. When the user clicks an item in the toolbar, the application reports which one was clicked. Not bad.

That gives you all the technology you need to create the Browser project, except for one item—the Browser object itself. That's coming up next.

Creating the Browser Project

As shown earlier in Figure 8.1, the Browser project uses ToolBar, Text, and Browser widgets. It starts by creating a good-sized shell to display the browser in:

```
import org.eclipse.swt.*;
import org.eclipse.swt.widgets.*;

public class BrowserProject
{
    Display display;
    Shell shell;
```

```
    public static void main(String[] args)
    {
        new BrowserProject();
    }

    BrowserProject()
    {
        display = new Display();
        shell = new Shell(display);
        shell.setText("The Browser Project");
        shell.setSize(600, 500);
            .
            .
            .
}
```

Then it creates the toolbar and buttons you see in Figure 8.1:

```
import org.eclipse.swt.*;
import org.eclipse.swt.widgets.*;

public class BrowserProject
{
    Display display;
    Shell shell;
    ToolBar toolbar;
    ToolItem go, forward, back, refresh, stop;

    public static void main(String[] args)
    {
        new BrowserProject();
    }

    BrowserProject()
    {
        display = new Display();
        shell = new Shell(display);
        shell.setText("The Browser Project");
        shell.setSize(600, 500);

        toolbar = new ToolBar(shell, SWT.NONE);
        toolbar.setBounds(5, 5, 200, 30);

        go = new ToolItem(toolbar, SWT.PUSH);
        go.setText("Go");
```

```
    forward = new ToolItem(toolbar, SWT.PUSH);
    forward.setText("Forward");

    back = new ToolItem(toolbar, SWT.PUSH);
    back.setText("Back");

    refresh = new ToolItem(toolbar, SWT.PUSH);
    refresh.setText("Refresh");

    stop = new ToolItem(toolbar, SWT.PUSH);
    stop.setText("Stop");
        .
        .
        .
}
```

You'll also need a Text widget to let the user enter URLs, and you'll need the Browser widget itself. Here's what that looks like:

```
import org.eclipse.swt.*;
import org.eclipse.swt.browser.*;
import org.eclipse.swt.widgets.*;

public class BrowserProject
{
    Display display;
    Shell shell;
    ToolBar toolbar;
    ToolItem go, forward, back, refresh, stop;
    Text text;
    Browser browser;

    public static void main(String[] args)
    {
        new BrowserProject();
    }

    BrowserProject()
    {
        display = new Display();
        shell = new Shell(display);
        shell.setText("The Browser Project");
        shell.setSize(600, 500);
            .
            .
            .
```

```
        stop = new ToolItem(toolbar, SWT.PUSH);
        stop.setText("Stop");

        text = new Text(shell, SWT.BORDER);
        text.setBounds(5, 35, 400, 25);

        browser = new Browser(shell, SWT.NONE);
        browser.setBounds(5, 75, 590, 400);
        .
        .
        .

}
```

You can find the significant methods of the SWT Browser class in Table 8.7. Note the methods—setUrl, back, forward, stop, and refresh—this project will use to make the browser do what the user wants.

TABLE 8.7   **Significant Methods of the** `org.eclipse.swt.widgets.Browser` **Class**

Method	Does This
void addCloseWindowListener (CloseWindowListener listener)	Adds a close-window listener to the browser
void addLocationListener (LocationListener listener)	Adds a location listener to the browser
void addOpenWindowListener (OpenWindowListener listener)	Adds an open-window listener to the browser
void addProgressListener (ProgressListener listener)	Adds a progress listener to the browser
void addStatusTextListener (StatusTextListener listener)	Adds a status listener to the browser
void addTitleListener(TitleListener listener)	Adds a close-title listener to the browser
void addVisibilityWindowListener (VisibilityWindowListener listener)	Adds a visibility listener to the browser
boolean back()	Navigates back to the previous web page in the browser's history
boolean forward()	Navigates forward to the next web page in the browser's history
String getUrl()	Returns the current URL
boolean isBackEnabled()	Returns true if the browser can navigate back to the previous web page in the history
boolean isForwardEnabled()	Returns true if the browser can navigate forward to the next web page in the history
void refresh()	Refreshes the current web page in the browser

TABLE 8.7   Continued

Method	Does This
void removeCloseWindowListener (CloseWindowListener listener)	**Removes the given close-window listener from the browser**
void removeLocationListener (LocationListener listener)	**Removes the given location listener from the browser**
void removeOpenWindowListener (OpenWindowListener listener)	**Removes the given open-window listener from the browser**
void removeProgressListener (ProgressListener listener)	**Removes the given progress listener from the browser**
void removeStatusTextListener (StatusTextListener listener)	**Removes the given status text listener from the browser**
void removeTitleListener (TitleListener listener)	**Removes the given title listener from the browser**
void removeVisibilityWindowListener (VisibilityWindowListener listener)	**Removes the given window visibility listener from the browser**
boolean setText(String html)	**Displays the given HTML text in the browser**
boolean setUrl(String url)	**Makes the browser navigate to the given URL**
void stop()	**Stops the current operation**

You can call the Browser widget's methods matching the various buttons in the toolbar. Here's what that looks like in code, making the toolbar buttons active (note that the Go button's code reads the URL the user entered into the Text widget and calls the browser's setUrl method to navigate to that URL):

```
import org.eclipse.swt.*;
import org.eclipse.swt.browser.*;
import org.eclipse.swt.widgets.*;

public class BrowserProject
{
    Display display;
        .
        .
        .
    public static void main(String[] args)
    {
        new BrowserProject();
    }

    BrowserProject()
    {
        display = new Display();
        shell = new Shell(display);
```

```
shell.setText("The Browser Project");
shell.setSize(600, 500);
.
.
.
browser = new Browser(shell, SWT.NONE);
browser.setBounds(5, 75, 590, 400);

Listener listener = new Listener()
{
    public void handleEvent(Event event)
    {
        try{
            ToolItem item = (ToolItem) event.widget;
            String string = item.getText();

            if (string.equals("Back")){
                browser.back();
            }

            else if (string.equals("Forward")){
                browser.forward();
            }

            else if (string.equals("Refresh")){
                browser.refresh();
            }

            else if (string.equals("Stop")){
                browser.stop();
            }

            else if (string.equals("Go")){
                browser.setUrl(text.getText());
            }
        }
        catch(Exception e)
        {
            System.out.println(e.getMessage());
        }
    }
};

go.addListener(SWT.Selection, listener);
forward.addListener(SWT.Selection, listener);
```

```
        refresh.addListener(SWT.Selection, listener);
        back.addListener(SWT.Selection, listener);
        stop.addListener(SWT.Selection, listener);
        .
        .
        .
}
```

That makes the toolbar active; all the user has to do is to click a button to make the browser do what he wants.

As with conventional browsers, you can also let the user navigate to a new URL simply by entering that URL in the text field and pressing Enter. Here's how that works in BrowserProject.java:

```
    text.addListener(SWT.DefaultSelection, new Listener()
        {
            public void handleEvent(Event e) {
                browser.setUrl(text.getText());
            }
        }
    );
    .
    .
    .
}
```

All that's left is to display the shell, including the Browser widget. When the browser first opens, it needs some default page to go to, and the Browser project simply uses http://www.sun.com:

```
import org.eclipse.swt.*;
import org.eclipse.swt.browser.*;
import org.eclipse.swt.widgets.*;

public class BrowserProject
{
    Display display;
    Shell shell;
        .
        .
        .
    public static void main(String[] args)
    {
        new BrowserProject();
    }
```

```
BrowserProject()
{
    display = new Display();
    shell = new Shell(display);
    shell.setText("The Browser Project");
    shell.setSize(600, 500);
    .
    .
    .


    shell.open();


    browser.setUrl("http://www.sun.com");


    while (!shell.isDisposed())
    {
        if (!display.readAndDispatch())
        {
            display.sleep();
        }
    }


    display.dispose();
    }
}
```

NOTE

You can also integrate this browser window into a standard, otherwise non-SWT Java project with ease if you want to—when you need this browser window, just call the `shell.open` method, and the browser window will open.

That completes the Browser project, BrowserProject.java. This browser features Go, Forward, Back, Refresh, and Stop buttons—and the user can even work with his Favorites folder, save images, print pages, and so on, simply by right-clicking the displayed web page, because what he's seeing in the browser control is Internet Explorer.

NOTE

Download the complete source code for the Browser project, BrowserProject.java, at the Sams website. After compiling the needed file (creating BrowserProject.class), you can run it, as detailed in this chapter, and get started browsing. You can also run the sample projects, ToolbarProject.java and LabelProject.java, following the instructions in this chapter.

Conclusion

This chapter presented the Browser project, a powerful custom browser that uses the Standard Widget Toolkit's Browser widget to display a browser from Java code. This project relies on the SWT, IBM's proposed successor to the Java AWT and Java Swing.

The SWT has a great deal of support written in native code for various platforms, which makes it fast and lets it take advantage of native resources such as built-in controls. To use the SWT, you have to make sure Java can reach that native support, so running programs that use the SWT take an extra step—you have to point Java at the right native-code library.

The Browser project presents the user with a toolbar full of buttons, a Text widget, and a browser window. The browser window in this case displays Internet Explorer and lets the user see the fully formatted text and images of web pages.

The user can also navigate to a new URL simply by entering that URL into the Text widget and clicking the Go button, or just by pressing Enter. He can navigate forward and backward in the browser's history with the Back and Forward buttons. The user can refresh the browser's display with the Refresh button, just as in a standard browser, and he can stop the browser's current operation with the Stop button.

All in all, an impressive and fun addition to any program. Want to direct the user to a location on the Internet? Don't just give him a URL and expect him to do the rest—take him there yourself with the Browser project.

CHAPTER 9
Typing Across the Internet: The Intercom Project

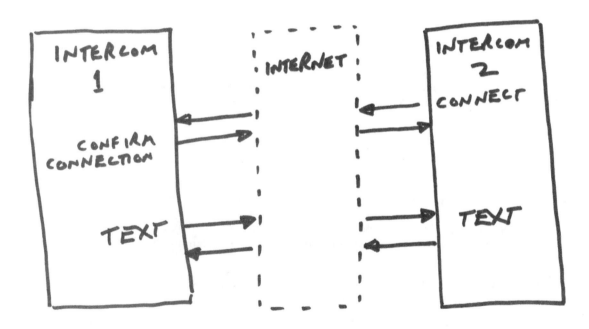

The Intercom.

Here's another fun one—the Intercom project, which lets two people type across the Internet. You just start up the project, connect with the click of a button, and you've got your own connection: Everything you type into the intercom, the other user can see; everything he or she types, you can see. Presto—your own private intercom over the Internet.

Using the Intercom, you can communicate between two machines anywhere in the world—just type your text, which will appear in the other person's intercom, and his or her reply text will appear in your window.

This one's much like the messenger programs you see all around, except that it's even better—no messenger service needed, no third-party site needed, no mysterious code to install. You don't even need an ISP that can run Java online—all the code is on your machines at home. You're running your own Internet server from your computer.

To run this project, all you need are two machines connected to the Internet, and Java. The only stipulation is that one intercom is able to find the other, which means you'll need a fixed Internet IP address for Intercom 1—which, if you're connected to the Internet via broadband, you almost certainly already have.

NOTE

There are two applications here—Intercom 1 and Intercom 2. Only Intercom 1 needs to be run on a machine with a fixed IP address of the kind you get with a broadband connection; you enter that IP address into Intercom 2 so it knows where to find Intercom 1. For example, you can find what your fixed IP address is in Windows by finding the Broadband icon in the Control Panel and double-clicking it; your IP address should be listed there. If you can't find that IP address on your machine, get in touch with your broadband provider and ask about it. They should be able to tell you how to find your IP address.

Using the Intercom

What does the intercom look like? You start Intercom 1 first (it functions as the server in this pair of applications, so it's necessary to start it first so Intercom 2 can find it), and it appears in Figure 9.1.

After starting Intercom 1, the person you're going to be typing with starts Intercom 2 on his or her machine, which you see in Figure 9.2.

How do you connect the intercoms? In Intercom 2, you enter the IP address of Intercom 1 in the text box, as shown in Figure 9.2; that IP address is 127.0.0.1 here, which is what you use if you're testing the two intercoms out on the same machine. If you're running the intercoms on different machines, enter the IP address of Intercom 1 here instead (in fact, even if you run the two intercoms on the same machine, you can enter the broadband IP address of your current machine here, and the two intercoms will connect over the Internet, even though they're on the same machine).

FIGURE 9.1   Intercom 1.

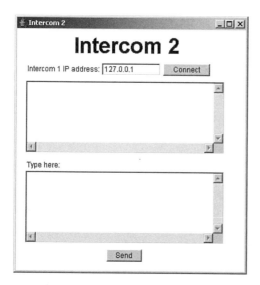

FIGURE 9.2   Intercom 2.

After entering the IP address of Intercom 1 into Intercom 2, click the Connect button in Intercom 2 to connect. If Intercom 1 isn't running, you'll see an error message, as shown in Figure 9.3.

If Intercom 1 is out there and ready to roll, Intercom 2 will connect, and you'll see the message "Connected" at the top of Intercom 2, as shown in Figure 9.4.

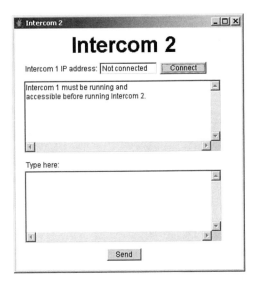

FIGURE 9.3   Trying to connect to Intercom 1.

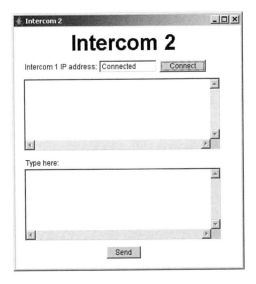

FIGURE 9.4   Connected to Intercom 1.

The two intercoms connect using built-in Java classes, with nothing extra needed. Now that you're connected, you can type back and forth—your text goes into the lower text area control, and the other user's into the upper text area. For example, in Intercom 2, you can enter the text "Are you there?" (see Figure 9.5).

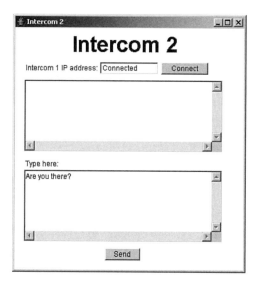

FIGURE 9.5   Entering text to send.

When you click the Send button in Intercom 2, the text you've entered is sent to Intercom 1, where it appears as you see in Figure 9.6. Not bad—that text can go across the Internet anywhere in the world, with no Java-enabled ISP needed, no messenger service to sign up with, and no ads to have to look at.

FIGURE 9.6   Receiving text in Intercom 1.

And, of course, you can enter text in Intercom 1, as you see in Figure 9.7.

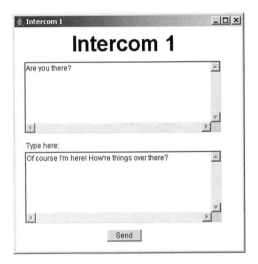

FIGURE 9.7   Entering text to send to Intercom 2.

When you click the Send button in Intercom 1, the text you've entered is sent to Intercom 2, as shown in Figure 9.8.

FIGURE 9.8   Receiving text in Intercom 2.

And that's it—now you can go back and forth between intercoms, typing what you want. When you do, any new text will be added to the text already typed, as you can see in Figure 9.9, where some new text has been sent by the Intercom 2 user back to Intercom 1.

FIGURE 9.9   Receiving additional text in **Intercom 1**.

These intercoms show off a lot of Java's power. Here's what they do:

- Intercom 1 acts as a server, and it accepts connections from Intercom 2.

- Intercom 2 acts as a client, and it lets you connect to Intercom 1.

- When connected, you can use standard Java streams to write back and forth between the intercoms.

When you want to hang up, just close the Intercom window—nothing more needed. As you can see, this is one cool application. So how do you create it?

Creating Intercom 1

The first thing to do in Intercom 1 is to create the window and controls you see in Figure 9.1. This works by creating a new object of the Intercom1 class in the main method:

```
import java.awt.*;
import java.awt.event.*;

public class Intercom1 extends Frame implements Runnable, ActionListener
{

    public static void main(String[] args)
    {
        new Intercom1();
    }
```

```
        .
        .
        .
}
```

Next, the code adds the Send button, connects it to an `ActionListener`, and adds the top
text area control (note that the text area controls in this project have only vertical scrollbars
so that the user doesn't have to stop to scroll horizontally with the mouse each time long
text appears or he's typing something longer than the text area can display on one line):

```java
import java.awt.*;
import java.awt.event.*;

public class Intercom1 extends Frame implements Runnable, ActionListener
{
    private Button button1;
    private TextArea textarea1;

    public static void main(String[] args)
    {
        new Intercom1();
    }

    public Intercom1()
    {
        setLayout(null);

        button1 = new Button("Send");
        button1.setBounds(160, 360, 60, 20);
        add(button1);
        button1.addActionListener(this);

        textarea1 = new TextArea("", 7, 45,
            TextArea.SCROLLBARS_VERTICAL_ONLY);
        textarea1.setBounds(20, 80, 340, 120);
        add(textarea1);
        .
        .
        .
}
```

You can find the significant methods of the Java AWT TextArea class in Table 9.1.

TABLE 9.1   Significant Methods of the java.awt.TextArea **Class**

Method	Does This
void append(String str)	Appends the specified text to the current text in the text area control
int getColumns()	Returns the number of columns in this text area as currently configured
Dimension getMinimumSize()	Returns the minimum size of this text area control
Dimension getMinimumSize (int rows, int columns)	Returns the minimum size needed for this text area control given the specified number of rows and columns
Dimension getPreferredSize()	Returns the preferred size of this text area control
Dimension getPreferredSize (int rows, int columns)	Returns the preferred size of the text area control given the specified number of rows and columns
int getRows()	Returns the number of rows currently in the text area control
void insert(String str, int pos)	Inserts the given text at a particular position in this text area control
void setColumns(int columns)	Sets the number of columns in this text area control
void setRows(int rows)	Sets the number of rows in this text area control

Next comes the bottom text area control, where you enter text to send to Intercom 2. To make it clear that this text area is for that purpose, the code also adds a label with the text "Type here:" above the second text area control:

```
import java.awt.*;
import java.awt.event.*;

public class Intercom1 extends Frame implements Runnable, ActionListener
{
    private Button button1;
    private TextArea textarea1, textarea2;
    private Label label1;

    public static void main(String[] args)
    {
        new Intercom1();
    }

    public Intercom1()
    {
        setLayout(null);
```

```
        button1 = new Button("Send");
        button1.setBounds(160, 360, 60, 20);
        add(button1);
        button1.addActionListener(this);
          .
          .
          .
        label1 = new Label();
        label1.setBounds(20, 210, 100, 20);
        label1.setText("Type here:");
        add(label1);

        textarea2 = new TextArea("", 7, 45,
            TextArea.SCROLLBARS_VERTICAL_ONLY);
        textarea2.setBounds(20, 230, 340, 120);
        add(textarea2);
          .
          .
          .
}
```

All that's left to create the Intercom 1 display is to add the label "Intercom 1" you see in
Figure 9.1, to set the window title, and to handle window-closing events, as you see here:

```
import java.awt.*;
import java.awt.event.*;

public class Intercom1 extends Frame implements Runnable, ActionListener
{
    private Button button1;
    private TextArea textarea1, textarea2;
    private Label label1, label2;

    public static void main(String[] args)
    {
        new Intercom1();
    }

    public Intercom1()
    {
        setLayout(null);
          .
          .
          .
```

```
        label2 = new Label("Intercom 1");
        label2.setFont(new Font("Times New Roman", Font.BOLD, 36));
        label2.setBounds(100, 35, 200, 30);
        add(label2);

        setSize(400, 400);

        setTitle("Intercom 1");

        setVisible(true);
        textarea2.requestFocus();

        this.addWindowListener(new WindowAdapter(){
            public void windowClosing(
                WindowEvent e){
                    System.exit(0);
                    try{
                        socket.close();
                    }catch(Exception ex){}
                }
            }
        );
        .
        .
        .

}
```

That's it for Intercom 1's GUI. The next step is to start the server and wait for a connection from Intercom 2. Intercom 1 acts as the server for the connection, waiting for connections from clients, so it's based on the Java java.net.ServerSocket class; Intercom 1 uses an object of this class to accept connections from Intercom 2.

Connecting to Intercom 2

ServerSocket connections let you create TCP/IP connections on the Internet, just as you would if you were writing your own web server. In fact, you *can* write a web server yourself in just a few lines, and you can host it yourself if you have a fixed IP address. Here's how: Just create a new ServerSocket object that will listen on port 80 (the port web browsers use), in a program called, say, Server.java. (More is coming up on how to use ServerSocket and what methods are available when this chapter develops the Intercom code next.)

```
import java.io.*;
import java.net.*;

public class Server
{
```

```
public static void main(String[] args )
{
    try {
        ServerSocket socket = new ServerSocket(80);
        .
        .
        .
    }
    catch (Exception e) {}
}
}
```

You can wait for connections to your new web server with the `ServerSocket` object's accept method and use a `PrintWriter` object to write to web browsers:

```
import java.io.*;
import java.net.*;

public class Server
{
    public static void main(String[] args )
    {
        try {
            ServerSocket socket = new ServerSocket(80);

            Socket insocket = socket.accept();
            PrintWriter out = new PrintWriter (
                insocket.getOutputStream(), true);
            .
            .
            .
        }
        catch (Exception e) {}
    }
}
```

After a browser connects to the web server, you can send a web page back to the browser, like this:

```
import java.io.*;
import java.net.*;

public class Server
{
    public static void main(String[] args )
```

```
{
    try {
        ServerSocket socket = new ServerSocket(80);

        Socket insocket = socket.accept();
        PrintWriter out = new PrintWriter (
            insocket.getOutputStream(), true);

        out.println("<!DOCTYPE HTML PUBLIC '-//W3C//DTD HTML 4.0 "
            + "transitional//EN'>");
        out.println("<html>");
        out.println("<head>");
        out.println("<title>");
        out.println("A new web page");
        out.println("</title>");
        out.println("</head>");
        out.println("<body>");
        out.println("<h1>");
        out.println("A custom web server! Not bad.");
        out.println("</h1>");
        out.println("</body>");
        out.println("</html>");
        insocket.close();
    }
    catch (Exception e) {}
}
}
```

After compiling Server.java, run it to start the server waiting for connections. In a browser on your or any Internet-connected machine, enter **http://nnn.nnn.nnn.nnn**, where *nnn.nnn.nnn.nnn* is your fixed IP address, and you'll see the web page Server.java creates, as shown in Figure 9.10.

FIGURE 9.10   A custom web server.

Congratulations, you've written your own custom web server, all using the built-in TCP/IP socket support in Java.

Intercom 1 centers around a `ServerSocket` object that Intercom 2 will connect to. Here's how that object is created in Intercom 1—note that this application communicates using port 8765, which is very rarely used by other applications (if you run across a conflict with other software, change this port number to some other four-digit number; using a value over 8000 helps avoid conflicts with most other software):

```java
import java.io.*;
import java.net.*;
import java.awt.*;
import java.awt.event.*;

public class Intercom1 extends Frame implements Runnable, ActionListener
{
    private Button button1;
    private TextArea textarea1, textarea2;
    private Label label1, label2;
    ServerSocket socket;

    public static void main(String[] args)
    {
        new Intercom1();
    }
}
```

REAL-WORLD SCENARIO: JAVA AND SOCKETS *continued*

Sockets are an unusually powerful part of Java. As you just saw, the socket support in Java is strong enough to let you write your own web server. And it's strong enough to let you write the whole Intercom project.

In the early days of Java, developers asked if there was some easy way to add socket support to Java, and Sun looked into the matter. The idea was to match Unix's way of working with sockets, which is to work with sockets much as you work with files—opening, writing, reading, and closing sockets just as you would files.

Developers liked that idea.

There are two main protocols for sockets: TCP/IP and UDP/IP. Thankfully, Sun chose the right one to support: TCP/IP.

User Datagram Protocol (UDP) operates in a connectionless way, and you send data using "datagrams." Because the connection isn't saved, you have to provide a socket descriptor each time you send a datagram, as well as the other socket's address. There's also a limit of

```
    public Intercom1()
    {
        .
        .
        .
        try {
            socket = new ServerSocket(8765);
            .
            .
            .
        }
        catch (Exception e)
        {
            textarea1.setText(e.getMessage());
        }
    }
    .
    .
    .
}
```

You can find the significant methods of the ServerSocket class in Table 9.2.

64 kilobytes per datagram. But the real issue with UDP is that it's unreliable—you can't assume that the datagrams you send are going to be received in the order you sent them, which has caused developers a lot of problems.

Transfer Control Protocol (TCP), on the other hand, is a streaming protocol that makes sure the packets you send arrive in the order you sent them. And once you make a connection, that connection is preserved unless it times out or is closed; there's no need to refresh the connection each time you want to send data, as in UDP. And there's no data size limit in TCP, as there is in UDP.

For all these reasons, Java sockets use the TCP/IP protocol by default, and that has made developers very happy. Just by using Java, you have a way to connect over the Internet with custom applications, such as the Intercom project. You don't need a browser if you don't want to use one. Using Java sockets, you can create your own entirely custom Internet applications like the ones that already have been developed—FTP, Telnet, SSH, and web browsers.

TABLE 9.2   **Significant Methods of the** `java.net.ServerSocket` **Class**

Method	Does This
`Socket accept()`	Listens for a connection attempt to this socket and accepts it if possible
`void bind(SocketAddress endpoint)`	Binds the `ServerSocket` object to the given address (which includes both an IP address and a port number)
`void close()`	Closes this socket's connection
`ServerSocketChannel getChannel()`	Returns the `ServerSocketChannel` object associated with this socket, if there is any
`InetAddress getInetAddress()`	Returns the local address of this server socket
`int getLocalPort()`	Returns the port on which this socket is set up to listen
`SocketAddress getLocalSocketAddress()`	Returns the address of the endpoint this socket is bound to. Returns `null` if it is not yet bound to an endpoint
`int getSoTimeout()`	Returns the `SO_TIMEOUT` setting
`boolean isBound()`	Returns `true` if the socket is bound
`boolean isClosed()`	Returns `true` if the socket is closed
`void setSoTimeout(int timeout)`	Sets the `SO_TIMEOUT` value to the given timeout (in milliseconds)

The `ServerSocket` object's accept method listens for and accepts connections, which is how you use a server socket. This method returns the `Socket` object you can use to communicate with Intercom 2. Here's what that looks like in code:

```java
import java.io.*;
import java.net.*;
import java.awt.*;
import java.awt.event.*;

public class Intercom1 extends Frame implements Runnable, ActionListener
{
    private Button button1;
    private TextArea textarea1, textarea2;
    private Label label1, label2;
    ServerSocket socket;
    PrintWriter out;

    Socket insocket;

    public static void main(String[] args)
    {
        new Intercom1();
    }
```

```
public Intercom1()
{
    .
    .
    .
    try {
        socket = new ServerSocket(8765);

        insocket = socket.accept();
        .
        .
        .
    }
    catch (Exception e)
    {
        textarea1.setText(e.getMessage());
    }
}
    .
    .
    .
}
```

You can find the significant methods of the `Socket` class in Table 9.3; these are the methods the code will use to communicate with Intercom 2.

TABLE 9.3   **Significant Methods of the** `java.net.Socket` **Class**

Method	Does This
void bind(SocketAddress bindpoint)	**Binds this** `Socket` **object to a local address**
void close()	**Closes this** `Socket` **object**
void connect(SocketAddress endpoint)	**Connects this** `Socket` **object to the given server**
void connect(SocketAddress endpoint, int timeout)	**Connects this** `Socket` **object to the given server, subject to the specified timeout**
SocketChannel getChannel()	**Returns the** `SocketChannel` **object for this socket, if there is one**
InetAddress getInetAddress()	**Returns the address to which the socket is connected**
InputStream getInputStream()	**Returns an input stream object for this socket for I/O operations**
InetAddress getLocalAddress()	**Returns the local address to which the** `Socket` **object is bound**
int getLocalPort()	**Returns the local port to which this** `Socket` **object is bound**

TABLE 9.3   Continued

Method	Does This
`SocketAddress getLocalSocketAddress()`	Returns the address of the endpoint this socket is bound to. Returns `null` if the `Socket` object is not yet bound
`OutputStream getOutputStream()`	Returns an output stream object for this socket for I/O operations
`int getPort()`	Returns the remote port to which this `Socket` object is connected
`SocketAddress getRemoteSocketAddress()`	Returns the address of the endpoint this socket is connected to. Returns `null` if it is not connected
`int getSoTimeout()`	Returns the value of the current SO_TIMEOUT setting
`boolean isBound()`	Returns `true` if the `Socket` object is bound
`boolean isClosed()`	Returns `true` if the `Socket` object is closed
`boolean isConnected()`	Returns `true` if the `Socket` object is connected
`boolean isInputShutdown()`	Returns `true` if the reading part of the `Socket` object is closed
`boolean isOutputShutdown()`	Returns `true` if the writing part of the `Socket` object is closed
`void setReceiveBufferSize(int size)`	Sets the receiving buffer size to the specified value in bytes
`void setSendBufferSize(int size)`	Sets the sending buffer size to the specified value in bytes
`void setSoTimeout(int timeout)`	Sets the SO_TIMEOUT setting to the specified timeout (in milliseconds)
`void shutdownInput()`	Shuts down the input stream
`void shutdownOutput()`	Shuts down the output stream

Sending Text to Intercom 2

Once the connection is made, you can use the `Socket` object's `getOutputStream` method to get an `OutputStream` object and create a `PrintWriter` object named out, which will let the user type to Intercom 2.

How do you handle both incoming and outgoing text in the same application, potentially at the same time? To do that, Intercom 1 is clever and launches a new thread for the incoming text. It creates the `PrintWriter` object named out first to handle outgoing text, and then it starts the new thread for the incoming text this way:

```
import java.io.*;
import java.net.*;
import java.awt.*;
import java.awt.event.*;
```

```java
public class Intercom1 extends Frame implements Runnable, ActionListener
{
    private Thread thread;
    private Button button1;
    private TextArea textarea1, textarea2;
    private Label label1, label2;
    ServerSocket socket;
    PrintWriter out;

    Socket insocket;

    public static void main(String[] args)
    {
        new Intercom1();
    }

    public Intercom1()
    {
        .
        .
        .
        try {
            socket = new ServerSocket(8765);

            insocket = socket.accept();

            out = new PrintWriter(insocket.getOutputStream(), true);

            thread = new Thread(this);
            thread.start();

        }
        catch (Exception e)
        {
            textarea1.setText(e.getMessage());
        }
    }
    .
    .
    .
}
```

You can find the significant methods of the PrintWriter class in Table 9.4; this is the class Intercom 1 will use to actually write text to Intercom 2 across the Internet.

TABLE 9.4   **Significant Methods of the** `java.io.PrintWriter` **Class**

Method	Does This
`PrintWriter append(char c)`	Appends the given character to this writer's stream
`PrintWriter append(CharSequence csq)`	Appends the given character sequence to this writer's stream
`PrintWriter append(CharSequence csq, int start, int end)`	Appends the given part of a character sequence to this writer's stream
`void close()`	Closes the stream connected to this writer
`void flush()`	Flushes the stream connected to this writer
`void print(boolean b)`	Prints a Boolean value using this writer object
`void print(char c)`	Prints a character using this writer object
`void print(char[] s)`	Prints an array of characters using this writer object
`void print(double d)`	Prints a double-precision floating-point number using this writer object
`void print(float f)`	Prints a floating-point number using this writer object
`void print(int i)`	Prints an integer using this writer object
`void print(long l)`	Prints a long integer using this writer object
`void print(Object obj)`	Prints an object using this writer object
`void print(String s)`	Prints a string using this writer object
`void println()`	Writes the line separator string using this writer object
`void println(boolean x)`	Prints a Boolean value followed by the line separator string using this writer object
`void println(char x)`	Prints a character followed by the line separator string using this writer object
`void println(char[] x)`	Prints an array of characters followed by the line separator string using this writer object
`void println(double x)`	Prints a double-precision floating-point number followed by the line separator string using this writer object
`void println(float x)`	Prints a floating-point number followed by the line separator string using this writer object
`void println(int x)`	Prints an integer followed by the line separator string using this writer object
`void println(long x)`	Prints a long integer followed by the line separator string using this writer object
`void println(Object x)`	Prints an object followed by the line separator string using this writer object
`void println(String x)`	Prints a string followed by the line separator string using this writer object
`protected  void setError()`	Reports that an error has occurred to the user

TABLE 9.4   Continued

Method	Does This
`void write(char[] buf)`	Writes an array of characters using this writer object
`void write(char[] buf, int off, int len)`	Writes a portion of an array of characters using this writer object
`void write(int c)`	Writes a single character using this writer object
`void write(String s)`	Writes a string using this writer object
`void write(String s, int off, int len)`	Writes part of a string using this writer object

The user enters his text in the bottom text area, `textarea2`, and clicks the Send button. That executes the `actionPerformed` method, which simply has to send the text in the text area to the out object, which in turn sends that text to Intercom 2 (note that the code also clears the text area of text):

```
public void actionPerformed(ActionEvent event)
{
    if(event.getSource() == button1){
        String text = textarea2.getText();
        textarea2.setText("");
        out.println(text);
        textarea2.requestFocus();
    }
}
```

Reading Text from Intercom 2

What about reading text from Intercom 2? Because the code is divided up between threads, Intercom 1 will be able to both read and send text at the same time. The worker thread in Intercom 1 will be run in Intercom 1's run method, and it will listen for text from Intercom 2.

To catch text from Intercom 2, you can use the `getInputStream` method of the `insocket` object of the `Socket` class to get an `InputStream` object. To make working with that input stream easier, the code uses that `InputStream` object to create a `BufferedReader` object, which lets you read whole lines of text at a time.

Here's how to create the `BufferedReader` object in the worker thread's run method:

```
public void run()
{
    try {

        BufferedReader in = new BufferedReader (new
            InputStreamReader(insocket.getInputStream()));
```

```
            .
            .
            .
    }catch (Exception e)
    {
        textarea1.setText(e.getMessage());
    }

}
```

You can find the significant methods of the BufferedReader class in Table 9.5.

TABLE 9.5   Significant Methods of the java.io.BufferedReader **Class**

Method	Does This
void close()	Closes the buffered stream object
int read()	Reads a single character using this object
int read(char[] cbuf, int off, int len)	Reads characters and stores them in a section of an array
String readLine()	Reads an entire line of text
boolean ready()	Returns true if this stream is ready to be read
long skip(long n)	Skips the specified number of characters

Now all you've got to do to read text from Intercom 2 is to use the BufferedReader object's readLine method, looping over that method repeatedly. Here's what that looks like in the run method, where the code waits until a line of text is ready and then appends it to the text in the top text area, textarea1:

```
public void run()
{
    String instring;
    try {

        BufferedReader in = new BufferedReader (new
            InputStreamReader(insocket.getInputStream()));

        while((instring = in.readLine()) != null){
            textarea1.append(instring + "\n");
        }

    }catch (Exception e)
    {
        textarea1.setText(e.getMessage());
    }

}
```

That completes all the tasks in Intercom 1—accepting connections from Intercom 2 on port 8765, reading text from Intercom 2, and sending text to Intercom 2.

Now it's time to get Intercom 2 working.

> **NOTE**
>
> The Intercom project is designed for two users only. Can you convert it into a multiuser chat program like the Chat project earlier? Yes, you can, but it would take some work.
>
> Each time a new connection is made, you'd have to store a different Socket object in Intercom 1 and listen for text from all of them. Also, you'd have to echo the text you got from one client to all the clients.
>
> In other words, you'd have to modify the server application, Intercom 1, to really act as a server for multiple clients, reading and sending text to all clients. This certainly can be done, but it would take some work to do it.

Creating Intercom 2

As with Intercom 1, the first item of business in Intercom 2 is to create its window, which you see in Figure 9.2. Here's how the code does it—note in particular the Connect button, which Intercom 1 (the server) doesn't have:

```java
import java.awt.*;
import java.awt.event.*;

class Intercom2 extends Frame implements Runnable, ActionListener
{
    private Button button1, button2;
    private TextArea textarea1, textarea2;
    private TextField textfield1;
    private Label label1, label2, label3;

    public static void main(String[] args)
    {
        new Intercom2();
    }

    public Intercom2()
    {
        setLayout(null);

        label1 = new Label("Server IP address:");
        label1.setBounds(35, 80, 105, 20);
        add(label1);
```

```java
textfield1 = new TextField("127.0.0.1");
textfield1.setBounds(145, 80, 100, 20);
add(textfield1);

button1 = new Button("Connect");
button1.setBounds(255, 80, 80, 20);
add(button1);
button1.addActionListener(this);

button2 = new Button("Send");
button2.setBounds(160, 390, 60, 20);
add(button2);
button2.addActionListener(this);

textarea1 = new TextArea("", 7, 45,
    TextArea.SCROLLBARS_VERTICAL_ONLY);
textarea1.setBounds(20, 110, 340, 120);
add(textarea1);

label2 = new Label();
label2.setBounds(20, 240, 100, 20);
label2.setText("Type here:");
add(label2);

textarea2 = new TextArea("", 7, 45,
    TextArea.SCROLLBARS_VERTICAL_ONLY);
textarea2.setBounds(20, 260, 340, 120);
add(textarea2);

label3 = new Label("Intercom 2");
label3.setFont(new Font("Times New Roman", Font.BOLD, 36));
label3.setBounds(100, 35, 200, 30);
add(label3);

setSize(400, 430);

setTitle("Intercom 2");
setVisible(true);
textarea2.requestFocus();

this.addWindowListener(new WindowAdapter(){
    public void windowClosing(
        WindowEvent e){
            System.exit(0);
        }
```

```
                }
        );
    }
```

That's all you need for the window, which you saw earlier in Figure 9.2. Creating that window is the easy part. Now how about connecting to Intercom 1?

Connecting to Intercom 1

To connect to Intercom 1, the user enters Intercom 1's IP address in Intercom 2's text field (you can leave it as the default 127.0.0.1 if you're testing the intercoms on the same machine) and then clicks the Connect button. This calls the `actionPerformed` method connected to the Connect button, which uses the `Socket` class's constructor to connect to that IP address on the port Intercom 1 is listening on, port 8765. The code also displays the message "Connecting...." in the text field, as you see here:

```
    public void actionPerformed(ActionEvent event)
    {
        if(event.getSource() == button1){
            try{
                socket = new Socket(textfield1.getText(), 8765);
                textfield1.setText("Connecting....");
                .
                .
                .
}
```

If the connection is made, the code uses the `getInputStream` and `getOutputStream` methods to get an object named `in` to handle incoming text from Intercom 1 and an object named `out` to handle outgoing text to Intercom 1:

```
    public void actionPerformed(ActionEvent event)
    {
        if(event.getSource() == button1){
            try{
                socket = new Socket(textfield1.getText(), 8765);
                textfield1.setText("Connecting....");

                in = socket.getInputStream();
                out = socket.getOutputStream();
            }
            .
            .
            .
}
```

The in object is an object of the InputStream class, and the out object is an object of the OutputStream class. You can find the significant methods of the InputStream class in Table 9.6 and the significant methods of the OutputStream class in Table 9.7.

TABLE 9.6   Significant Methods of the java.io.InputStream **Class**

Method	Does This
int available()	Returns the number of bytes available from this input stream
void close()	Closes this input stream object
abstract int read()	Reads and returns the next byte from the input stream object
int read(byte[] b)	Reads bytes from the input stream object, storing them into the given buffer array
int read(byte[] b, int off, int len)	Reads up to a specified number of bytes from the input stream object and stores them in an array of bytes
long skip(long n)	Skips over the given number of bytes in this input stream object

TABLE 9.7   Significant Methods of the java.io.OutputStream **Class**

Method	Does This
void close()	Closes the output stream
void flush()	Flushes the output stream. This also makes sure that buffered output will be written out object
void write(byte[] b)	Writes bytes from the specified byte array to the output stream object
void write(byte[] b, int off, int len)	Writes bytes from the specified byte array, using the given offset into the array and length of data to write, to the output stream object
abstract void write(int b)	Writes the given byte to this output stream object

All that's left is to start the worker thread that Intercom 2 uses to handle the incoming text from Intercom 1:

```
public void actionPerformed(ActionEvent event)
{
    if(event.getSource() == button1){
        try{
            socket = new Socket(textfield1.getText(), 8765);
            textfield1.setText("Connecting....");

            in = socket.getInputStream();
            out = socket.getOutputStream();

            thread = new Thread(this);
            thread.start();
```

```
        }
        .
        .
        .
}
```

If there is an IOException, the most likely cause is that Intercom 1 wasn't set up and running. Here's how the code displays a message to that effect:

```
public void actionPerformed(ActionEvent event)
{
    if(event.getSource() == button1){
        try{
            socket = new Socket(textfield1.getText(), 8765);
            textfield1.setText("Connecting....");

            in = socket.getInputStream();
            out = socket.getOutputStream();

            thread = new Thread(this);
            thread.start();
        }
        catch (IOException ioe){
            textarea1.setText("Intercom 1 must be running and\n"
            + "accessible before running Intercom 2.");
            textfield1.setText("Not connected");
        }
        .
        .
        .
    }
```

If there is any other exception, you can display the message in a general catch statement. If the Socket object is not null and its isConnected method returns true, on the other hand, the intercoms are connected, and the code displays the message "Connected" in the text field:

```
public void actionPerformed(ActionEvent event)
{
    if(event.getSource() == button1){
        try{
            socket = new Socket(textfield1.getText(), 8765);
            textfield1.setText("Connecting....");
```

```
                    in = socket.getInputStream();
                    out = socket.getOutputStream();

                    thread = new Thread(this);
                    thread.start();
                }
                catch (IOException ioe){
                    textarea1.setText("Intercom 1 must be running and\n"
                    + "accessible before running Intercom 2.");
                    textfield1.setText("Not connected");
                }
                catch (Exception e){
                    textarea1.setText(e.getMessage());
                }

                if(socket != null && socket.isConnected()){
                    textfield1.setText("Connected");
                }
            }
            .
            .
            .
        }
```

Okay, we're connected. What about sending text to Intercom 1 when the user enters some?

Sending Text to Intercom 1

When the user enters text in the bottom text area in Intercom 2, `textarea2`, and clicks the Send button, that text is supposed to be sent to Intercom 1. Sending that text isn't difficult; you can simply use the `write` method of the `out` object created when the connection was established:

```
public void actionPerformed(ActionEvent event)
{
    .
    .
    .
        if(event.getSource() == button2){
            try{
                String str = textarea2.getText() + "\n";
                byte buffer[] = str.getBytes();
                out.write(buffer);
                textarea2.setText("");
                textarea2.requestFocus();
```

```
            }
        catch(Exception ex)
            {textarea1.setText(ex.getMessage());}
    }
  }
}
```

And that's all you need; now the text in the bottom text area is sent to Intercom 1. What about reading any text sent to Intercom 2 from Intercom 1?

Reading Text from Intercom 1

Intercom 2 uses a worker thread to read text from Intercom 1. The idea of using a new thread, as in Intercom 1, is to let both text reading and sending happen at the same time. Intercom 2 simply uses the InputStream class's read method to read characters, one by one, this way:

```
public void run()
{
    try{
        while ((character = in.read()) != -1) {
            .
            .
            .
        }
    }
}
```

This lets you read from Intercom 1, character by character. To make that kind of input into a string that you can append to the top text area's text, you can use the String class's constructor, but note that that constructor won't take char variables. To fix that, you can simply store the just-read character in a char array and convert that into a string, which is then appended to the text area's text this way:

```
public void run()
{
    try{
        while ((character = in.read()) != -1) {
            chars[0] = (char)character;
            textarea1.append(new String(chars));
        }
    }
}
```

And you can handle exceptions in a `catch` statement that displays the exception's message:

```java
public void run()
{
    try{
        while ((character = in.read()) != -1) {
            chars[0] = (char)character;
            textarea1.append(new String(chars));
        }
    }
    catch(Exception ex)
        {textarea1.setText(ex.getMessage());}
}
```

That completes Intercom 2, the client application.

And that's all you need. To get everything started, you run Intercom 1, then Intercom 2, and you use Intercom 2 to connect to Intercom 1. After being connected, both parties can type back and forth freely. Very cool.

> **NOTE**
>
> Download the complete source code for the Intercom project, Intercom1.java and Intercom2.java, at the Sams website. After compiling these files, run Intercom1.java first, followed by Intercom2.java, as detailed in this chapter, and get started writing back and forth.

Conclusion

This chapter presented the Intercom project, a fun application that uses its own connection over the Internet, as well as Java methods, to communicate.

All you have to do is to start up Intercom 1 on one machine. Intercom 1 functions as the server, and after you start it, it'll wait for a connection from Intercom 2 over the port the Intercom project uses (in this case, 8765, but you can change it simply by editing the code).

After Intercom 1 is running, start Intercom 2. Enter the IP address of Intercom 1 into the text field in Intercom 2 (if you're using broadband, you should have a fixed IP address; take a look in the Control Panel in Windows, for example, and open the Broadband icon, or ask your broadband ISP how to determine your IP address). Then you just click the Connect button, and Intercom 2 connects to Intercom 1.

When the two intercoms are connected, you can simply type in the lower text area control in either one and click the Send button—your text will appear in the upper text area in the other intercom. It's as simple as that—your own personal connection over the Internet. You don't have to host any code on web servers—all you've got to do is to connect and play using the Intercom project.

CHAPTER 10

Getting a Graphical Weather Forecast: The Forecaster Project

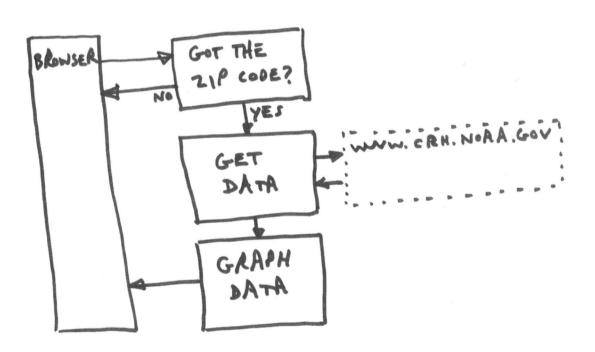

The Forecaster.

Here's a cool one—the Forecaster project. It displays a four-day weather forecast for your area, starting with today's high and low temperatures. All you've got to do is to tell the Forecaster your ZIP Code, and it'll give you the forecast.

The Forecaster does its thing by getting the weather data from the National Weather Service, whose website is http://www.crh.noaa.gov. When the Forecaster knows your ZIP Code, it'll fetch your weather forecast from the National Weather Service, create a JPEG image online with the high and low temperatures plotted, and send your browser that graph. You can see what this looks like in Figure 10.1. The forecasted high temperatures are the upper figure (in red, although you can't tell that here), and the low temperatures are the lower figure (in blue in real life).

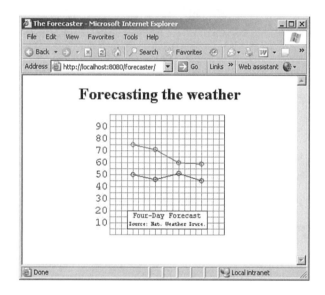

FIGURE 10.1   The forecaster in a browser.

This project is written as a JSP, forecast.jsp, partly to show how you can create JPEG images on a server interactively and send them back to a browser—an impressive technique that online programmers should have in their arsenals. But this one's too good to miss just because you might not have access to a Java-enabled ISP that can run JavaServer Pages. For that reason, the Forecaster project also comes as a standalone Java application you can run on a desktop machine (as long as you're connected to the Internet so the code can get the needed weather data), as you see in Figure 10.2.

NOTE

The Forecaster project depends on the National Weather Service website for its data, and it extracts its data from the forecast page for your ZIP Code. Although the format of these pages has been the same for years, there's always the possibility that it may change by the time you read this. In that case, you'll have to update the way the Forecaster project searches those pages for its data—just find the new way the temperatures are displayed, and update the search text in the Forecaster accordingly.

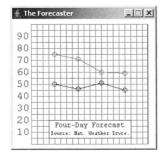

FIGURE 10.2   **The standalone forecaster.**

This chapter starts by creating the Forecaster JSP, complete with the technology to create JPEG images online and send them back to the browser. After creating the JSP (forecast.jsp), you'll continue by creating the standalone Java application, Forecast.java, in case you want to use that application instead of the online JSP page.

Creating the Forecaster JSP

In this project, the first task is to get the user's ZIP Code. You're going to need the ZIP Code in order to get the National Weather Service's high and low temperature forecasts, so that's the first order of business. After getting that ZIP Code, the code will concentrate on getting the forecast and graphing it.

Getting the ZIP Code

In the JSP, there are two ways to get the ZIP Code. First, you can supply a ZIP Code as part of the URL encoded as ?zip=*nnnnn*, this way, which sets the URL to 94707:

```
http://www.yourjsphost/username/forecast.jsp?zip=94707
```

This way is handy in case you want to embed the JPEG image this JSP creates in a web page, as you see in Figure 10.1. You can use the URL to the JSP, with the encoded ZIP Code, in an HTML <IMG> tag's SRC attribute to display the forecast in a web page like this (this is the page you see displayed in Figure 10.1—forecast.jsp just sends a JPEG back to the browser, but by using an HTML <IMG> tag, you can neatly embed that JEPG in a web page):

```
<HTML> tag;SRC attribute>;SRC attribute> tag> tag>
    <HEAD>
        <TITLE>
            The Forecaster
        </TITLE>
    </HEAD>
```

```
<BODY>
    <CENTER>
        <H1>
            Forecasting the weather
        </H1>
            <IMG SRC="forecast.jsp?zip=94707">
    </CENTER>
</BODY>
</HTML>
<IMG SRC="" />
```

Here's the second way the code can get the ZIP Code: If you don't supply a URL this way, forecast.jsp will ask you for your URL with an HTML text field, and it'll store that URL in a cookie on your machine.

NOTE
_____

If you want to use the Forecast.java standalone application, on the other hand, it'll ask you the first time you run it what your ZIP Code is and then store it in a file named zip.txt, which it uses from then on.

The forecast.jsp page begins with the JSP page directive, which it uses both to import the needed Java classes and to set the type of the content it will send back to the browser. Setting the content type is particularly important, because this is how you tell the browser that you're not sending it HTML, but a JPEG image instead.

Here is the syntax for the JSP page directive:

```
<%@ page
            [ language="java" ]
            [ extends="package.class" ]
            [ import="{package.class ¦ package.*}, ..." ]
            [ session="true ¦ false" ]
            [ buffer="none ¦ 8kb ¦ sizekb" ]
            [ autoFlush="true ¦ false" ]
            [ isThreadSafe="true ¦ false" ]
            [ info="text" ]
            [ errorPage="relativeURL" ]
            [ contentType="mimeType [ ;charset=characterSet ]"
                ¦   "text/html ; charset=ISO-8859-1" ]
            [ isErrorPage="true ¦ false" ]
%>
```

Here are the attributes that are important in this case:

- `import="{package.class ¦ package.* }, ..."`—You assign this attribute a comma-separated list of Java packages that you want to import. Once imported, the packages, and their contents, will be available to scriptlets, expressions, and declarations in the JSP.

- `contentType="mimeType [ ;charset=characterSet ]" ¦ "text/html;charset=ISO-8859-1"`—You assign this attribute the MIME type (including, if you want to, the character encoding) the JSP code will use in the response it sends to the browser. Note that the default MIME type is "text/html," and the default character encoding is "ISO-8859-1."

In this case, the code needs to import the java.io.*, java.awt.*, java.awt.image.*, java.net.*, and com.sun.image.codec.jpeg.* packages, which looks like this in the page directive:

```
<%@ page import="java.io.*, java.awt.*,
➥java.awt.image.*,java.net.*,com.sun.image.codec.jpeg.*" %>
          .
          .
          .
```

To tell the browser that you're sending back a binary image in JPEG format, you can set the `contentType` attribute to the "image/jpeg" MIME type:

```
<%@ page contentType="image/jpeg" import="java.io.*, java.awt.*,
java.awt.image.*,java.net.*,com.sun.image.codec.jpeg.*" %>
          .
          .
          .
```

How do you recover the ZIP Code if the user has supplied one? He might have URL-encoded a ZIP Code, like this:

```
http://www.yourjsphost/username/forecast.jsp?zip=94707
```

Encoding data this way is often how the data in HTML controls is sent back to the server, so you can recover the ZIP Code by pretending that it was entered by the user into an HTML control named "zip." To recover that data, you'd use this code in forecast.jsp:

```
<%@ page contentType="image/jpeg" import="java.io.*, java.awt.*,
java.awt.image.*,java.net.*,com.sun.image.codec.jpeg.*" %>

<%
    String zip = "";
```

```
    if(request.getParameter("zip") != null){
        zip = request.getParameter("zip");
            .
            .
            .
    }
        .
        .
        .
}
```

If the ZIP Code was found this way, the code only needs to call the drawImage method (covered in a few pages) that will perform the data gathering and drawing:

```
<%@ page contentType="image/jpeg" import="java.io.*, java.awt.*,
java.awt.image.*,java.net.*,com.sun.image.codec.jpeg.*" %>

<%
    if(request.getParameter("zip") != null){
        zip = request.getParameter("zip");
        drawImage(zip, response);
        return;
    }
        .
        .
        .
}
```

So far, so good. But what if the ZIP Code hasn't been URL-encoded? In that case, perhaps it was already encoded in a cookie set by forecast.jsp earlier. The cookie that forecast.jsp sets is called zipCookie, and the code checks if it already exists and sets a Boolean variable named foundCookie to true if it does.

Here's how that works. First, the code uses the request object's getCookies method to get the current cookies passed to the code by the browser as an array of Cookie objects:

```
<%@ page contentType="image/jpeg" import="java.io.*, java.awt.*,
java.awt.image.*,java.net.*,com.sun.image.codec.jpeg.*" %>

<%
    Cookie[] cookies = request.getCookies();
    boolean foundCookie = false;
    String zip = "";
        .
        .
        .
}
```

This is the first time code in this book has worked with cookies, and you can find the significant methods of the Java Cookie class in Table 10.1. Being able to use cookies is a powerful technique, and JSP is up to the task.

TABLE 10.1 Significant Methods of the `javax.servlet.http.Cookie` **Class**

Method	Does This
`java.lang.String getComment()`	Returns a comment that describes the purpose of this cookie
`java.lang.String getDomain()`	Returns the domain name for the cookie
`int getMaxAge()`	Returns the maximum age of the cookie (given in seconds). The default value is -1, which means the cookie should be deleted when the browser is closed
`java.lang.String getName()`	Returns the name of the cookie as text
`boolean getSecure()`	Returns a value of `true` if the browser is sending cookies using only a secure protocol
`java.lang.String getValue()`	Returns the value of the cookie as text
`int getVersion()`	Returns the version of the protocol this cookie uses
`void setComment (java.lang.String purpose)`	Sets a comment that describes this cookie and/or its purpose
`void setDomain (java.lang.String pattern)`	Sets the domain associated with this cookie
`void setMaxAge(int expiry)`	Sets the maximum age of the cookie (given in seconds)
`void setSecure(boolean flag)`	Specifies to the browser whether or not the cookie should only be returned to the server using a secure protocol
`void setValue (java.lang.String newValue)`	Assigns a text value to the cookie
`void setVersion(int v)`	Sets the version of the cookie protocol this cookie uses

Now the code loops over the cookie array in order to search for the cookie named zipCookie:

```
<%@ page contentType="image/jpeg" import="java.io.*, java.awt.*,
java.awt.image.*,java.net.*,com.sun.image.codec.jpeg.*" %>

<%
    Cookie[] cookies = request.getCookies();
    boolean foundCookie = false;
    String zip = "";

    if(request.getParameter("zip") != null){
        zip = request.getParameter("zip");
        drawImage(zip, response);
        return;
    }

    if(cookies != null){
        for(int loopIndex = 0; loopIndex < cookies.length; loopIndex++)
        {
```

```
                .
                .
                .
            }
        }
        .
        .
        .
}
```

It can determine if the current cookie in the loop is named `zipCookie` by using the cookie's `getName` method:

```
if(cookies != null){
    for(int loopIndex = 0; loopIndex < cookies.length; loopIndex++)
    {
        Cookie cookie1 = cookies[loopIndex];
        if (cookie1.getName().equals("zipCookie")) {
            .
            .
            .
        }
    }
}
    .
    .
    .
}
```

If the `zipCookie` object was found, you can get the ZIP Code from it with the `Cookie` object's `getValue` method, and you can also set the `foundCookie` Boolean to `true`:

```
if(cookies != null){
    for(int loopIndex = 0; loopIndex < cookies.length; loopIndex++)
    {
        Cookie cookie1 = cookies[loopIndex];
        if (cookie1.getName().equals("zipCookie")) {
            zip = cookie1.getValue();
            foundCookie = true;
        }
    }
}
    .
    .
    .
}
```

If you've found the cookie, you've also got the ZIP Code, so you're ready to go. But what if the cookie didn't exist? In that case, you've got to ask the user for his ZIP Code and store it in the cookie. The Forecaster project does that with the web page you see in Figure 10.3.

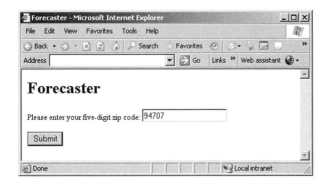

FIGURE 10.3   **Asking for the user's ZIP Code.**

So how do you handle the case where the user enters his ZIP Code this way? The text field you see in Figure 10.3 is named "textField," and you can check if the user has filled his ZIP Code in that text field this way, if the cookie doesn't exist:

```
if(cookies != null){
    for(int loopIndex = 0; loopIndex < cookies.length; loopIndex++)
    {
        Cookie cookie1 = cookies[loopIndex];
        if (cookie1.getName().equals("zipCookie")) {
            zip = cookie1.getValue();
            foundCookie = true;
        }
    }
}

if (!foundCookie) {
    if(request.getParameter("textField") != null){
        .
        .
        .
    }
    .
    .
    .
}
```

If there's text waiting for you in the textField parameter, that text is the user's ZIP Code. The code stores that ZIP Code in the zipCookie cookie first:

```
if (!foundCookie) {
    if(request.getParameter("textField") != null){
        Cookie cookie1 = new Cookie("zipCookie",
            request.getParameter("textField"));
            .
            .
            .
        .
        .
        .

    }
```

Then you can set the maximum age of the cookie—in this case, the code sets it to 365 * 24 * 60 * 60 seconds, or one year, before it expires. To set that cookie in the user's machine, you can use the response object's addCookie method this way:

```
if (!foundCookie) {
    if(request.getParameter("textField") != null){
        Cookie cookie1 = new Cookie("zipCookie",
            request.getParameter("textField"));
        cookie1.setMaxAge(365 * 24 * 60 * 60);
        response.addCookie(cookie1);
        .
        .
        .

    }
```

At this point, you can also display the forecast using the ZIP Code the user has entered into the text field in Figure 10.3 by using the drawImage method, which will be created in a few pages:

```
if (!foundCookie) {
    if(request.getParameter("textField") != null){
        Cookie cookie1 = new Cookie("zipCookie",
            request.getParameter("textField"));
        cookie1.setMaxAge(365 * 24 * 60 * 60);
        response.addCookie(cookie1);
        drawImage(request.getParameter("textField"), response);
    }
    .
    .
    .

}
```

On the other hand, what if there is no text waiting for you in the `textField` parameter? In that case, the user hasn't seen the input page that appears in Figure 10.3 yet, and you should display it. Here's how that looks: (Note that this is where the input text field named "textField" is created.)

```
if (!foundCookie) {
    if(request.getParameter("textField") != null){
        Cookie cookie1 = new Cookie("zipCookie",
            request.getParameter("textField"));
        cookie1.setMaxAge(365 * 24 * 60 * 60);
        response.addCookie(cookie1);
        drawImage(request.getParameter("textField"), response);
    }
    else{

%>
    <HTML>
        <HEAD>
            <META HTTP-EQUIV="Expires" CONTENT="-1">
            <TITLE>
                Forecaster
            </TITLE>
        </HEAD>

        <BODY>
            <H1>
                Forecaster
            </H1>
            <FORM NAME="form1" METHOD="POST">
                Please enter your five-digit zip code:
                <INPUT TYPE="TEXT" NAME="textField"></INPUT>
                <BR>
                <BR>
                <INPUT TYPE="SUBMIT" VALUE="Submit">
            </FORM>
        </BODY>
    </HTML>
        .
        .
        .
```

If the user doesn't need to see the input page, you already have his ZIP Code at this point, so you're ready to call the method that does all the work, drawImage:

```
if (!foundCookie) {
    if(request.getParameter("textField") != null){
        .
        .
        .
    }
    else{

%>
    <HTML>
        <HEAD>
            <META HTTP-EQUIV="Expires" CONTENT="-1">
            <TITLE>
                Forecaster
            </TITLE>
        </HEAD>
        .
        .
        .
    </HTML>
<%
        }
    }
    else{
        drawImage(zip, response);
    }
%>
```

Excellent, you've gotten the user's ZIP Code, whether it's from URL-encoding, a cookie, or the text field. Now it's time to start the real business of the Forecast project—displaying the forecast.

Gathering the Weather Data

Next on the list is writing the drawImage method, which does the actual work, now that you have the user's ZIP Code at hand. You pass this method the ZIP Code and response object (you need the response object so the code can send the JPEG back to the browser). Because this is a new method, you need to declare it in a JSP declaration (not a scriptlet, which can't support method declarations). This is created with the markup <%! and %>:

```
<%!
public void drawImage(String zip, HttpServletResponse response)
{
```

```
        .
        .
        .
        .
}
%>
```

The `drawImage` method starts by getting the weather data from the National Weather Service. The National Weather Service has a web page at http://www.srh.noaa.gov that allows you to enter the ZIP Code you're interested in. By taking a look at the web page, you find that the ZIP Code is sent to a PHP file named zipcity.php and that the text field containing the ZIP Code is called "inputstring." To automate the submission process to include the user's ZIP Code, then, you can create a Java URL object like this:

```
public void drawImage(String zip, HttpServletResponse response)
{
    try {

        URL url = new URL
            ("http://www.srh.noaa.gov/zipcity.php?inputstring="
            + zip);
            .
            .
            .
}
```

To connect to the National Weather Service's website, you can use a `URLConnection` object this way:

```
public void drawImage(String zip, HttpServletResponse response)
{

    try {

        URL url = new URL
            ("http://www.srh.noaa.gov/zipcity.php?inputstring="
            + zip);

        URLConnection urlconnection = url.openConnection();
            .
            .
            .
}
```

You can find the significant methods of the Java URLConnection class, which is terrific for downloading web pages in code, in Table 10.2.

TABLE 10.2   Significant Methods of the java.net.URLConnection **Class**

Method	Does This
void addRequestProperty (String key, String value)	Sets a request property as given by this key-value pair
abstract void connect()	Connects to the resource referenced by this URL
int getConnectTimeout()	Returns the value of the connection timeout (given in seconds)
Object getContent()	Returns the contents of this URL connection as an object
String getContentEncoding()	Returns the current value of the content-encoding header
int getContentLength()	Returns the current value of the content-length header
String getContentType()	Returns the current value of the content-type header
long getDate()	Returns the current value of the date header
boolean getDoInput()	Returns the current value of this URLConnection object's doInput setting
boolean getDoOutput()	Returns the current value of this URLConnection object's doOutput setting
long getExpiration()	Returns the current value of the expires header field
String getHeaderField(int n)	Returns the value for a given header
String getHeaderField (String name)	Returns the value of a header specified by name
long getHeaderFieldDate (String name, long Default)	Returns the value of the named field treated as a date
int getHeaderFieldInt (String name, int Default)	Returns the value of the named field treated as an int
String getHeaderFieldKey(int n)	Returns the key for a given header field
Map<String,List<String>> getHeaderFields()	Returns a Java map containing the headers
InputStream getInputStream()	Returns an input stream that lets you read from this connection
long getLastModified()	Returns the value of the last-modified header
OutputStream getOutputStream()	Returns an output stream that you can use to write to this URL connection
Permission getPermission()	Returns an object giving the permission you need to connect using this object
int getReadTimeout()	Returns the current setting for the timeout length (given in milliseconds)
Map<String,List<String>> getRequestProperties()	Returns a Java map containing request properties for this connection
String getRequestProperty (String key)	Returns the value of the named request property
URL getURL()	Returns the value of this URLConnection object's URL
void setConnectTimeout (int timeout)	Sets a timeout value, in milliseconds, used when opening a connection

TABLE 10.2   Continued

Method	Does This
void setDoInput(boolean doinput)	Sets the value of the doInput **setting for this** URLConnection **object to the given value**
void setDoOutput (boolean dooutput)	Sets the value of the doOutput **setting for this** URLConnection **object to the given value**
static void setFileNameMap (FileNameMap map)	Sets the FileNameMap **setting for this connection**
void setReadTimeout(int timeout)	Sets the timeout for reading operations to the given value (given in milliseconds)
void setRequestProperty (String key, String value)	Sets a request property to the given value

How do you read the National Weather Service page that's returned by this URL, letting you recover the weather data? You can open an InputStream object to the URL using the URLConnection class's getInputStream method this way in the code:

```
public void drawImage(String zip, HttpServletResponse response)
{

    try {

        URL url = new URL
            ("http://www.srh.noaa.gov/zipcity.php?inputstring="
            + zip);

        URLConnection urlconnection = url.openConnection();

        InputStream in = urlconnection.getInputStream();
            .
            .
            .

}
```

So far, so good. Now that you have an InputStream object connected to the National Weather Service's web server, you can read in the target web page to a temporary buffer, which in this case is a String object named input:

```
public void drawImage(String zip, HttpServletResponse response)
{

    try {

        URL url = new URL
            ("http://www.srh.noaa.gov/zipcity.php?inputstring="
            + zip);
```

```
URLConnection urlconnection = url.openConnection();

InputStream in = urlconnection.getInputStream();

String input = "";
String inchar;
char[] cc = new char[1];

while ((character = in.read()) != -1) {
    char z = (char)character;
    cc[0] = z;
    inchar = new String(cc);
    input += inchar;
}

in.close();
    .
    .
    .
}
```

At this point, you've got the weather data, and you can start searching it for high and low temperature predictions. You can see a representative National Weather Service forecast in Figure 10.4; notice the "Hi" numbers (these are displayed in red) and the "Lo" numbers (these are displayed in blue) at the bottom of the page. These numbers give the forecast.

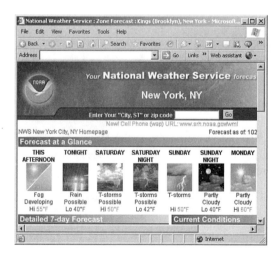

FIGURE 10.4   A representative National Weather Service forecast.

To retrieve the high temperature forecasts for the next four days, you can search for the formatting text that immediately precedes the high temperatures. The National Weather Service pages use either the HTML Hi `<font color="#FF0000">` or Hi: `<span class="red">` right in front of the high temperature forecast values. You can determine which HTML is used in the page you've retrieved by searching for these HTML strings and then storing named hiSearch:

```
public void drawImage(String zip, HttpServletResponse response)
{
    try {

        URL url = new URL
            ("http://www.srh.noaa.gov/zipcity.php?inputstring="
            + zip);

        URLConnection urlconnection = url.openConnection();
        .
        .
        .
        in.close();

        if(input.indexOf("Hi <font color=\"#FF0000\">") >= 0){
            hiSearch = "Hi <font color=\"#FF0000\">";
        }
        else{
            hiSearch= "Hi: <span class=\"red\">";
        }
        .
        .
        .
}
```

Now that you know what HTML to search for, you can retrieve the four-day high temperature forecasts and store them in an array named hiTemperature this way:

```
public void drawImage(String zip, HttpServletResponse response)
{
    String hiTemperature[] = new String[4];

    try {

        URL url = new URL
            ("http://www.srh.noaa.gov/zipcity.php?inputstring="
            + zip);
```

```
URLConnection urlconnection = url.openConnection();
    .
    .
    .
if(input.indexOf("Hi <font color=\"#FF0000\">") >= 0){
    hiSearch = "Hi <font color=\"#FF0000\">";
}
else{
    hiSearch= "Hi: <span class=\"red\">";
}

    int currentPosition = 0;

    for(int loopIndex = 0; loopIndex < 4; loopIndex++){
        int location = input.indexOf(hiSearch,
            currentPosition);
        int end = input.indexOf("&deg;", location);
        hiTemperature[loopIndex] = input.substring(location +
            hiSearch.length(), end);
        currentPosition = end + 1;
    }
    .
    .
    .
}
```

That fills the `hiTemperature` array with the highs. Now what about the lows? The National Weather Service pages use either `Lo <font color="#0033CC">` or `Lo: <span class="blue">` as the HTML to format the low temperature forecasts, so you can determine which format the current page uses and fill an array named `loTemperature` with the forecasted low temperatures this way:

```
public void drawImage(String zip, HttpServletResponse response)
{
    String hiTemperature[] = new String[4];
    String loTemperature[] = new String[4];
        .
        .
        .
    if(input.indexOf("Lo <font color=\"#0033CC\">") >= 0){
        loSearch = "Lo <font color=\"#0033CC\">";
    }
    else{
        loSearch= "Lo: <span class=\"blue\">";
    }
```

```
        currentPosition = 0;

        for(int loopIndex = 0; loopIndex < 4; loopIndex++){
            int location = input.indexOf(loSearch,
                currentPosition);
            int end = input.indexOf("&deg;", location);
            loTemperature[loopIndex] = input.substring(location +
                loSearch.length(), end);
            currentPosition = end + 1;
        }
        .
        .
        .

    }
```

Excellent. You've now stored the high temperature forecasts in the hiTemperature array and the low temperature forecasts in the loTemperature array. You've got your data—the next step is to graph that data and send it back to the user.

Graphing the Data

The problem now breaks down to graphing the data in the hiTemperature and loTemperature arrays and then sending it back to the browser.

The code in the drawImage method continues by drawing the image that will be sent back to the browser, using a BufferedImage object, and creating a Graphics2D object, called g, to draw in that image:

```
        BufferedImage image = new BufferedImage(225, 201,
            BufferedImage.TYPE_INT_RGB);
        Graphics2D g = image.createGraphics();
        .
        .
        .
```

You can start by filling the image with a white background (when first created, it's black):

```
        g.setColor(Color.white);
        g.fillRect(0, 0, 224, 200);
        .
        .
        .
```

Here's how to draw the grid lines you see in Figure 10.1, in gray:

```
g.setColor(Color.gray);

for(int loopIndex = 0; loopIndex < 21; loopIndex++){
    g.drawLine(25, loopIndex * 10, 224, loopIndex * 10);
    g.drawLine(loopIndex * 10 + 25, 0, loopIndex * 10
        + 25, 199);
}
.
.
.
```

Next come the temperature labels, 10 to 90 degrees, you see along the left in Figure 10.1. Here's how to draw them in blue:

```
g.setColor(Color.blue);
Font font = new Font("Courier", Font.PLAIN, 18);
g.setFont(font);

for(int loopIndex = 20; loopIndex < 200; loopIndex += 20){
    g.drawString(String.valueOf(100 - loopIndex / 2), 0,
        loopIndex + 5);
}
.
.
.
```

Okay, what about drawing the high and low temperature forecasts? First the highs, which are displayed in red. As you can see in Figure 10.1, each temperature forecast is drawn with a circle, and then the circles are connected. In the evening, the National Weather Service's forecasts omit the day's high, starting instead with the evening's low. For that reason, the code determines if it's evening by checking whether the low or high forecast appears first:

```
boolean evening = false;

if(input.indexOf(loSearch) < input.indexOf(hiSearch)){
    evening = true;
    hiTemperature[3] = hiTemperature[2];
    hiTemperature[2] = hiTemperature[1];
    hiTemperature[1] = hiTemperature[0];
}
.
.
.
```

After you determine whether this is the evening, here's how to draw those circles, each corresponding to a high temperature forecast (note that the code checks if it's evening in order to determine whether today's high value is no longer available):

```
g.setColor(Color.red);

if(!evening){
    g.drawOval(65 - 4, 200 - (Integer.parseInt(
        hiTemperature[0]) * 2) - 4, 8, 8);
}
g.drawOval(105 - 4, 200 - (Integer.parseInt(hiTemperature[1]) *
    2) - 4, 8, 8);
g.drawOval(145 - 4, 200 - (Integer.parseInt(hiTemperature[2]) *
    2) - 4, 8, 8);
g.drawOval(185 - 4, 200 - (Integer.parseInt(hiTemperature[3]) *
    2) - 4, 8, 8);
.
.
.
```

Then you connect those circles with lines to get the upper figure you see in Figure 10.1:

```
if(!evening){
    g.drawLine(65, 200 - (Integer.parseInt(
        hiTemperature[0]) * 2), 105, 200 -
        (Integer.parseInt(hiTemperature[1]) * 2));
}
g.drawLine(105, 200 - (Integer.parseInt(hiTemperature[1]) * 2),
    145, 200 - (Integer.parseInt(hiTemperature[2]) * 2));
g.drawLine(145, 200 - (Integer.parseInt(hiTemperature[2]) * 2),
    185, 200 - (Integer.parseInt(hiTemperature[3]) * 2));
.
.
.
```

Okay, now what about the low temperature forecasts? Here's how that works:

```
g.setColor(Color.blue);

g.drawOval(65 - 4, 200 - (Integer.parseInt(loTemperature[0]) *
    2) - 4, 8, 8);
g.drawOval(105 - 4, 200 - (Integer.parseInt(loTemperature[1]) *
    2) - 4, 8, 8);
g.drawOval(145 - 4, 200 - (Integer.parseInt(loTemperature[2]) *
    2) - 4, 8, 8);
```

```
g.drawOval(185 - 4, 200 - (Integer.parseInt(loTemperature[3]) *
    2) - 4, 8, 8);

g.drawLine(65, 200 - (Integer.parseInt(loTemperature[0]) * 2),
    105, 200 - (Integer.parseInt(loTemperature[1]) * 2));
g.drawLine(105, 200 - (Integer.parseInt(loTemperature[1]) * 2),
    145, 200 - (Integer.parseInt(loTemperature[2]) * 2));
g.drawLine(145, 200 - (Integer.parseInt(loTemperature[2]) * 2),
    185, 200 - (Integer.parseInt(loTemperature[3]) * 2));
.
.
.
```

Finally, here's how to create the label box with the text "Four-Day Forecast" and the attribution "Source: Nat. Weather Srvce." that you see in Figure 10.1:

```
g.setColor(Color.white);
g.fillRect(55, 160, 140, 30);
g.setColor(Color.blue);
g.drawRect(55, 160, 140, 30);

font = new Font("Courier", Font.PLAIN, 12);
g.setFont(font);
g.drawString("Four-Day Forecast", 65, 172);

font = new Font("Courier", Font.PLAIN, 9);
g.setFont(font);
g.drawString("Source: Nat. Weather Srvce.", 58, 185);
.
.
.
```

That completes the image. However, all this work will have gone for nothing if you can't send the image back to the browser. You've already indicated in the JSP page's page directive that you're going to be sending back a JPEG image, but how do you actually do that?

This turns out to be simpler than you might imagine. You can create a com.sun.image.codec.jpeg.JPEGImageEncoder object that will encode the image and send it back to the browser. To create that object, you use the createJPEGEncoder method of com.sun.image.codec.jpeg.JPEGCodec, passing it the OutputStream object you want to send the data to.

You can get an `OutputStream` object that will send data back to the browser using the JSP response object's `getOutputStream` method. Here's what that looks like (note that this code opens a binary output stream to the browser):

```
JPEGImageEncoder encoder = JPEGCodec.createJPEGEncoder
    (response.getOutputStream());
    .
    .
    .
}
```

You can find the significant methods of the Java `JPEGCodec` class in Table 10.3 and the significant methods of the Java `JPEGImageEncoder` class in Table 10.4. Both these classes come bundled with Java, no extra downloads needed.

TABLE 10.3   **Significant Methods of the** `com.sun.image.codec.jpeg.JPEGCodec` **Class**

Method	Does This
`static JPEGImageDecoder createJPEGDecoder(InputStream src)`	**Creates a** `JPEGImageDecoder` **object that you can use to decode JPEG data**
`static JPEGImageDecoder createJPEGDecoder (InputStream src, JPEGDecodeParam jdp)`	**Creates a parameterized** `JPEGImageDecoder` **object that you can use to decode JPEG data**
`static JPEGImageEncoder createJPEGEncoder (OutputStream dest)`	**Creates a** `JPEGImageEncoder` **object that you can use to encode image data as JPEG data**
`static JPEGImageEncoder createJPEGEncoder (OutputStream dest, JPEGEncodeParam jep)`	**Creates a parameterized** `JPEGImageEncoder` **object that you can use to encode image data as JPEG data**
`static JPEGEncodeParam getDefaultJPEGEncodeParam (BufferedImage bi)`	**Lets you create** `JPEGEncodeParam` **objects given a buffered image to hold parameter settings**
`static JPEGEncodeParam getDefaultJPEGEncodeParam (int numBands, int colorID)`	**Lets you create** `JPEGEncodeParam` **objects, given the number of bands and a color ID to hold parameter settings**
`static JPEGEncodeParam getDefaultJPEGEncodeParam (JPEGDecodeParam jdp)`	**Lets you create** `JPEGEncodeParam` **objects, given a** `JPEGDecodeParam` **object to hold parameter settings**
`static JPEGEncodeParam getDefaultJPEGEncodeParam (Raster ras, int colorID)`	**Lets you create** `JPEGEncodeParam` **objects, given raster and color ID to hold parameter settings**

TABLE 10.4 Significant Methods of the *com.sun.image.codec.jpeg.JPEGImageEncoder* Class

Method	Does This
void encode(BufferedImage bi)	**Encodes a buffered image into JPEG data**
void encode(BufferedImage bi, JPEGEncodeParam jep)	**Encodes a buffered image as JPEG data, using a** JPEGEncodeParam **object**
void encode(Raster ras)	**Encodes a** Raster **object as a JPEG data stream**
void encode(Raster ras, JPEGEncodeParam jep)	**Encodes a** Raster **object as a JPEG data stream using a** JPEGEncodeParam **object**
static JPEGEncodeParam getDefaultJPEGEncodeParam (BufferedImage bi)	**Lets you create** JPEGEncodeParam **objects given a buffered image to hold parameter settings**
static JPEGEncodeParam getDefaultJPEGEncodeParam (int numBands, int colorID)	**Lets you create** JPEGEncodeParam **objects, given the number of bands and a color ID to hold parameter settings**
static JPEGEncodeParam getDefaultJPEGEncodeParam (JPEGDecodeParam jdp)	**Lets you create** JPEGEncodeParam **objects, given a** JPEGDecodeParam **object to hold parameter settings**
static JPEGEncodeParam getDefaultJPEGEncodeParam (Raster ras, int colorID)	**Lets you create** JPEGEncodeParam **objects, given raster and color ID to hold parameter settings**
JPEGEncodeParam getJPEGEncodeParam()	**Returns a copy of the current** JPEGEncodeParam **object**
OutputStream getOutputStream()	**Returns the output stream the encoder is associated with**
void setJPEGEncodeParam (JPEGEncodeParam jep)	**Sets the** JPEGEncodeParam **object used for encoding operations**

REAL-WORLD SCENARIO: INTERACTIVE ONLINE IMAGES

Creating interactive online images and sending them to the browser in real time is one of the exciting things you can do with Java. But most Java programmers don't know that they can do this—let alone that it's so easy, just two lines of code.

All the functionality you need is packed into the com.sun.image.codec.jpeg packages, and more programmers have been putting this technology to work over the years. However, the fact that these classes are not in the standard Java packages has made adoption of these auxiliary classes slower than it should have been.

On the other hand, developers who know how to make this work know that the potential is great. You can put together real-time stock tickers, financial reports, system resource usage charts, and, as shown in this chapter, up-to-date weather forecasts. You can add your picture to your data or charts, display photos of current users, and even interact with the users if you track their mouse movements using JavaScript event handling to let them draw JPEG images.

Now that you've created a `JPEGImageEncoder` object, you can encode and send the image to the browser as a JPEG image this way:

```
JPEGImageEncoder encoder = JPEGCodec.createJPEGEncoder
    (response.getOutputStream());
```

```
encoder.encode(image);
    .
    .
    .
}
```

That's all it takes. Now you've created the forecast graph and have sent it back to the browser. If you want to embed the image in an HTML page, use an HTML `<IMG>` element like this (change this to supply your correct ZIP Code):

```
<IMG SRC="forecast.jsp?zip=94707">
```

Congratulations, you've written your own online daily temperature forecaster in Java, forecast.jsp. This JSP is ready to go. Just store it in the webapps directory of a JSP-enabled Internet server.

What about writing the standalone desktop version? That's coming up next.

Creating the Desktop Version

The Forecaster project can also be written as a standalone desktop Java application, Forecast.java. To display the weather graph, as you see in Figure 10.2, you can create the Forecast class by extending the `Frame` class:

```
import java.io.*;
import java.awt.*;
import java.net.*;
import java.awt.image.*;
import java.awt.event.*;
```

```
public class Forecast extends Frame
    .
    .
    .
```

This application will also need a way of asking the user his ZIP Code, so it'll use the `OKCancelDialog` class introduced in Chapter 2, "Slapshot! The Interactive Hockey Game":

```
import java.io.*;
import java.awt.*;
```

```
import java.net.*;
import java.awt.image.*;
import java.awt.event.*;

public class Forecast extends Frame
{
    OkCancelDialog textDialog;
         .
         .
         .
```

The main method will call the Forecast constructor, where the real action takes place:

```
import java.io.*;
import java.awt.*;
import java.net.*;
import java.awt.image.*;
import java.awt.event.*;

public class Forecast extends Frame
{
    OkCancelDialog textDialog;

    public static void main(String[] args)
    {
        new Forecast();
    }

    public Forecast()
    {
            .
            .
            .
    }
}
```

In the Forecast constructor, the first order of business is to get the user's ZIP Code. This application stores that information in a file named zip.txt, so it checks to see if zip.txt already exists, and if so, it reads in the user's ZIP Code:

```
    public Forecast()
    {
        String zip ="";
        File zipFile = new File("zip.txt");
```

```
        try {

            if(zipFile.exists()){
                FileReader filereader = new FileReader("zip.txt");
                BufferedReader bufferedreader = new
                    BufferedReader(filereader);
                zip = bufferedreader.readLine();
            }
            .
            .
            .

    }
```

If zip.txt doesn't exist, Forecast.java uses an OKCancelDialog object to ask the user for his ZIP Code and stores it in zip.txt:

```
    public Forecast()
    {
        String zip ="";
        File zipFile = new File("zip.txt");

        try {

            if(zipFile.exists()){
                FileReader filereader = new FileReader("zip.txt");
                BufferedReader bufferedreader = new
                    BufferedReader(filereader);
                zip = bufferedreader.readLine();
            }
            else
            {
                textDialog = new OkCancelDialog(this,
                    "Enter your five-digit zip code", true);
                textDialog.setVisible(true);
                zip = textDialog.data.trim();
                FileOutputStream fileoutputstream = new
                    FileOutputStream("zip.txt");
                fileoutputstream.write(zip.getBytes());
            }
            .
            .
            .

    }
```

After you have the user's ZIP Code, you can fetch the weather data as before:

```
URL url = new URL
    ("http://www.srh.noaa.gov/zipcity.php?inputstring="
    + zip);

URLConnection urlconnection = url.openConnection();
    .
    .
    .
```

After fetching the data and filling the hiTemperature and loTemperature arrays, you can create the forecast graph as in the JSP version of this project:

```
image = new BufferedImage(225, 201,
    BufferedImage.TYPE_INT_RGB);
Graphics2D g = image.createGraphics();

g.setColor(Color.white);
g.fillRect(0, 0, 224, 201);
    .
    .
    .
```

Finally, you can set up the window with a title and size, and you can make it visible:

```
setTitle("The Forecaster");

setResizable(false);

setSize(250, 240);

setVisible(true);

this.addWindowListener(new WindowAdapter(){
    public void windowClosing(
        WindowEvent e){
            System.exit(0);
        }
    }
);
    .
    .
    .
```

Now that the image is ready, you can draw it in the `paint` method this way:

```
public void paint(Graphics g)
{
    if(image != null){
        g.drawImage(image, 10, 30, this);
    }
}
}
```

And that completes Forecast.java, the desktop version of this application. To run it, just compile it and you're ready to go.

> **NOTE**
>
> **Download the complete source code for the Forecaster project, forecast.jsp and Forecast.java, at the Sams website. If you have a JSP-enabled server around, you can use forecast.jsp on it as you'd use any other JSP page. If you want to run the desktop version, just compile Forecast.java and run it as you'd run any other Java program (making sure you have a connection to the Internet available).**

Conclusion

This chapter presented the Forecaster project, the finale to the 10 projects presented in this book for some Java fun. This was a particularly powerful project, reading weather forecast data from the National Weather Service, graphing it, and reporting it to you.

There are two versions of this project: a JSP, forecast.jsp, for online use, and Forecast.java, for desktop use. One or the other of these files is all you need. The JSP file runs like any other JSP file on a Java-enabled server, whereas you can run the .java file on your desktop.

This project starts by getting the user's ZIP Code. The online version uses cookies, URL encoding, and an HTML form to get and store the user's ZIP Code; the desktop version uses a dialog box and a file, zip.txt, to get and store the ZIP Code.

Forecaster then passes the ZIP Code to the National Weather Service website and reads the web page that is returned to scan for weather forecast data. The high and low forecasts for four days, starting with today, are stored in arrays.

That data is then graphed and displayed to the user. In the online version, the forecast graph is encoded as a JPEG image and sent to the browser; in the desktop version, the image is drawn using standard Java graphics techniques.

Index

Numerics

3D rectangle, 14
8765 port, ServerSocket class, 268-269

A

Abstract Windowing Toolkit. *See* AWT
access, WebLogger project
    access restriction
      by password, 180-186
      by time of day, 175-179
    discussed, 164
    FileWriter object, 192-195
    FilterConfig object, 190-192
    filters, 165-174
    java.io.Writer class, 192
    log report information, 165
    roles, 186-187
    source code, 195
    user data collection, 188-190
ACTION attribute, 144-145
action listeners, 52
ActionEvent object, 37
ActionListener class, 202
    dialog box buttons, 51
    Send button, 262
addresses (IP), 256, 267-268
alignment, labels, 36
AlphaComposite class, 113
Apache Tomcat server
    directory structure, 138
    installing, 138
    localhost, 138
    main page, 138
    port numbers, 138
    starting, 138
    WEB-INF directory, 139
    webapps directory, 139
application creation, 231-233
application objects, 153-154
arcs, 14-15
attributes
    ACTION, 144-145
    CONTENT, 155
    contentType, 289
    getAttribute() method, 150-151

    import, 289
    METHOD, 145
    sessions, 148-150
    setAttribute() method, 150
    SRC, 287
authentication, 184
AWT (Abstract Windowing Toolkit)
    Frame class, 7-8
    Graphics class, 14-15
    Image class
      GIF images, 9-10
      methods, 11-13
    listener classes, 9
    Toolkit class, 11

B

background images, 47, 303
backgrounds, transparent, 9
beeping sound, 221
blurring images, 88-89
Boolean flags, 37
bounding rectangles, 7
brightening images, 87-88
Browser class, 230, 246-250
Browser project
    built-in browser control, 226
    button features, 228
    InputStream class, 226-227
    source code, 253
    SWT (Standard Widget Toolkit)
      advantages of, 228-229
      application creation, 231-233
      as AWT replacement, 229
      Browser class, 230, 246-250
      browser control, 227
      Button class, 236-239
      controls, 229-230
      Event object, 244-246
      Internet Explorer and, 229
      Label class, 234-236
      precompiled support, 231
      Shell class, 233
      swt.jar file, 231
      Text class, 239-240
      Toolbar class, 241-243
      ToolItem class, 243-244